# GOD-TALK

# THE SEABURY LIBRARY OF CONTEMPORARY THEOLOGY

# GOD-TALK

## An Examination of the Language and Logic of Theology

John Macquarrie

**A Crossroad Book**
The Seabury Press • New York

1979
The Seabury Press
815 Second Avenue
New York, N.Y. 10017

Published 1967 by SCM Press Ltd.
Seabury paperback edition 1979

Library of Congress Catalog Card Number: 78-68577
ISBN: 0-8164-2205-2

Printed in the United States of America

*To Edward Schouten Robinson*

# Contents

# Preface

ONE OF THE most pervasive problems in contemporary theology is the problem of language. What does theological discourse mean? How does it refer? What is its logic? Can such language communicate to the people of our time?

The problem first impressed me when I was working in the area of demythologizing, and I resolved to study it more closely when an opportunity should offer itself. But the same kind of problem is raised by what is called the 'new hermeneutic' and also by the exchanges between theology and logical analysis. Thus the problem of language has become a point of convergence for different approaches to theology.

An invitation to give the Hastie Lectures at Glasgow University in 1962 allowed me to begin this book. The theme of the lectures was 'The Problem of Theological Language' and the substance of these lectures has been incorporated into Chapters 1–4 and Chapter 6. I was able to develop the theme in further lectures given in the United States, and the material from these lectures has been incorporated into the later chapters of the book. These lectures were: a Cooper Lecture at Swarthmore College, Pennsylvania, in 1962 on 'The Language of Myth' (Chapter 8); two Lilly Lectures at DePauw University, Indiana, in 1963 on 'The Language of Existence and Being' (Chapter 12); a Calder Lecture at Marquette University, Milwaukee, in 1964 on 'Light as a Religious Symbol' (Chapter 9); a John XXIII Lecture at St Xavier College, Chicago, in 1965 on 'Heidegger and

Hermeneutics' (Chapter 7); and a Page Lecture at the Berkeley Divinity School, New Haven, in 1966 on 'The Problem of Analogy in Contemporary Theology' (Chapter 10). I wish to express my thanks to all those who invited me to give these various lectures.

I also wish to express thanks for permission to use in Chapter 5 material taken from two articles which I wrote on the subject of theology and analytical philosophy for *The Expository Times*, published in volumes LXVIII and LXXV. The poem 'Das Wort', by Stefan George, originally published in *Stephan George Werke*, Ausgabe in zwei Bänden, Verlag Helmut Küpper vormals Georg Bondi, Munich–Dusseldorf 1958, and printed on p. 165, is included by kind permission of Verlag Helmut Küpper, Munich.

JOHN MACQUARRIE

*Union Theological Seminary,*
*New York City*

# I

## The Problem Introduced

IF WE SUBSTITUTE Anglo-Saxon roots for Greek ones, the word 'theology' would seem to be equivalent to 'God-talk'. It is a form of discourse professing to speak about God. Not all God-talk would qualify as theology, for we reserve this name for the most sophisticated and reflective ways of talking about God. Moreover, only a very little sophistication is needed to see that talking about God must be very different from talking about the ordinary things and persons that we come across in the world, and that, in spite of the similarity of their names, theology must be something very different from geology. So right away we can acknowledge that theology is rather a strange kind of language. It is a special form of God-talk, and God-talk itself seems to be different from our everyday discoursing about what is going on in the world.

Theology is not only strange; it has become problematical in the modern world. What does it mean to talk about God at all? Impressed with the difficulty of returning a clear answer to this question, some theologians have proposed a theology without God. According to Paul van Buren, it is not only the case that, as Nietzsche said, God is dead; 'the problem now is that the *word* "God" is dead'.[1] To meet this problem, he argues that theology should give up talking about God, and be reduced to talking about the areas of history and ethics; and he claims that

[1] *The Secular Meaning of the Gospel* (New York: Macmillan and London: SCM Press, 1963), p. 103.

such a reduction would parallel what has taken place in other branches of inquiry that have become completely scientific, mentioning specifically how astrology has been reduced to astronomy, and alchemy to chemistry.[1] But such arguments merely muddy the waters. Astronomy and chemistry have *replaced* astrology and alchemy among modern educated people, and are different pursuits, with quite different aims from those of the old occult pseudo-sciences. Because these modern sciences are different, the difference is made clear by giving them different names. No one would dream of calling them 'reduced astrology' and 'reduced alchemy', whatever these expressions might mean. If the word 'God' is dead, then obviously God-talk and theology are dead, and we may as well replace them with ethics or whatever is considered appropriate. But let us not confuse the issue by talking about a 'reduced theology' which is no theology at all.

Actually, much God-talk probably is dead. When we consider some of the theological disputes over which men got excited in the past, we find that perhaps most of them mean little or nothing to us. Was monothelitism correct in holding that Christ had only one will; or did he, as orthodoxy eventually decided, have both a human will and a divine will? Is there, as Western Christianity maintains, a double procession of the Holy Spirit from the Father and the Son; or is the Eastern Church more accurate in holding that the Holy Spirit proceeds from the Father alone? Is the real presence of Christ in the eucharist to be understood in terms of the Roman Catholic doctrine of transubstantiation, whereby it is believed that the whole substance of the bread and wine is converted into the whole substance of Christ's body and blood, though the sensible accidents remain; or are we to follow rather the Lutheran doctrine of consubstantiation, whereby it is supposed that, the accidents still remaining, the substance of the bread and wine coexists in union with the substance of Christ's body and blood? Among the Calvinists, does the truth lie with the supralapsarian

[1] *Op. cit.*, pp. 197–8.

view that the divine decree allotted to individual men their several destinies before the fall of Adam; or should one rather give assent to the infralapsarian view that the divine decree was subsequent to the fall?

These questions have been picked out almost at random from a thousand years of theological debate and from the whole broad expanse of Christendom. Perhaps some comparable questions could be found in contemporary and recent theological discussion. We may recall the famous debate over natural theology between Karl Barth and Emil Brunner. It resolved into the question whether man has lost the image of God in its entirety, or whether he has lost the content of this image while retaining its form.

When we are confronted with such questions as those that have been mentioned, we are nowadays likely to react in a different way from that in which men reacted when the questions were first debated. Even if we happen to belong to a tradition that accepted one or other of the answers in such a matter, we probably sit rather lightly to it. We are not likely to identify ourselves passionately with one or other of the alternatives presented in each question, for the questions seem pretty dead and do not stir us any more. Certainly, we are not likely to think that our well-being, either here or hereafter, is in any way dependent on our ability to give correct answers to such questions. We are more likely to wonder whether there are any correct answers at all, and our first step today would be to take a harder look at the questions themselves. Are they genuine questions? Can we attach sense to the terms in which they have been formulated? Is any question of fact or reality involved? Or must we conclude that these questions that confront us have arisen out of sophistry, misconception and empty debate?

It is perhaps not too fantastic to imagine something like the following discussion between an ancient Egyptian and a follower of Shinto. The Egyptian might say: 'The sun is of the male sex, for he is none other than the great god Ra.' To this, the Japanese might reply: 'No, you are mistaken. The sun is female, for she is a goddess and her name is Amaterasu.' Possibly there would take place a heated argument over the question of whether the sun is a god or a goddess. But we should consider such an argument to be entirely empty, for there is no real question here. The sun does not belong to the class of entities of which one can significantly assert a sex. Of course, it is open to anyone who pleases to exercise his poetic imagination by giving the sun a proper name, whether masculine or feminine; but this seems to be a matter of private taste, and not something about which you can argue for its truth or falsity. Actually, different languages have assigned different genders to the sun and the moon. This may tell us something of the mythology or the psychology of the peoples who expressed themselves in these languages, but surely it gives no objective information about the sun and moon.

Were the theological disputes which we mentioned just as unrealistic or subjective as a dispute over the sex of a celestial body? This question cannot be easily or quickly answered, for obviously those theological disputes were much more sophisticated than a simple-minded argument as to whether the sun is male or female. Behind the theological disputes stand highly complex ideas. The dispute about one or two wills presupposes the idea of the 'God-man' who combines in himself two 'natures'. The dispute about the single or double procession of the Holy Spirit presupposes the idea of the 'triune God'. The dispute about transubstantiation and consubstantiation presupposes both the belief in a 'real presence' and the philosophical notions of 'substance' and 'accident'. The dispute between supralapsarians and infralapsarians presupposes the ideas of a 'predestinating decree' of God and of a 'fall' of man, and presupposes further that these, if not exactly datable, can at least somehow be placed in an order of before and after. The dispute between Barth and Brunner presupposes the idea of a 'divine image' which may or may not be present in man, and Brunner's position seems to carry the further presupposition that the 'form' of this image can subsist in the absence of its 'content'.

In their turn, all of these complex ideas presuppose others, and indeed a whole 'universe of discourse', as logicians used to call it, opens up behind each of these particular debates. A long and arduous process of unravelling would be required to find out whether some or all of the ideas in question make sense, and whether some or all of the disputes in which they play a part are genuine arguments or merely empty sophistries.

It is probable enough that under strict logical analysis some of the theological disputes mentioned might well collapse into heaps of meaningless verbiage. Yet the fact that some of these matters were, in the situations in which they arose, argued with passionate conviction, may make us wonder whether some real issues were at stake, even though these were obscured by the abstruse speculative language. These real issues, if there were any, could scarcely be revealed by a cold formal analysis, especially if it considered the particular dispute in isolation. But the issues might begin to show themselves if we first of all saw each dispute in the context of a whole theology, and if we could next think ourselves into the concrete situation in which the dispute arose, seeking to understand what the participants were trying to say in that situation.

Here we may call to mind still another theological dispute— the celebrated Arian controversy. As we learn about it nowadays, it appears to have been a dispute over metaphysical essences. We all hear about one episode in the controversy, the distinction between *homoousios* and *homoiousios*, and this is presented as having to do with the abstract question about the difference between 'sameness' and 'likeness'. But it is surely very significant that in his three undoubtedly genuine *Orationes contra Arianos*, St Athanasius only once uses the famous word, *homoousios*. This is a strange fact indeed, if the argument was about essences. Actually, as historians have often pointed out, for St Athanasius the real issue underlying the metaphysical language was the question of whether any finite entity, however exalted, can properly lay claim to man's ultimate concern, without bringing him into a distorting idolatry; or, in other words, whether Christ can be given the allegiance of faith unless he really is God. Exactly what is the logical status of questions like these, we cannot at this point say. Clearly, however, these questions are much more concrete and existentially rooted than the talk of metaphysical essences would at first have led us to expect. It may be the case that underlying many abstruse and speculative theological debates, and quite undisclosed by formal syntactical analysis, there are concrete issues of the kind that stirred St Athanasius.

But I do not want to suggest that every theological debate could yield issues of this kind. It would surely be hard to show that any such issues were at stake in, let us say, the debate between monothelitism and dyothelitism, or in that between supralapsarianism and infralapsarianism. It may be worth observing that both of these debates came at the end of long periods of theological controversy, when the original issues had been buried and forgotten and the discussion was petering out in sterile speculations and unreal distinctions. If the two debates which we have in mind served any useful purpose at all, perhaps it was only to stand as a warning to future generations of how silly theological talk can become, and how far it can wander from the concrete experiences that it is supposed to bring to expression.

The examples of theological talk that we have so far had before us are drawn from controversies in which, admittedly, the theologian gets involved in his most abstruse and technical jargon. But these examples serve nevertheless to focus our attention in a forcible way on the problem which is to occupy us—the problem of theological language. What does the theologian mean when he talks, even in simpler ways than those so far considered, about God, angels, immortality, sin, grace, salvation and all the rest? Can we find an intelligible sense for his utterances? This is surely one of the most crucial problems in contemporary religious thought. In one form or another, the problem is raised both by the major types of theology that are current today and by contemporary philosophical considerations of religion. We are being forcibly reminded that the question of meaning is prior to the question of truth. Before one can discuss whether a statement is true or false, one must have at least some idea of what the statement means.

I say, 'at least some idea', in order to avoid suggesting that the meaning of a statement must always be crystal-clear before one can hold it for true or false. The early Wittgenstein did in fact maintain that 'what can be said at all can be said clearly'.[1] But there are degrees of clarity, and it may be the case that some things can be said only obscurely or obliquely, without the consequence that they are therefore meaningless. For instance, when Freud writes that 'the study of dream-work affords us an excellent example of the way in which unconscious material from the id forces itself upon the ego',[2] I would claim to have some idea of what is meant, and I would even think that the statement is likely to be true. But if questioned as to precisely what kind of entities are intended by the somewhat obscure expressions 'unconscious material', 'id' and 'ego', or what kind of process is intended by the expression 'forces itself', I could not return any clear answers. Perhaps, as some logical analysts have claimed, the language of psychoanalysis stands in need of clarification. Perhaps, on the other hand, the language would resist clarification, expecially if this meant reducing it to the language of physics in the interests of the 'unity of science', as was urged by some of the more positivist-minded analysts. In any case, the presence of some obscurities in the language does not seem to preclude us from having a tolerable idea of what is meant. Certainly, it is by no means obvious that we would have to deny any meaning to the passage if it proved impossible to eliminate entirely its obscurities.

I have stressed this point because the user of religious language has himself been aware for centuries or millennia that his statements have some peculiarities and do not possess the clarity

[1] *Tractatus Logico-Philosophicus*, trans. C. K. Ogden (London: Kegan Paul, 1922), p. 27.

[2] *An Outline of Psychoanalysis*, trans. James Strachey (London: Hogarth Press, 1949), p. 27.

that belongs to such assertions as 'The sky is blue' or 'The cat sat on the mat'; but he would claim that even if an obscure or oblique character is inseparable from some of the expressions that he uses, nevertheless we can form some idea of what is meant. His language is logically odd. Yet it may be the case, as the Bishop of Durham suggests, that the questions that concern us most demand the oddest kind of language;[1] and if indeed this language gives us *some* idea of the matters talked about, however obliquely, then its use is surely legitimate and is to be preferred to that silence which Wittgenstein once enjoined by declaring that the questions that matter to us most (*unsere Lebensprobleme*) are inexpressible.[2]

Of course, if one insists that meaning must be tied up with verification by sense-experience, or if one upholds the doctrine of physicalism—the doctrine that any statements which are not tautologies or definitions, and which claim to convey genuine knowledge, must in principle be translatable into the universal language of physics—then the possibility of any meaningful theological language would seem to be excluded from the start. God-talk just does not fit into such a scheme. But the days of iconoclastic logical positivism seem to have passed, and it is now more customary to say that the meaning of statements is to be sought in the way they get used, or something of the sort. However, this reprieve in no way lessens the urgency of the problem of meaning in theology. It is the business of the theologian (and here he might have to speak for users of religious language in general) to show in what way God-talk, in spite of its admitted obscurities, does have a meaning, and perhaps a very important one. Indeed, the task is inescapable if theology claims to be an intellectual discipline which sets out to explore and elucidate a given area of subject-matter.

Not all God-talk, we said, is theology, and at this point we may draw more sharply the line between theological language and the wider phenomenon of religious language. The latter

[1] Ian T. Ramsey, *Religious Language* (London: SCM Press, 1957), p. 48.
[2] *Op. cit.*, pp. 186–7.

expression would be used to include such diverse kinds of utterances as praying, praising, exhorting, blessing, cursing, and perhaps many other things besides. Furthermore, faith or religion may express itself in ways which are not verbal but which might nonetheless be regarded as 'language' of some sort— ritual acts, and deeds of love as well; crucifixes, paintings, statues; music, poetry, and even silence. Theological language arises out of religious language as a whole, and it does so when a religious faith becomes reflective and tries to give an account of itself in verbal statements. What is done (ritual) perhaps came before what is said (myth), but the myth and the ritual go together in a reciprocal interpretation of each other, and one can say that the myth is already implicit in the ritual. Again, an immediate and unreflective utterance of faith may imply some theological belief; for instance, when we read about St Stephen's addressing a prayer to Jesus,[1] this seems to point to some christological conviction in the primitive Church, though presumably as yet that conviction had been very little elucidated in explicit terms. What we wish to indicate is the close connection between theology and the living faith out of which it comes by a process of reflection. Theology itself lives and has its meaning only in relation to the wider religious matrix from which it arises. When it strays too far from its source or when it gets separated from other modes of expression in worship and ethics, it degenerates into empty and arid disputes; and of course, if it has become detached from its living background and then gets subjected in an artificial way to some formal analysis, we must not be surprised if it begins to appear senseless.

But when we urge that theological statements are to be understood in the context of the faith of a religious community, does this really take us anywhere? Where today are we to find the living religious context that gives meaning to theological statements? The great religions arose at a time when the world was still supposed to be filled with divine manifestations, and these could be plainly pointed out. Theophanies took place

[1] Acts 7.59.

—or so it was believed—and even when the gods did not appear in person, they might manifest themselves in sensible effects which, since they could not be understood in any other way, were assigned to divine agency.

Thus Moses and the elders are said to have seen God directly on the summit of Mount Sinai.[1] At other times, Yahweh's presence was visibly manifested by the appearance of smoke or fire or cloud.[2] Yahweh might be heard, as well as seen, as when he answered Moses in thunder;[3] and even when he was not directly seen or heard, he might show himself by some sensible effects, such as the fiery serpents that he is said to have sent among the people on one occasion.[4]

It is interesting to notice that in early times a religious teacher was expected to give some sensible demonstration in support of his message, so that the demand for verification by sense-experience is certainly no new thing. Thus we read that Elijah demonstrated the truth of his teaching as against that of the pagan priests by setting up a public contest wherein, in response to his prayer, the fire of Yahweh fell from heaven and was seen by all the people, who thereupon acknowledged Yahweh as God. 'And when all the people saw it, they fell on their faces; and they said, "The Lord, he is God; the Lord, he is God." '[5] In the New Testament, the Pharisees are said to have come to Jesus seeking a sign from heaven.[6] Their request was discouraged. It is, of course, true that miracles were in fact attributed to Jesus, and that in St Mark's Gospel and elsewhere, they were cited as signs of the inbreaking of the kingdom of God. Yet a study of the most ancient apologists shows that, for the most part, they based their claims for the Christian faith on quite different grounds.

Appeals to empirical evidences are to be found in many religions. When the Buddha met with a cold reception from his kinsfolk, he is said to have performed the spectacular miracle of

[1] Ex. 24.9-11.
[2] Ex. 19.18; 20.21.
[3] Ex. 19.19.
[4] Num. 21.6.
[5] I Kings 18.39.
[6] Mark 8.11.

the pairs,[1] and the only purpose of this seems to have been to provide a sensible demonstration of the truth of his claims. Mohammed was reproached for his inability to work a miracle. The reproach was, in the eyes of his followers, removed at the battle of Badr. There he defeated a Meccan force that outnumbered his own troops by two to one. Such a remarkable and unexpected victory could be explained only on the supposition that angels had intervened on the side of the Muslims, and so had provided empirical verification of Mohammed's claims.[2]

But these ways of arguing belong to the past. The world nowadays has become for us a non-religious secularized environment, a self-regulating cosmos in which we have learned to describe the events that take place within it in terms of other events that are equally immanent in the world. And if there are gaps that remain mysterious, then we expect that science will in time fill them in, and, if we are wise, we do not rush forward to postulate these gaps as points of entry for the supernatural. We no longer look for sensible manifestations of the divine, whether they be theophanies, miracles, signs from heaven, or angelic interventions. 'The world,' writes Hans Urs von Balthasar, 'is not God. This much is clear today, to the theist as well as to the atheist. Nor is the world open to God in such a way that he would have to intervene in it at every moment to keep it going. Christian apologetics has probably by now learned from its past mistakes.'[3] Perhaps most theologians would agree with the view expressed in this quotation, and it is surely somewhat ironical that just at the time when religious apologists have ceased to look for sensible manifestations of the divine in the world and have outgrown the ways of argument that belonged to an earlier period, some philosophers should come forward with the demand for verification by sense-experience.

[1] E. J. Thomas, *The Life of Buddha as Legend and History* (London: Kegan Paul, 1931), p. 98. The miracle gets its name from the fact that its impressive performances were arranged in complementary pairs.

[2] D. S. Margoliouth, *Mohammed* (London: G. P. Putnam's Sons, 1923), p. 269.

[3] *Science, Religion and Christianity* (London: Burns & Oates, 1958), p. 93.

But although the problem of theological language is one that is attracting special interest at present, we would be utterly mistaken if we thought that this problem had arisen suddenly, or that only with the development of modern techniques of logical analysis has the man of religious faith been driven to recognize the problems that are inherent in his ways of talking. I have already said that the spokesmen of religion have long been aware of the obscure and oblique elements in their language, and this awareness arose at a very early stage, as soon as religion began to be reflective. We find that the archaic naive ways of talking about the gods came to be criticized. Gradually the gods themselves were withdrawn from the realm of the sensible, though they might still be considered to produce sensible effects. However, it might happen, as in mystical religion all over the world, that attention was directed away from sense-experience altogether. In any case, new ways of talking were demanded, and as soon as men began to depart from the mythical mentality which thought that the gods and their doings showed themselves as sensible phenomena, religious teachers became aware of the difficulty of talking about the gods at all. It may be worth our while to take note of a few examples illustrating how, even in ancient times, the main problems of theological language were already recognized.

In many religions there appeared the belief that what is most important in the religious experience is inexpressible; or that the reality which impinges on man's life in religion is so different from everyday objects of experience and so transcends our power of understanding that we are reduced to silence about it. Thus while, as we have noted, one passage in the Pentateuch tells us that Moses and the elders actually 'saw the God of Israel', another passage from a different source represents Yahweh as saying to Moses: 'You cannot see my face; for man shall not see me and live.'[1] The passage goes on to relate how Yahweh promises that although Moses may not see his face, he shall see his back. The language here is still mythological, but

[1] Ex. 33.20.

whatever may be meant by talking about Yahweh's 'face' and Yahweh's 'back', it seems to be clearly recognized that there is something in God that cannot be seen or known or described in any direct way, and that God shows himself only indirectly. Philo of Alexandria has a comment on this passage: 'Everything which is subsequent to God, the virtuous man may grasp: God alone cannot be grasped. That is to say, God cannot be grasped by a direct frontal approach, for this would imply that he is disclosed as he is. But God can be grasped through the powers that are subsequent to his being, for these powers do not present his essence but only his existence from the effects resulting from it.'[1]

Of course, the most developed thought of the Old Testament finds repellent the idea that God can be seen at all, or adequately described. Deutero-Isaiah asks: 'To whom then will you liken God, or what likeness compare with him?'[2] This whole passage on the divine transcendence is a far cry from the naive ideas of the creation story where Adam and Eve 'heard the sound of the Lord God walking in the garden in the cool of the day'.[3]

The notion of inexpressibility is even more forcibly propounded outside the tradition of biblical religion, and especially in eastern religions. One well-known example will be sufficient here. Lao-tse begins his treatise by saying: 'The *tao* that can be trodden is not the enduring and unchanging *tao*. The name that can be named is not the enduring and unchanging name.'[4] There could, of course, be several reasons for maintaining the essential inexpressibility of what is encountered in religious experience. In the Hebrew scriptures, the reason would seem to be the utter transcendence of God over all creaturely beings, and transcendence is in fact the theme of the passage from deutero-Isaiah, quoted above. On the other hand, in Lao-tse and in eastern mysticism generally, the thought seems to be rather of

[1] *Opera*, ed. L. Cohn and P. Wendland (Berlin: 1896ff.), vol. ii, p. 237.
[2] Isa. 40.18.          [3] Gen. 3.8.
[4] *The Texts of Taoism*, trans. James Legge (New York: Dover Publications, 1962), Part I, p. 47.

a primal undifferentiated Being, which one cannot even name without giving it a determinate character, and so making it some particular thing. In Philo, perhaps both reasons are operative, for although he is ostensibly talking of the God of the Old Testament, he thinks of this God quite in the mystical manner as *apoios*, 'without qualities'. But whatever the underlying reasons may have been, there has been from the earliest times a widespread and conscious acknowledgement that at the core of religion lies something that language cannot express, or at least cannot express in any adequate way.

If the religious experience were absolutely inexpressible, then it would follow that the reflective attempt, called 'theology', to explicate the content of religious faith in words, is an altogether mistaken endeavour, and that those who hold such a faith ought to remain silent. 'Whereof one cannot speak, thereon one must be silent.'[1] This assertion was made by Wittgenstein in the positivistic phase of his philosophizing, and according to Thomas McPherson, a positivistic philosophy is quite compatible with religion, which ought to remain silent.[2] But it has to be acknowledged that adherents of religious faiths are almost notorious for their habit of talking and writing at great length. Perhaps the urge to verbalize is more characteristic of the West than of the East. W. P. Paterson wittily remarked that the Indian sage's career culminates when he retires to the forest to meditate in silence, while his western counterpart is more likely to be invited to give a course of lectures embodying his mature reflections on life![3] But the fact that Friedrich Max Müller's series, *The Sacred Books of the East*, ran to fifty volumes, shows us that the contrast cannot be pushed too far.

Have religious thinkers been right in seeking to express themselves in words, or ought they to have held their peace? I have already rejected the idea that everything that can be said can be said clearly, and have claimed that discourse cannot be dis-

---

[1] L. Wittgenstein, *op. cit.*, p. 189.
[2] 'Religion as the Inexpressible', in *New Essays in Philosophical Theology*, ed. A. Flew and A. MacIntyre (London: SCM Press, 1955), pp. 131ff.
[3] *The Nature of Religion* (London: Hodder & Stoughton, 1925), pp. 1–2.

missed as simply pointless or meaningless because some of the words used in it have elements of obscurity. If there is any cognitive element in religion and if there is any knowledge of what we call the 'divine', then the attempt must be made to put this knowledge, as far as possible, into words. We need not try to decide the question whether there could be any genuine knowledge at all without words. But even if there were such knowledge, it would seem to be without structure or pattern, and it is hard to see how it could be either communicated or brought into relation with other knowledge. W. M. Urban writes: 'It is perhaps conceivable that we may have a direct apprehension or intuition of life, but the meaning of life can be neither apprehended nor expressed except in language of some kind.'[1] Elsewhere the same writer remarks: 'Reality is, in a sense, doubtless beyond language, as Plato felt so deeply, and cannot be wholly grasped in its forms, but when in order to grasp reality we abandon linguistic forms, then reality, like quicksilver, runs through our fingers.'[2] So the man of religious faith, if he believes that some kind of knowledge has been revealed to him, must look for some way of expressing it in words.

The way that lies closest to a sense of the ineffability of the divine is the *via negationis*. Infinite or transcendent Being is to be described by denying of it every character that implies finite or creaturely being. In some ways, the *via negationis* is a great safeguard against ways of speaking or thinking about God that reduce him to some manipulable entity, and so a great safeguard also against idolatry. But as far as the problem of expressing the knowledge of God in words is concerned, it is doubtful whether the *via negationis* permits us to advance very far out of silence. It is significant that one of the exponents of this way, Clement of Alexandria, mentions with approval the five years of silence that are said to have been enjoined on the disciples of Pythagoras. For Clement, 'God is above both space and time

[1] *Language and Reality* (London: Allen & Unwin, 1939), p. 21.
[2] *Op. cit.*, p. 49.

and name and conception.' But if we proceed by 'abstracting all that belongs to bodies, and to things called "incorporeal"', we are told that 'we may reach somehow to the conception of the Almighty, knowing not what he is, but what he is not.'[1]

No doubt in certain contexts a denial may imply some quite definite assertion. If there are a limited number of possibilities, then to eliminate one of them is to make what remains appreciably more definite. For instance, in a game of chess, where there are only two colours of pieces, 'not white' is equivalent to 'black'. In any particular case, the definiteness of what is indirectly asserted when something is denied will vary according to the context of the discussion in which the denial has been made. Now it does not seem that there is any clearly delimited context or universe of discourse which would yield any very definite assertions when it is denied that God possesses certain characteristics. To say, for instance, that God is not corporeal implies simply that he is non-corporeal, and so, of course, are numbers, grammar, scientific theories and many other things. It may indeed be the case that we are very much in danger of smuggling some positive content into a word like 'incorporeal', when applied to God. When we say God is 'incorporeal' or 'without a body', perhaps we interpret this in some positive kind of way, as meaning, let us say, that he is a 'spiritual' as distinct from a 'bodily' substance. But this positive element (which remains vague enough in any case) is not deducible from the simple denial of corporeality. Similarly, we may import some positive content into such apparently negative words as 'immortal' or 'immutable' in applying them to God, but again, this element of affirmation is not justified by the *via negationis* alone. Actually Clement, in commending the way of negation, says that 'we cast ourselves into the greatness of Christ, and thence advance into immensity by holiness,'[2] and this remark, with its appeal to Christ and its allusion to holiness, clearly adds something quite affirmative to the way of simple negation. If one adhered strictly to the *via negationis*, it is hard to see how the

[1] *The Miscellanies*, V, 11.  [2] *Ibid.*

knowledge of God said to be reached in this way could be other than wholly vacuous. It would scarcely be distinguishable from agnosticism, and while indeed we hinted that a measure of reverent agnosticism is entirely proper in any discourse that respects the mystery and uniqueness of God, faith is possible only on the basis that God has granted some positive knowledge of himself.

This talk of inexpressibility, to be found from the earliest stages of religious development, and the tendency to remain silent about the content of religious faith or to confine oneself to negative statements, point to an awareness that our familiar speech is adapted to talking about the everyday world. According to P. F. Strawson's analysis,[1] our ordinary language has two basic categories for particulars—material bodies and persons. Since persons are themselves embodied, it would seem then that our language is basically adapted to talking about the entities that encounter us within the sensible world. When the myths began to break and the gods were gradually extruded from the sensible world, it might seem that they had also receded beyond the limits of language. Yet we have seen that if religious faith is to maintain its claim to have some cognitive character, it cannot rest content either with silence or with a strict *via negativa*, but must try to articulate in words what it claims to know. In other words, the attempt must be made to stretch language beyond its normal (or 'logically primitive') usages, so that—if we may so speak—it may pursue the gods whither they have gone. Even in ancient times, those who attempted to stretch language in one way or another were quite clearly aware of the obscurities and difficulties involved in their ways of talking.

One of the Hebrew psalmists says: 'I will open my mouth in a parable; I will utter dark sayings from of old.'[2] The Hebrew word here translated as 'parable' is *māshal*. The root expressed the idea of 'similarity' or 'likeness', though the noun *māshal*

---

[1] In *Individuals: an Essay in Descriptive Metaphysics* (Garden City, N.Y.: Doubleday, 1963 and London: Methuen (University Paperbacks), 1964).
[2] Ps. 78.2.

came to have a very wide semantic range, and was used generally of proverbs and wise sayings, perhaps because these were often expressed in two parallel or similar sentences.[1] It is not indeed obvious that the psalm quoted, taken as a whole, could be called a 'parable', but it does abound in 'likenesses' or 'similes' of one kind or another. For instance, Yahweh is said to be a rock and a champion; he is compared to a man waking out of sleep; and also to a warrior shouting because of wine. The question of how appropriate or inappropriate such comparisons may be does not specially concern us at present. We may well think that some of them are less appropriate than others that are to be found in the psalms and that have commended themselves more to later generations, as, for instance, the assertion: 'As a father pities his children, so the Lord pities those who fear him.'[2] But the whole question of what would be an appropriate comparison for God or what kind of 'likeness' there could be, is a very difficult one. 'To whom will you liken God?' Here, however, we are only concerned to notice that one of the most obvious ways of stretching language is by the use of likenesses, or by the metaphorical transfer of words. A less well-known object or situation can in some respects be elucidated through comparison with an object or situation that is better known.

The use of likenesses or similes was early seized upon in religious talk so as to stretch everyday language in such a way that it might—so it was hoped—embrace the gods, at least in some manner. This way of talking eventually developed into a full-blown doctrine of analogy, much discussed and elaborated in the Middle Ages. Thus the *via negationis* is supplemented by the *via eminentiae*. Both ways contrast the infinite with the finite, or creative Being with creaturely being, but whereas the *via negativa* simply denies the infinite all characteristics of the finite, the *via eminentiae* claims that every positive characteristic of the finite bears some affinity to a corresponding characteristic of the

---

[1] W. O. E. Oesterley translates the verse we have quoted as follows: 'I would open my mouth in wise sayings, pour out riddles from the past.' See *The Psalms* (London: S.P.C.K., 1939), vol. II, p. 359.

[2] Ps. 103.13.

infinite, in which, so to speak, the positive characteristics of finite being are raised to a pre-eminent degree. Thus, every analogous predication involves the assertion both of likeness and unlikeness. The possibility which this way offers of talking intelligibly about God clearly depends on just how wide the gulf between God and created beings is taken to be, and on just how far language can be stretched without coming to a breaking-point. This is a question which must be deferred for the present.

It is worth looking also at the second hemistich of the verse of the psalm quoted earlier: 'I will utter dark sayings.' The English expression 'dark sayings' represents the Hebrew word *hīda*, which is commonly translated 'riddle'. It is the word used, for instance, of Samson's well-known riddle: 'Out of the eater came something to eat.'[1] A riddle is a dark or obscure saying because it gives a deliberately obscure and puzzling description of something, a description which at first sight may well seem nonsensical, but is not nonsensical when one hits upon the correct solution. Here again, we have a stretching of language beyond its ordinary uses, though it is less easy to see in this case how the stretching functions, or what part it could play in theological discourse.

The oblique, partial or fragmentary knowledge of God which the Christian has in his earthly existence is frankly characterized as a riddle (*ainigma*) by St Paul.[2] Christian writings abound in riddling passages of the kind which we call 'paradoxes'. St Paul himself provides illustrations of this, such as: 'We are afflicted in every way, but not crushed; perplexed, but not driven to despair; persecuted, but not forsaken; struck down, but not destroyed ... for while we live, we are always being given up to death for Jesus' sake.'[3] These paradoxes of the Christian life may be compared with the paradox of Christ himself, as it finds expression in a well-known passage of St Ignatius: 'Of flesh and spirit, generate and ingenerate, God in man, true life in death, son of Mary and son of God, first passible and then impassible '[4] Notable examples of paradox are also to be found outside the

[1] Judges 14.14.   [2] I Cor. 13.12.   [3] II Cor. 4.8, 9, 11.   [4] *Epistles*, Eph. 7.

tradition of biblical religion. A striking instance is the Vedic hymn of creation: 'Then was not non-existent or existent . . . Death was not then, nor was there anything immortal . . . That one thing, breathless, breathed by its own nature.'[1]

These utterances all contain some contrasts so violent that, on any formal logical analysis, they would have to be branded as self-contradictory and senseless. Yet many people believe that such sayings are expressing something of importance, and that they convey an understanding of some kind and are not merely sophisticated ways of evincing some subjective emotional attitude. Moreover, it might well be claimed that there is no other way that quite expresses what is being said in these paradoxes. Is it possible then that language can be stretched in such apparently illogical ways, so as to enable us to see something that language in its ordinary usages would miss? And if so, how is this possible?

Perhaps we should first of all ask whether it was right to use the word 'illogical' here. Paradoxes may indeed be illogical if the criterion is the logic of ordinary usage, but are we being too hasty in demanding that all language should conform to a single logic? Are there perhaps other logics, or other modes of syntax, that have their legitimate uses?

The question is raised here only in a provisional way, but the direction in which an answer may be sought is suggested by D. T. Suzuki in a passage[2] where he considers the important part played by the riddle or *koan* in Zen Buddhism. A learner is given a *koan* on which to meditate. A familiar example is: 'What is the sound of one hand clapping?' The question is apparently senseless. However, according to Suzuki, it is by striking at everyday logic that the Zen master introduces his student to 'a new order of things'. The purpose of the riddle is to make the learner question the dualistic subject-object structure of everyday experience, and to bring him to the point where there opens up to him a new dimension of experience with a logic of its own.

[1] *Rigveda*, x, 129.
[2] *An Introduction to Zen Buddhism* (London: Rider, 1949), p. 105.

I have mentioned Zen Buddhism, and perhaps its riddles are more than ordinarily obscure, and certainly they would strike the Western mind as more violently illogical than the paradoxes of Christian theology. (Perhaps to the Eastern mind this judgment would be reversed!) Yet there may be a basic similarity and a common function in all these 'illogical' ways of talking. D. M. Baillie has suggested that the paradoxes of Christian theology represent the diffracted expression in an objectifying language of an experience that takes place in the dimension of direct interpersonal relations.[1] We cannot at this stage determine the adequacy of such a suggestion, and still less can we answer the question of how successful paradox may be in achieving its purpose, but we can at least see the possibility that its riddling utterances may provide a way of stretching ordinary language so as to illuminate some dimension of experience other than the realm of objects presented to the senses.

It has become abundantly clear to us that the problem o theological language has long been recognized, and that as soon as men began to emerge from purely mythical ways of talking, they became aware that discourse about the gods has in it an oblique and even obscure character. We have not as yet made any serious attempt to see how such theological language functions, or indeed to see whether it can function adequately at all. The 'grammar' of this language appears to have grown up in a somewhat haphazard fashion. But it is surely rather striking that we find similar ways of talking in quite different religions, and it was to draw attention to this that I introduced a few illustrations from outside the biblical tradition. The fact that common patterns of talk may be seen in widely scattered faiths suggests that there is some universal logical structure that characterizes theological discourse.

From time to time the awareness of the problematical character of theological language or God-talk has risen to the level of an explicit investigation into such language, notably in the medieval study of analogy. We have said, however, that the

[1] *God was in Christ* (London: Faber & Faber, 1948), p. 108.

whole issue has become particularly crucial today. In the twentieth century, there is a specially pressing demand that theological language should, so to speak, produce its credentials and make clear what it is all about. So our next step will be to turn to some of the theologians of our time, and see how they respond to the problem of language.

## 2

---

## *How Some Contemporary Theologians View Language*

THE PURPOSE OF the present chapter is to show that the problem of theological language, long recognized in various ways, has come to occupy a key position in contemporary theological discussion. In one form or another, this problem is raised by all the major trends within current theology. It is already implicit in theologies which lay stress on the word (or language) of God; it figures more or less prominently in discussions about demythologizing, existential interpretation and the problem of hermeneutics; it becomes the major issue where Christian apologists find themselves engaged in debate with philosophers of the analytical school. Upon the way in which one is able to respond to this problem will depend not only the question of how one is going to decide among the rival views of competing theological schools, but also the question of whether one can assent to the claim of theology to be a genuine reflective discipline, with an assured place as a reputable branch of inquiry.

The problem is that of God-talk. To put it briefly, this problem is to show how in a human language one can talk intelligibly about a divine subject-matter. There are two obvious approaches to the problem. One would begin from the side of human language in its ordinary, intelligible usages, and would inquire whether and how this language can be legitimately stretched so that one can use it to talk about God. The obvious advantage of this approach is that it sets out from the solid ground of something that is familiar and intelligible. The second line of approach would begin by positing the reality of God, and would then bear in mind that if we do concede God's reality, then we must think of him as coming before everything else and as making possible everything else, including any knowledge of him or talk about him. So the inquiry would begin from God, and would ask what conditions would have to be fulfilled if the divine reality is to fall, at least to some extent, within the scope of human language. This second approach would seem to suffer from the disadvantage of trying to begin from the further side, as it were; but, on the other hand, it has the advantage of conforming to the universal pattern of religious experience, in which God is said to be known by revelation, that is to say, by an approach from the divine to the human, with the initiative on the side of the divine.

It is possible, however, that neither of these approaches, if taken in isolation, could be successful. Whether we set out from human language with the intention of talking about God, or whether we set out from the reality of God in order to discover how he can be expressed in human language, we might come to an impassable gulf. If we found ourselves in this embarrassment, we should have to look for a third approach, one that would somehow combine the merits of the other two but that would provide a bridge over the gulf—and a bridge strong enough to bear the very considerable volume of traffic that theologians want to send across.

What has been said here in a summary and abstract way will now be illustrated in more concrete detail by considering some representatives of the various possible approaches. Chiefly, we shall examine what has been said on this theme of theological language by three of the leading Protestant theologians of our time—Rudolf Bultmann, Karl Barth and Paul Tillich.

Let us begin with Bultmann. As everyone knows, he is a stern critic of every mythological way of talking about God. Mythology represents the divine as part of the objective world, as publicly manifesting itself in sensible phenomena, and as constantly intervening in the course of nature and history. In New Testament times, mythological ways of talking were still widely prevalent, although for a long time, among both Hebrews and Greeks, the cruder forms of myth had been subject to criticism and refinement. Nevertheless, the New Testament message has come down to us clothed, to some extent, in mythological garments. It is set in a framework of signs and wonders, of supernatural interventions actual or anticipated, and, above all, in the context of a vivid eschatology. In so far as the Church continues to proclaim the message with this mythological apparatus combined with it, then, Bultmann argues, the message is made something unintelligible for modern minds. Mythology has, in the scientific age, become a dead language, as mysterious and indecipherable as the linear scripts of the ancient Minoans—unless someone finds a key to break the code.

We should notice, of course, that the border between mythological and non-mythological tends, in practice, to be somewhat blurred. We find both ways of looking at the world together in the same person, and it may be that they have always been found side by side. H. J. Rose gives an interesting illustration of this.[1] He tells us that the ancient Italian farmer took care, at the appropriate season, to sacrifice a cow upon his land to the earth-goddess, Tellus Mater. The idea was that the goddess must be using up her stock of *numen*, on which the fertility of the land was supposed to depend, and so this stock had to be replenished by the sacrifice of an animal which had shown itself to possess fertility. Thus the farmer understood the fertility of his land in a mythical or crudely supernatural way, and performed the appropriate ritual act. But it would be a mistake to imagine that the farmer's ideas moved within the horizons of a religious or mythical mentality. What is interesting is the further point that Rose goes on to mention, namely, that the same farmer, from the earliest times of which there has survived any evidence, was by no means ignorant of the principles of

[1] *Religion in Greece and Rome* (New York: Harper & Row, 1959), pp. 166–7.

good agriculture. He was as careful to manure his fields regularly as he was to maintain the numinous power of the goddess! Presumably he saw no conflict between these actions, nor did he suppose that either of them rendered the other superfluous.

No doubt there are many people today who live in the modern world and perhaps even play their part in it as scientists or technicians, and who yet manage to go on talking about their religion in the mythological or quasi-mythological language of a past age. Almost certainly, the hard-headed, self-sufficient 'secular man' is much more of a *rara avis* than many of the books about him would lead us to believe. But is the double-think, that combines religious and matter-of-fact views of the world, logical? Or is it, as Bultmann says, 'a curious form of schizophrenia and insincerity' which leads to 'accepting a view of the world in our faith and religion which we should deny in our everyday life'?[1] Even if we have not arrived at the explicit *thought* of the world as a self-regulating cosmos, at least we all *act* as if the world were such that one event or set of events in it can be explained in terms of other events that are also within the natural world. And we do not need two explanations. Just as the modern farmer fertilizes his fields but does not waste money in sacrificing a cow besides, so, in the interests of logical economy, Occam's razor cuts away the mythological understanding of the world. No doubt mythology has a toughness that will keep it alive for a long time yet, and very likely this toughness is due to some inherent truth which mythology conceals in itself and which would be lost in any shallow positivistic understanding of the world. But Bultmann is right in maintaining that if modern man is to talk of God at all, it must be in some other language than that of myth.

To go on talking mythologically in the profane or secularized world which science discloses to us means in effect to maintain a superstition, in the sense of an *Aberglaube* or superfluous belief. But if the old myths contained some hidden insights, what language is now available for their expression? Bultmann, as is

[1] *Kerygma and Myth*, ed. H.-W. Bartsch (London: S.P.C.K., 1957), p. 4.

well known, recommends the way of demythologizing or existential interpretation. The meaning of the myths lies in what they obliquely express concerning our own existence. Thus, on his view, the story of creation is not an account of how things began, but an expression of man's understanding of his own finite and dependent status. The story of the fall does not recall some primal sin of humanity, the consequences of which are still working themselves out, but is an expression of man's awareness that his existence is not in order. The 'primitive mythology', to use Bultmann's own description,[1] of a divine Being who becomes incarnate and atones by his blood for human sins, is interpreted as the reorientation of human existence away from a world in which it has been scattered and broken up, toward the genuine selfhood from which it had been estranged. The myth of the resurrection expresses the new being which arises out of the reorientation. The eschatological myths of judgment and the end set forth the urgency of man's situation as one who is responsible for an unrepeatable existence lived always in the face of death.

All of this makes very good sense, salvaging the genuine insights of mythology and re-expressing them in an intelligible and convincing language. The new language, however, is intelligible precisely because it does not stray from the familiar territory of our own human existence and experience. So far, we have come no nearer to seeing how we can talk about God, and it is this talk about God that constitutes the problem for us. Indeed, it may already have occurred to us to ask whether, in the light of Bultmann's success in making sense of myth through existential interpretation, the idea of God should not be regarded as itself the last stronghold of myth, and subjected to the solvents of demythologizing. When, for instance, Bultmann tells us that 'God is the incomprehensible, enigmatic power that surges through my concrete life and sets limits to it',[2] what exactly differentiates this conception of God from what

[1] *Op. cit.*, p. 7.
[2] *Essays—Philosophical and Theological*, trans. James C. G. Greig (London: SCM Press, 1955), p. 8.

Bultmann elsewhere criticizes as a mythological understanding of the Holy Spirit in the New Testament, when he asserts that 'biological man cannot see how a supernatural entity like the *pneuma* can penetrate within the close texture of his natural powers and set to work within him'?[1] Should we not abandon altogether the notion of mysterious powers that break in upon our human existence? Or, if we do indeed have experiences of this kind, should we not explain them in terms of forces rising out of the subconscious depths of existence itself?

Or, to put the question differently, should God not go the way that the demons go in Bultmann's own demythologizing treatment of them? If the demonic can be understood in terms of factors operating within existence, so that one does not need to posit independently existing 'principalities and powers', cannot we do the same with the idea of God? In that case, the word 'God' would not be taken to denote some mysterious entity that is supposedly independent of human existence but would be simply a factor in existence itself, an archetypal idea or an imaginary focus of values or something of the sort. Some philosophers have in fact used the word 'God' in such ways. Examples are Herrmann Cohen in his neo-Kantian version of Judaism, and John Dewey in his sketch of a humanistic faith. If the word 'God' is understood in these ways, then God-talk presents no special difficulties. Language about God has become as thoroughly secularized as language about the world.

Bultmann, of course, does not demythologize God in the sense of making him simply an ideal of existence or a focus of value. On the contrary, Bultmann stresses the transcendence and initiative of God, and seems to think of autonomy (*Eigenständigkeit*) as the cardinal sin on man's part. But if God cannot be assimilated as a factor within human existence itself, then how do we talk about him? This question has troubled Bultmann for a long time. As early as 1935, he wrote an essay with the title, 'What Sense is there in Talking of God?'[2] Here he tells us

---

[1] *Kerygma and Myth*, p. 6.

[2] There is an. English translation by Franklin H. Littell in *The Christian Scholar*, vol. XLIII, pp. 213–22.

that one cannot talk about God as if he could be an object of thought, to be examined in detachment like other possible objects. 'God does not permit himself to be spoken of in general propositions, universal truths which are true without reference to the concrete existential situation of the one who is talking.' But in such a concrete situation, so it is maintained, if we have the experience of God's word directed to us or of his acting upon us, we can speak of him, though in doing so we must at the same time speak of ourselves. Bultmann quotes with approval a sentence from his old teacher, Wilhelm Herrmann: 'Of God we can tell only what he does to us.' Thus our talk of God cannot be considered in abstraction, but has sense only in the context of those concrete moments of experience in which he impinges on our existence. The allusion to Herrmann reminds us that Bultmann is not saying anything new here, for many theologians of the past have maintained that one cannot speak of God as he is in himself, but only as he relates himself to us. But then the question must arise as to whether God is anything other than a name for a factor in human existence itself. Is God a transcendent Other, who in his saving act or kerygmatic address comes to us from beyond our human existence? Or are such ideas simply a remnant of mythology, and what we call 'God' is simply the ideal possibility of existence that at once rebukes and attracts us as it confronts our actual disordered existence? When Bultmann himself uses the much-quoted sentence, 'The question of God and the question of myself are identical,'[1] he might seem to be lending countenance to a humanistic interpretation of the word 'God', though when the sentence is read in its context, it is clear that he had no such reductionist intention. One of Bultmann's disciples, Herbert Braun, has pushed the correlation of God-language and man-language so far as to get himself accused of atheism by Helmut Gollwitzer,[2] though I think myself that Gollwitzer has exaggerated his case.

[1] *Jesus Christ and Mythology* (New York: Scribners, 1958 and London: SCM Press, 1960), p. 53.
[2] *The Existence of God as Confessed by Faith* (London: SCM Press, 1964), pp. 81–97.

Nevertheless, the problem is an acute one both for Bultmann and for those who follow him in existential interpretation. Bultmann himself maintains, as I have mentioned, that the *seemingly* independent existence of alien demonic powers is a mythological expression for the state of affairs when man, by his own sinful decisions, enslaves himself to the world.[1] Heidegger points out that the call of conscience *seems* like a call from some power beyond ourselves, but it can be adequately described in terms of our own authentic selfhood, and if the call appears to come from beyond our own existence, this is only because for the most part we live so far from authentic selfhood that nothing could seem stranger to us.[2] Should not talk of God be interpreted in similar fashion? Are we not invited or even compelled to do so by Bultmann's own policy of demythologizing and existential interpretation, if we are going to take these seriously?

The problem of how to speak of God has continued to exercise Bultmann's mind, and in his later writings his solution takes the form of a distinction between the language of mythology and the language of analogy.[3] When we speak of God as acting, says Bultmann, we speak analogically, and the analogy is that of a personal encounter. We may agree that this way of talking about God is different from mythology, where God is spoken of as manifesting himself in natural events of a publicly observable character. We may agree also that when God in something like a personal encounter addresses a man in his responsibility and freedom, this is something different from the notion of a Spirit which takes possession of a man and causes him, let us say, to 'speak with tongues'. Thus analogy is itself a kind of demythologizing which has broken away from the objectifying language of myth. But what remains unclear is the question of how this analogical kind of demythologizing is related to the other kind— the kind in which mythology is translated into statements that refer to our own human existence. Obviously, there is a major

[1] *Theology of the New Testament* (London: SCM Press, 1952), vol I, p. 230.
[2] *Being and Time*, trans. J. Macquarrie and E. S. Robinson (London: SCM Press, 1962), pp. 319ff.
[3] *Jesus Christ and Mythology*, p. 68; cf. *Kerygma and Myth*, p. 196.

logical difference between existential language which refers directly to its proper subject (human existence), and existential language which is said to refer analogically to God as its subject. Bultmann nowhere seems to have paid sufficient attention to this logical difference, so that it remains as an unexplained leap or hiatus in his thought.

We are not, of course, asking for some *proof* that God acts on any particular occasion, for Bultmann rightly recognizes that such proof would be possible only if we could know God in some other way than through those acts of his that are recognized by faith, and his own view is that we know God only through his acts and that he is never accessible as some objective phenomenon. Nevertheless, we have a duty to ask about the logical structure of talking about God's acts. Especially when we remember that the call of conscience and the experience of the demonic appear to be adequately elucidated in terms of the structures of human existence itself, it becomes a burning question why God should be regarded differently, and taken for a transcendent power acting upon us from beyond the borders of our own existence. Surely the decision about this question cannot be just an arbitrary one. In so far as Bultmann fails to give a satisfying answer, we must conclude that the approach to theological language considered so far in this chapter, the approach that sets out from the side of human language, while it undoubtedly illuminates many things, comes to a halt at the crucial point where we want to extend it to God.

Let us turn next to Barth, and see whether he can help us. The very fact that Barth's theology is often called a 'theology of the Word' is itself indicative of the importance of language in his treatment of the theological theme. He says explicitly in the opening section of his *Church Dogmatics* that theology, in the strictest signification of the word, is a task for the Church, namely, 'the task of criticizing and revising her language about God'.[1] Bultmann too may be said to think of theology as the

---

[1] *Church Dogmatics*, trans. G. W. Bromiley, T. F. Torrance and others, 'The Doctrine of the Word of God' (Edinburgh: T. & T. Clark, 1936), vol. I/1, p. 2.

criticism and revision of the Church's language about God, but we should notice at once that Barth understands this task in a different and indeed almost contrary way from Bultmann. For Bultmann, the task is to revise and criticize the obsolete, unintelligible, mythological language, in order to express it, so far as possible, in a contemporary meaningful language about human existence. For Barth, the task is to revise and criticize the human language of theology so that, as near as possible, it becomes a vehicle for the divine word. He writes elsewhere: 'The subject of theology is the "Word of God". Theology is a science and teaching which *feels itself responsible* to the living command of this specific subject and to nothing else in heaven or in earth, in the choice of its methods, its questions and answers, its concepts and language, its goals and limitations.'[1]

The difference between Barth and Bultmann on this matter is brought out very sharply in what Barth has written in his little book on Bultmann. There he maintains that Bultmann, as an interpreter, feels himself primarily responsible to his contemporaries, that is to say, to those for whom his interpretation is intended. Bultmann must speak their language and use their concepts. Barth, on the other hand, holds that the interpreter's first responsibility is to the text which he interprets, and we have seen that in the case of theology, this means responsibility to the Word of God.[2] Of course, these two responsibilities are both real ones and they need not be thought to exclude one another,[3] but obviously there can be considerable differences of emphasis, and there is in fact a major difference in this matter between Barth and Bultmann. A further important criticism which Barth makes of Bultmann is to the effect that we mistake the character of myth if we attempt to submit it to an *exclusively* existential interpretation. This point, however, raises large

[1] See the foreword to the new edition of *Dogmatics in Outline* (New York: Harper & Row, 1959), p. 5.

[2] *Rudolf Bultmann: ein Versuch ihn zu verstehen* (Zürich: Evangelischer Verlag, 1952), p. 31. An English translation is available in *Kerygma and Myth*, vol. II (London: S.P.C.K., 1962), pp. 83ff.

[3] See my comments in *The Scope of Demythologizing* (London: SCM Press, 1960), pp. 35-36.

questions which will more properly call for discussion later in this book.

For the present, we note that for Barth the primary datum is the Word of God. To this alone, he tells us, the theologian is responsible. This seems to imply that any genuine discourse about God must come from the side of God himself. It is, of course, a first principle of Barth's epistemology that there is no way from man's natural understanding to the understanding of God. There is no 'natural theology', no path that leads from our everyday knowledge of things and persons in the world to the knowledge of God. Rightly or wrongly, Barth believes that Bultmann represents the Christian faith as the 'truly natural' understanding of human existence; and Barth himself would say that even the understanding of man's sin and fallen condition cannot be obtained from existential analysis alone, without the knowledge of what God has done about sin, in his saving activity.[1] Thus for Barth the problem of theological language resolves itself into the question of how the words of man can bring to expression the primary Word of God.

What then is this Word of God, which Barth holds to be the primary datum for all theological discourse? Barth tells us that the Word of God meets us in a threefold form—as the revealed Word, which centres on the person of Jesus Christ; as the written Word of the Holy Scriptures; and as the proclaimed Word of the Church. The revealed Word is foundational; it is prior to the other two forms of the Word, and engenders them. In saying this, Barth rightly focuses the revealing Word in the living person of Jesus Christ, rather than in any propositions about him. Yet we meet the foundational Word only through the mediacy of scripture and proclamation, and these three forms constitute a unity, from which, presumably, we must not isolate any single form. This unitary Word of God is, we are told, God's language.

Obviously, scripture and proclamation are language, but Barth insists that revelation too is language. Presumably this

[1] *Op. cit.*, pp. 14–15.

is not just the language of words and sentences, that is to say, the revelation is not given in the form of propositions or statements. But in a wider sense, perhaps one can say that revelation is language. If, in revealing, a person brings himself to expression and communicates himself, then these are the kind of activities that go on in language too. Moreover, it would seem that language, in the strictly verbal sense, is required if that which is revealed is to be understood and to become accessible to reflection. Hence it is right to insist that the foundational form of the Word must be held in unity with the derivative verbal forms of scripture and proclamation.

Something more should be said about the place of scripture in this doctrine of the Word of God. Barth has, of course, a very high regard for scripture, and the Bible is definitely integrated into the concept of the Word. This implies that the particular language of the Bible, rather than just any human language, has a special place. In fact, Barthian theology has been closely associated in the present century with biblical theology. But I do not think that this point can be pushed too far. Barth himself, in the development of his dogmatic system, has come to show an increasing respect for language which, though not itself biblical, has been adopted by classical Christian theology. Examples are trinitarian and christological language. The more extreme exponents of biblical theology, on the other hand, have tended to absolutize the language of the Bible and what they suppose to be the conceptuality of the Hebrew mind, as expressed in Semitic linguistic forms. In doing this, they have come near to setting up a new kind of 'verbal inspiration'. Barth, as it seems to me, while certainly claiming a special status for the Word of scripture, avoids giving to the biblical language a monopoly.

But to return to his doctrine of the Word of God, we note that he writes: 'We have no reason for not taking the concept "Word of God" in its primary and literal sense. "God's Word" means "God speaks". "Speaks" is not a symbol.'[1] Here Barth explicitly dissociates himself from the view of Tillich that to say 'God

[1] *Church Dogmatics*, vol. I/1, p. 150.

speaks' must be understood not literally but symbolically. Yet, on the other hand, Barth recognizes that because of the inadequacy of human language, the proposition 'God speaks' corresponds only in a broken way with the nature of the Word of God. And his subsequent analysis of the language of God suggests that there is a considerable element of metaphor in the expression, though he says that he is concerned only with the exegesis and not with the limitation or negation of the proposition, 'God speaks'.

Barth's elucidation of the proposition, 'God speaks', can only be summarized here. It seems to me that there are three salient points. The first is the spirituality of the Word of God. Its operation and its content are on the level of spirit, though Barth rightly notes that, as with all language, there is no Word of God without a physical event to embody it. The second point has to do with the personal character of the Word. The Word indeed is a person, Jesus Christ, though this personal character is said not to make the word any less verbal. This last point may seem strange, but it is, I think, acceptable if we accept that language is one of the most essential characteristics of personal being, so that to claim that the Word is personal is to acknowledge a fundamentally linguistic character belonging to it. The third salient point about the Word is its purposiveness. It is a reconciling Word addressed to man, a Word which, as it were, brings man into his true being.

Barth tells us furthermore that God's language has to be understood as God's act. Perhaps, in the terminology used by some linguistic analysts, we could say that this is a 'performative' language—a language not so much concerned with imparting information as with getting things done. Finally, the Word is to be understood as God's mystery. This is a Word (and again it could be said that this holds for any language) which at once reveals and veils him who speaks it.

Enough has been said to make it clear to us that God's Word is no ordinary word, and his language no ordinary language. The proposition 'God speaks', though we are asked to take it literally, is not to be understood like the proposition 'Socrates speaks'. By asking us to take the proposition literally, Barth does not mean that we are to expect to hear a 'voice from heaven' or anything of the sort. But it does not follow that propositions about God's speaking are therefore symbolic. If God does speak, then one would expect his speech to be of a unique and incomparable kind. I have suggested above that if one thinks of language in terms of self-expression and self-communication, then in this very wide sense, God's revelatory acts may be called 'language'. We may be reminded here of the even wider claim made by Bishop Berkeley, who thought of the whole creation as the language of God—an idea that has reappeared in various forms in idealist philosophy.

But if we are going to use the word 'language' in a very wide sense—and there would be justification for this, since we often talk of the 'language of the dance' and the like—then we would have to be very careful to keep this meaning of 'language' distinct from its more common meaning, where it refers to verbal language, to words and sentences. We would have to be specially careful not to move from statements about language in the wide sense to statements about language in its more specific sense. And as soon as we say this, we see that Barth's discussion has not really advanced us very far. We are still confronted with the difficulty of how this unique and exalted divine speech could possibly be expressed in human words and sentences. The difficulty is especially acute for Barth, for during most of his career his stress was upon the distance between the divine and the human, and even if he came to modify this and to recognize what he has called the 'humanity' of God, he has not relinquished his insistence on the utter inaccessibility of the divine from the human side. If he did, his whole system would collapse. We must ask then whether the breadth of the gulf does not make impossible the task of theology as Barth himself understands it, namely, the criticizing and revising of our language about God in obedience to the criterion of God's own language.

It might seem as if we were being driven to retreat into the *via negationis* and to an ultimate silence, listening to God's language but not attempting to reproduce it in any affirmations of our own. We have already seen the unsatisfactory nature of such a solution, and Barth's voluminous writings plainly testify that he does not accept it. Of course, we are to remember that, in Barth's theology, there is a great difference between the natural man who is indeed remote from God and the man who has been seized by divine revelation and grace, and made receptive to the truth of God by the Holy Spirit. Yet such a man continues to speak the same language as the natural man, or at least a language having the same basic structure. Is he then to confine himself to paradoxical utterances, as the divine language gets diffracted into the alien medium of our broken human speech? Everyone knows that Barth's own dialectical theology abounds in such paradoxes, and we have already come across some of them in considering what he says about language. Indeed, one of the major difficulties in the way of understanding, expounding and criticizing Barth's thought is just the fact that one can never take an isolated sentence or paragraph at face value without seeking to discover whether its assertion is not modified or corrected elsewhere by another sentence or paragraph of a seemingly contrary sense. Yet obviously the subtle and imposing structure of the *Church Dogmatics* is something much more than a collection of paradoxes, and, for that matter, theology could hardly claim to be an intellectual discipline if it did not attempt somehow to interpret and elucidate its paradoxes.

Barth does in fact offer a solution to the problem of how our human language can express God's own self-revealing Word and, just as we found in the case of Bultmann, the proffered solution leads us to a consideration of analogy. However, Barth's treatment of analogy is quite different from Bultmann's. Barth's fundamental principle that there is no way of access from the human side to the divine excludes the possibility that human language can be stretched so as to reach out to God. The kind of procedures described by the Bishop of Durham, whereby human 'models' are developed by means of 'qualifiers' to a point at which some 'disclosure' of the divine takes place,[1] are not permissible on Barth's view. As he sees it, there can be no progress along the *via eminentiae*, no matter to what degree of pre-eminence we seek to raise any human predicate: the ice will never break, the penny will never drop, the disclosure will never occur, to use the Bishop's expressions. Barth gives illustration after illustration of the impossibility of such disclosure. For instance, we cannot arrive at the understanding of God as Creator by stretching the language that refers to the ordinary human activity of making things, or of bringing them into being. 'We know,' writes Barth, 'originators and causes. We can extend their series into the infinite. When we reach the point at which we grow tired of extending it, we can call that point "God" or "Creator". But we cannot attain to the idea of the real Creator or the real creation. What we can represent to ourselves lies in the sphere of our own existence, and of existence generally, as distinct from God. If we do know about God as the Creator, it is neither wholly nor partially because we have a prior knowledge of something that resembles creation. It is only because it has been given to us by God's revelation to know him, and what we previously thought we knew about originators and causes is contested and converted and transformed.'[2] Of course, Ramsey too does not believe that there is a continuity between human analogues and the divine reality, and he posits a leap; but Barth denies that any such leap is possible. Thus he strictly preserves the initiative from the divine side.

But how then does our human language ever come to express a truth about God? Barth's final answer to this question is quite simple, and cuts straight through the knot. God graciously confers upon our human language the capacity to speak about himself. Just as God has condescended to become flesh in Jesus Christ, so he permits his divine speech to be expressed in human speech. This analogy is an *analogia gratiae*. It depends not on the characteristics of our human language but rather on what God

[1] Ian T. Ramsey, *Religious Language* (London: SCM Press, 1957), pp. 66ff.
[2] *Church Dogmatics*, 'The Doctrine of God' (Edinburgh: T. & T. Clark, 1957), vol. II/1, pp. 76–77.

does with that language. According to Barth, God *makes* our language about him *veridical*. He confers on it the capacity to speak meaningfully and truly about him.

But is this really a solution? We are inquiring about what meaning can be given to such sentences as 'God gives us his revelation' or 'God has made the world out of nothing', and we are told 'God gives meaning to these words' or 'God makes this language veridical', although the very expressions which trouble us are of the type 'God gives . . .' and 'God makes . . .' It may indeed be true that God is ontologically prior to everything else, that everything gets its meaning from him, that language too is his creation. These points are not to be ignored, but they do not answer the kind of question that has been engaging our attention. Barth's proffered solution of the problem of how we talk about God has been aptly described by Frederick Ferré as the 'logic of obedience',[1] and perhaps it is the only solution open to Barth, once his presuppositions have been accepted. Just as the Word becomes flesh in Jesus Christ, so God condescends to let his language be expressed in human speech, and how this happens is a mystery, to inquire into which too critically might even be esteemed a mark of sinful pride. When we remember, however, that the Barthian solution is only one of several that are offered by contemporary theologians, perhaps we shall not be deterred from pressing on with our inquiry, and seeing whether any further elucidation can be obtained about the logic of God-talk.

The position now reached is that we have seen both Bultmann and Barth building out from opposite sides, Bultmann from the side of human language, Barth from the side of divine language. But neither of them has been able to get to the other side, save by an arbitrary leap, and the logic of this remains quite obscure, except that it is supposed to have something to do with analogy. Bultmann's leap occurs when he gives up talking about possibilities of human existence and applies the language of such existence analogically to God. Barth's leap occurs when he

---

[1] *Language, Logic and God* (London: Eyre and Spottiswoode, 1962), p. 84.

appeals to the *analogia gratiae,* whereby the incomparable divine language becomes expressible in broken human words by a mysterious act of divine grace. I believe that both of these theologians have important and instructive things to say about language, but there seems to be something missing in each case. What is missing is a firm logical bridge, that can unite language about man and language about God; or perhaps I should say that what is missing is the central span of the bridge, Barth and Bultmann having built the opposite ends of it.

We now call our third theological witness, Paul Tillich. He too has much to say about language, and of course he has much in common with both Bultmann and Barth. Tillich's method of correlation, whereby theology sets out from the questions posed by man's existence, links him closely with Bultmann. His insistence that the answers are to be sought in revelation relates him to both Barth and Bultmann, and indeed to a whole generation of Protestant theologians. Tillich, however, takes up a much more positive attitude towards symbolism and imagery than does Bultmann, and believes that such symbolism is both valuable and irreplaceable, provided its symbolic character is recognized. We have already noted that Tillich differs also from Barth in this matter of symbolism, for he insists on the symbolic character of such an expression as 'God speaks', which Barth wants to take in a direct literal sense.

But the important contribution which Tillich makes to the problem of theological language is that he seems to provide the logical bridge (or one span of such a bridge) that was missing in Barth and Bultmann. It is true that at first sight the bridge may appear to us a very slender and shaky one. The bridge consists in the language of 'being' and, implicit in this language, a version of the traditional doctrine of an *analogia entis.*

Let us begin from an often quoted passage of Tillich's writing: 'The statement that God is Being-itself is a non-symbolic statement. It does not point beyond itself. It means what it says directly and properly; if we speak of the actuality of God, we first assert that he is not God if he is not Being-itself. Other assertions about God can be made theologically only on this basis.'[1]

Admittedly, this passage presents great difficulties of interpretation. My own suspicion is that the statement that 'God is Being-itself', along with the similar statement that 'he is not God if he is not Being-itself,' is simply a definition, that is to say, an announcement of the way in which Tillich proposes to use the word 'God'. This word is to stand for Being, not for some being or for something that is. If this is a correct analysis of the language, then to say that God is Being-itself is not to make a non-symbolic statement about God or indeed to make any kind of statement about him at all; it is simply to make a statement about how the word 'God' is to be understood.

Tillich himself had second thoughts about the passage quoted, and he later declared that the only non-symbolic assertion we can make about God is 'the statement that everything we say about God is symbolic'.[2] However, he immediately goes on to make a vigorous and, on the whole, successful defence of his use of the expression 'being' in speaking of God. Although his initial attempt to explicate the use of 'Being-language' in respect of God was confused, and although this confusion was compounded through his use of such ambiguous expressions as 'ground of being,' 'power of being' and the like, his insight into the role of this language was essentially correct. In summary fashion, one could express his insight somewhat as follows. 'Being' is the word which bridges the gap between ordinary talk and God-talk. We *are*, the world *is*, and God 'is' Being-itself. Moreover, since every symbol participates in the being of that which it symbolizes, the notion of 'being' serves also as the basis for all indirect symbolic statements which may be made about God, after one has defined 'God' as 'Being-itself'. For everything that is participates in Being-itself (God) and has therefore the possibility of functioning as a symbol of God.

These remarks help us to see more clearly where Tillich's

[1] *Systematic Theology*, vol. I (London: Nisbet, 1953), pp. 264–5.
[2] *Op. cit.*, vol. II (London: Nisbet, 1957), p. 10.

understanding of theological language differs from the views of Bultmann and Barth. Tillich himself distinguishes his theological position from that of Bultmann chiefly in respect of its ontological character. It is a curious fact that Bultmann, who owes so much to Heidegger's existential analytic, shows no apparent interest in following him into his ontological researches, to which the existential analytic was intended to be only a preliminary. Barth, on the other hand, is strongly opposed to acknowledging any *analogia entis*, and, presumably with a view to upholding the divine transcendence, explicitly denies that 'being' can provide a basis on which to talk about God.[1]

We have said that at first sight the ontological bridge which Tillich offers seems to be somewhat slender or even shaky. Can such an apparently abstract and even vacuous concept as 'being' bear the weight which we are invited to lay upon it? Nietzsche thought that this word is merely a haze, and many contemporary philosophers would agree that talk of 'being' is sheer mystification. Critics of Tillich usually fasten somewhere on his use or misuse of the expression 'being',[2] so it might seem as if I had chosen the weakest element in Tillich's system to supplement the deficiencies that we found in Bultmann and Barth!

I think, however, that most of these criticisms of Tillich have completely missed the mark. They simply repeat ancient nominalist prejudices without seeing that these do not even remotely apply to Tillich's talk about 'Being-itself'. If this expression were supposed to refer to some highly abstract universal, at which we arrive by abstracting every determinate characteristic from the sum total of whatever is, then the criticisms might be just. But Tillich makes it abundantly clear that his expression 'Being-itself' is no abstraction, but something entirely concrete, namely in his words the 'power of being in everything that has being'.[3] I have already indicated that the expression 'power of being' is an unfortunate and ambiguous one, but in this same passage

[1] *Church Dogmatics*, vol. II/1, p. 243.
[2] E.g., J. Heywood Thomas, *Paul Tillich: an Appraisal* (London: SCM Press, 1963), p. 36.
[3] *Systematic Theology*, vol. II, p. 12.

Tillich mentions Heidegger as one who has in recent times re-discovered the significance of the expression 'Being'. Although Tillich himself probably owes more to Schelling and to Boehme than to Heidegger, it is to the last named that we must turn if we want to get clarification of this talk about 'Being'. Heidegger is much more careful in his language than Tillich, and I have tried to show elsewhere[1] that his talk about 'Being' is so far from having an abstract or speculative character that it is rooted in the most concrete existential experience—the experience of finitude as possible ceasing-to-be, which for the first time awakens the wondering awareness of being. But it may readily be conceded that Being-talk calls for much more elucidation and we shall try to give this in due course. For the present, however, it has seemed necessary to offer this provisional rebuttal of nominalist criticisms.

While Tillich has been cited as the third theologian whose views on language might help to bridge over the gaps left by the other two, we have already seen that the philosophical thought of Martin Heidegger lies behind Tillich's understanding of Being and thus of God. It is not surprising that Heidegger's influence exerts itself very powerfully in current theological discussions concerning language and hermeneutics.[2] In these discussions, an attempt is made to give a place both to an existential dimension of understanding and to the priority of God in any 'Word of God'. Heinrich Ott has undertaken the specific task of mediating between Bultmann and Barth on the basis of Heidegger.[3] But it seems to me that he has not been nearly radical enough in his appropriation of Heidegger. If he had been, he would have acknowledged that Heidegger's philosophy provides the material for a new kind of 'natural' theology; and he would have seen that, in Heidegger, Being is sufficiently divine to make any other kind of God superfluous. Indeed,

[1] 'The Language of Being' in *Studies in Christian Existentialism* (London: SCM Press, 1966), pp. 79ff.
[2] Cf. *New Frontiers in Theology*, ed. J. M. Robinson and J. B. Cobb: vol. I, 'The Later Heidegger and Theology'; vol. II, 'The New Hermeneutic' (New York: Harper & Row, 1963 and 1964).
[3] Cf. *Denken und Sein* (Zollikon: Evangelischer Verlag, 1959).

Heidegger's philosophy has no room for a substantial God, any more than it has for a substantial self. At the same time, it points the way toward reconceiving God and the self without the notion of substantiality.

Our study of the conceptions of language to be found in three of the leading Protestant theologians of our time must certainly have convinced us of the centrality and importance of the issue in current debate. But it has also become clear that the whole subject is a confused one, with wide divergencies of opinion. Bultmann has shown admirably that language about the possibilities of human existence can play a major part in the elucidation of theological statements, but he leaves us in doubt as to whether God-talk is going to collapse completely into talk about ourselves. Barth is true to the pattern of Christian (and religious) experience in insisting on the primacy of revelation, a Word that comes from God to man, but he gives no satisfactory account of how such a word could ever be expressed in a human language. Tillich introduces a mediating conception in the notion of 'being' which may somehow link God (Being-itself) to the multiplicity of finite persons and things that *are* in the world, but many obscurities still surround this talk.

If we are to make any progress toward resolving these conflicts and toward arriving at a more satisfactory account of theological language, we shall have to leave for a while the area of theological debate and turn to an inquiry into the nature of language in general. This is one of many cases in which the theologian, whether he is willing or unwilling, is constrained to enlist the help of the philosopher. The theologian talks about language, and he must have some idea, explicit or implicit, of what language is. If he is wise, he will pay attention to what has been said on the subject by those who have made language the specific theme of their researches. So we must turn now to philosophers and others who have studied these matters, and see what we can learn about the nature and functions of language, its scope and its limitations.

# 3

## Some General Reflections on Language

THE WIDE DISAGREEMENTS among theologians as to how they think they must construct their theological discourse has compelled us to take up the problem of language in a more general way. Indeed, we could hardly have any adequate understanding of theological language or any other specialized kind of language unless we had some grasp of language in general. What are its nature and functions, its scope and limitations, its varieties and its universal characteristics? These are far-reaching questions, and certainly we cannot embark upon a task so vast and complex as that of attempting to construct a philosophy of language. Yet we must try to get light on some of the fundamental issues.

It is at once obvious that the question, 'What is language?', is a highly peculiar one. It is so because, in order to ask the question, we have to make use of the very language about which we are asking. This implies that before we ask the question, we must already have some understanding of language in order to be able to ask the question at all. So perhaps the answering of the question consists in no more than making explicit and clarifying as far as possible the understanding of language which we already have. To ask the question of language is possible only for one who, so to speak, exists linguistically. This question about language might be compared with Heidegger's question, 'What is the meaning of "being"?', where the question already employs the verb 'to be'; or possibly with Frege's question,

'What is the number one?', for unity also would seem to be presupposed in even the simplest kind of discourse.

It would seem that little is to be gained by spending time over speculations concerning the empirical question about the origin of language. We are confronted with language as a distinctively human phenomenon—at least, in ordinary experience, and leaving aside the question of whether there could be, as Barth thinks, anything that might properly be called 'divine language'. Very probably it is the case that human language evolved out of animal cries through a process in which these cries received form and structure and so were made capable of bearing meaning. But this process must have included a step of the kind which some philosophers call an 'emergence', that is to say, a step which results in the appearance of a characteristic possessing a novel qualitative unity, such that it is not explicable simply in terms of the antecedent elements out of which it has arisen.

It is true enough that in some sense the germ of the emergent characteristic was already present in the antecedent elements, but this is something which we do not perceive from the elements themselves, but only by looking back upon them as they appear in the light of the new characteristic that has emerged. We do not understand the higher in terms of the lower; rather, it is only in the light of the higher that for the first time we perceive the latent potentialities of the lower. The warning cry of a bird, for instance, is presumably an instinctive emotional reaction on the part of the bird when perhaps it sees a cat coming into the garden, and the reaction of other birds in the neighbourhood is similarly instinctive. But from the point of view of a human observer, the warning cries can be seen as pointing the way toward language, because they have an indicative and even an informative potential. We interpret the lower levels by abstraction from what we already know about the higher levels; we do not understand these higher levels by trying to piece them together from the factors operating on lower levels.

These brief remarks on the question of the origin of language have tended to confirm our suspicion that the study of this particular question would turn out to be a blind alley for any investigation into the nature of language. At the same time, we have also been put on our guard against any naturalistic accounts of language, such as attempts to explain human language in terms of subhuman factors. (In this chapter, I am using the word 'naturalistic' in its traditional sense, as referring to naturalism of the reductionist type, and clearly my remarks would not apply to the naturalism of such philosophers as A. N. Whitehead.)

A good example of such a naturalistic account of the matter is afforded by the view of language once put forward very persuasively by Bertrand Russell.[1] Pressing into service the behaviouristic psychology, he described language in terms of a causal interaction between the organism and its environment. On this view, the laws of logic are, at bottom, connected with the laws of physics. Spoken words are physical events in the speech organs, and have an arrangement in time; similarly, written words are physical markings on paper or some other material, and they have an arrangement in space. In each case, according to Russell, the arrangement copies or pictures the structure of some fact in the physical environment. The meaning of the words is the behavioural response which they produce in the hearer, and this is said to be analogous to a conditioned reflex in an animal.

It will not surprise us that Russell is eventually able to draw from his theory the conclusion that our language and therefore our knowledge is confined to the physical world. He writes: 'I am inclined to think that quite important metaphysical conclusions, of a more or less sceptical kind, can be drawn from simple considerations as to the relation between language and things. A spoken sentence consists of a temporal series of events; a written sentence is a spatial series of bits of matter. Thus it is not surprising that language can represent the course of events in the physical world; it can, in fact, make a map of the physical world, preserving its structure in a more manageable form, and

[1] *An Outline of Philosophy* (London: Allen & Unwin, 1927), pp. 46–60.

it can do this because it consists of physical events. But if there were such a world as the mystic[1] postulates, it would have a structure different from that of language, and would therefore be incapable of being verbally described.'[2]

The criticism of this naturalistic account of language is the same kind of criticism that may be made of any type of reductive naturalism—namely, that it proceeds by a one-sided abstraction which utterly distorts the phenomenon that is to be described. Russell is right in drawing attention to the fact that words and sentences, whether written or spoken or perhaps even thought (spoken inwardly), can be considered as physical entities, and probably this fact has too often been overlooked in speculations about language. But while words and sentences have their physical substratum, what is distinctive about them is not their physical but their human aspect, as bearers of understanding and meaning in the intelligent and evaluating community of human beings. It is precisely this distinctive characteristic of language—admittedly one which has almost certainly 'emerged' from a physical background—that Russell minimizes or ignores in his attempt to give an account of language in physical terms. However, like naturalistic philosophies in general, Russell's account of language is more easily held in theory than in practice, and his own uses of language make clear the inadequacy of his theory of language. Wilbur M. Urban has shrewdly pointed out that when Russell writes on political or social problems, he conveniently sets aside his ingenious theories about language.[3]

It is even doubtful whether the 'copy' or 'picture' theory of language has validity in talking about the physical world itself. It may indeed have a rough-and-ready applicability to much of our everyday talk about perceptible facts, but it is questionable how far it would apply to scientific descriptions of the physical

[1] Russell uses the term 'mystic' in a very general and imprecise way for anyone holding a religious belief, or for anyone who believes in a reality somehow transcending the physical world.

[2] *Op. cit.*, p. 275.

[3] *Language and Reality* (London: Allen & Unwin, 1939), p. 306.

world. According to some of the ablest exponents of modern physics, this science does not 'picture' the constituents of the physical worlds, for they cannot be pictured at all. The language 'symbolizes' them. At least some physicists are prepared to recognize that this new way of understanding the language of physics opens the way to a wider understanding of reality than the old-style naturalism permitted.[1]

If physical scientists themselves no longer think that their language 'pictures' the physical world, then Russell's theory is in serious trouble. In particular, his argument that because language itself is a physical occurrence, it can picture the physical world but not what Russell is pleased to call the 'world of the mystic', falls to the ground. We seem nowadays forced to recognize that ordinary language can 'picture' neither the one world nor the other; and it remains a question whether language, in some stretched or specialized usage, may be as well or as little able adequately to symbolize the world of the physicist or the world of the mystic.

The truth is that Russell's argument has nothing to do with drawing 'metaphysical conclusions' from 'simple considerations' about language. His argument really goes the other way round. It rests on the presupposition that the real is the physical, and it is on the basis of this prejudice that Russell constructs his theory of language. Then, of course, his eventual 'conclusion' that language is limited to talking of the physical is seen to be nothing but the assumption from which he started out.

These criticisms of a naturalistic theory of language should be borne in mind in any attempt to evaluate the logical positivism[2] which, however Russell may eventually have thought about it, owed very much to him in its early stages. The thesis of logical positivism was that informative propositions are restricted to the physical world, and that sentences that purport

[1] See the chapter 'Language and Reality in Modern Physics' in Werner Heisenberg, *Physics and Philosophy* (New York: Harper & Row, 1958 and London: Allen & Unwin, 1959), pp. 167ff.

[2] For a discussion of logical positivism and logical analysis, see below, Chapter 5, pp. 102ff.

to tell us about anything beyond the world of the senses are, strictly speaking, nonsense; and this thesis was supposed to be based on the logic of language itself. But in the light of all that has happened in the world of philosophy since, one may ask: 'The logic of what language?' And when this question is asked, it is easy to see that the logical positivists already presupposed a naturalistic theory of language, in which the primacy of the physical has been conceded. Ludwig Wittgenstein, for instance, expounds in the *Tractatus Logico-Philosophicus* a 'picture' or 'copy' theory of language of the kind that we have already met in Russell; and he too concludes that we can talk about the world of the senses but must be silent about the 'mystical'.

The sceptical conclusions of logical positivism did not flow, as was sometimes naively supposed, from an unbiased examination of the logic of language, but from arbitrarily assuming that one kind of language has a paradigmatic character; or, to put the matter differently, from naturalistic presuppositions about language—presuppositions which turn out to be themselves of a definitely metaphysical kind. Thus logical positivism, so far from ending metaphysics, had its own metaphysical presuppositions. This is particularly evident in the case of the famous verification principle, the doctrine that a sentence can be regarded as a meaningful assertion only if some sense-experience is relevant to its verification. 'The fact is,' writes John Wisdom, 'the verification principle is a metaphysical proposition—a "smashing" one, if I may be permitted the expression.'[1]

If, as we have said, a distorting abstraction is the principal vice of naturalism, one may say that this abstraction is carried to extreme lengths in logical positivism. Language was treated by the positivists as something that could exist and be studied in a vacuum, cut off from the personal existence and the concrete world in which language arises and has its life. This error may be described as the failure to distinguish language and discourse, and to this distinction we shall return in due course.

But someone may think we have spent too much time in

[1] *Philosophy and Psychoanalysis* (Oxford: Blackwell, 1953), p. 245.

flogging dead horses. Few philosophers nowadays seem willing to be called 'logical positivists' and perhaps few would subscribe to the behaviouristic theories of language that were once popular. Everyone knows that the logical positivism of an earlier time has passed into logical analysis or logical empiricism. The later Wittgenstein of the *Philosophical Investigations* himself made it clear that one cannot lay down in advance that one kind of language is meaningful and other kinds nonsense, but that one must recognize that there are many kinds of languages, and that the meaning of each is to be studied from the way in which it gets used. One welcomes this broadening of horizons among the adherents of this school of philosophy, but perhaps it is easy to exaggerate its significance. It does not mean, for instance, that the philosophical movement stemming from Wittgenstein has suddenly become more friendly towards the claims of theological or religious language, even if it is now less violently iconoclastic. It is true that theological language is no longer summarily dismissed as nonsense. It has, so to speak, been granted a reprieve and an opportunity to show its credentials. But it is noticeable that even those members of the school who are favourably disposed toward religion tend to find the meaning of theological language in practical and social terms, and are very hesitant about allowing for the possibility that God-talk may indeed refer to some transhuman reality, as people have always naively supposed. That is to say, these philosophers give to theological language a much more positivistic sense than the theologian himself would normally claim for it. There seem to be some grounds for the fear expressed by Carl Michalson who, on looking at contemporary empiricism, told us that he got 'the sense of the ghost of logical positivism lingering in its procedures.'[1]

Over against the views of language which we have so far considered stands an alternative tradition. This may be broadly described as the idealist tradition. In this way of looking at things, primacy belongs not to the physical but to the mental.

[1] 'The Ghost of Logical Positivism' in *The Christian Scholar*, vol. XLIII/3, p. 226.

Language is seen not as a product of the physical environment's interaction with the organism, but as a creation of the thinking subject which, by means of language, goes out into the world and gives it form and order—indeed, one might almost say, makes a *world* out of the manifold of sense-data. Language can be regarded as 'objectified spirit'.

Such views are not much in evidence today, for almost everywhere the idealism of an earlier time has been superseded by empiricism, existentialism or other contemporary styles of philosophy. Yet the idealist view of language would seem to have had in it some elements needed for the correction of the onesidedness of naturalistic accounts. The idealists were, within limits, justified in stressing the active and creative aspects of language, which get overlooked in naturalistic theories. On the other hand, idealist theories may readily fall into a one-sidedness of their own through their preoccupation with the thinking subject. If naturalism suffers from abstractness, one must also say that the pure subject is an abstraction from the concrete reality of being-in-the-world. As far as our special problem, that of language, is concerned, it is hard to see how there could be thought, or at least thought that has any degree of coherence and logical structure, without the physical medium of language. Again, while it is true that language shapes and even, in a sense, creates our world, it is equally true that the physical environment shapes our language. To give an example, it is stated that African tribes which live by hunting have a rich vocabulary for distinguishing the finest shades of difference in the colour of the vegetation, but that they have no words at all for distinguishing between, let us say, red and blue.[1] It is easy to give a distorted account of language and to overlook inconvenient facts if one starts out with a prejudice in favour of the primacy either of the physical or of the mental. Surely language is a phenomenon that shows as clearly as any the interaction and interdependence of mental and physical in concrete existence.

[1] See the article 'Sprache' in *Philosophisches Wörterbuch*, ed. Heinrich Schmidt and Georgi Schischkoff (Stuttgart: Alfred Kröner, 1957), p. 567.

While both naturalism and idealism have no doubt something of value to teach us about language, the initial presuppositions of these viewpoints introduce distortions into their accounts of the matter. If we are to avoid the dangers inherent in their respective accounts, we must put their presuppositions into brackets and attempt a purely phenomenological analysis of language. This means in effect that we take developed human speech as we find it, and endeavour to discern what phenomena go to constitute it and what conditions must be fulfilled for its functioning. As I indicated at the beginning of the chapter, this may amount to no more than making explicit that understanding of language which is already implied in our own linguistically constituted existence, evidenced in our ability to use language so that we can ask the question, 'What is language?'

What then do we have in mind when we use such words as 'saying', 'speaking', 'talking' and the like? It may be helpful as a beginning to consider the etymology of verbs of saying, although to introduce etymological considerations can have only a limited value and one would certainly not wish to base an argument upon them.[1] Nevertheless, one can hardly fail to be impressed on noticing how many verbs of saying can be traced back to roots signifying 'light', so that to 'say' something seems originally to have meant to 'bring it into the light'. The English word 'say' is a causative form cognate with 'see', and was thus originally 'cause to see' or 'let see'. The Greek *phēmi*, 'say', is connected with *phaino*, 'show, bring to light', and so with *phōs*, 'light'. The Latin *dicere*, 'say' is cognate with Greek *deiknūmi* and with German *zeigen*, both meaning 'show'; while all three words probably go back to an old Indo-European root, *di*, signifying 'bright' or 'shining'. These connections with light are not confined to Indo-European verbs of saying. When we turn to the Semitic languages, we are told that the common Hebrew verb *'āmar*, 'say', is likewise connected with the idea of 'showing',

---

[1] James Barr has shown some of the errors into which theologians have fallen through an uncritical appeal to the etymologies of words. See his *Semantics of Biblical Language* (London: Oxford University Press, 1961), pp. 107ff.

and eventually with such simple notions as 'prominent', 'bright', 'visible'.

The list of words could be expanded, but we already have quite an impressive accumulation of evidence as to what men had in mind when they first used verbs of saying. This strongly suggests that at least one characteristic of saying anything, and perhaps even the fundamental characteristic, is that what is talked about is brought into the light. That is to say, what is talked about is made to stand out from the undifferentiated background of all that may be vaguely present to our minds at any given time, or even what may be in our memory or our anticipation. It is brought into the focus of attention and is shown for what it is. To put it in another way, that which is talked about is manifested and made unhidden; and, as Heidegger never tires of pointing out,[1] 'unhiddenness' or *alētheia* is precisely the expression which the Greeks used to express the notion of 'truth'. We speak truly if we make what we are talking about unhidden.

Now, if 'saying' means something like 'causing to see' or 'letting see', it is at once obvious that the kind of relationship involved in saying anything is considerably more complex than what is involved in seeing anything. When I see something, only two terms are involved—myself, and whatever is seen. Of course, we all know that a very complex mechanism is required for an act of seeing. Nevertheless, the relation of seeing as we actually experience it, the relation between myself and what is seen, is one of the most direct that we know. To see something or someone, so we believe, is to stand in a direct and intimate relation to that thing or person. But saying shows itself to be a phenomenon that implies a much more intricate kind of relation. In the first place, it typically involves three terms instead of only two. Thus it consistutes a three-cornered or triadic relation. The three terms are, of course, the person who says something, the matter about which he says it, and the person or persons to whom he says it. Ideally, this threefold structure is always dis-

[1] *Being and Time*, p. 265, etc.

cernible, even on occasions when two or even three of the terms of the relation happen to coincide, as on the rare occasions on which I say something to myself, or the still rarer occasions on which I say something to myself about myself. In the second place, the relation involved in saying does not have the directness of an act of seeing, for we have still to take account of a fourth factor—what is said, namely, the words and sentences,

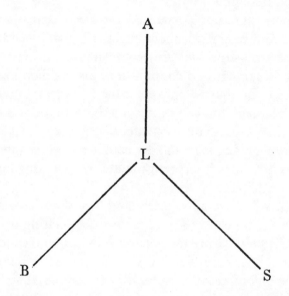

or the language. It is language which mediates the triadic relation, and indeed constitutes it. If A stands for the person who says something, B for the person to whom something is said, S for the matter about which something is said, and L for what is actually said, then we may represent an act of saying as shown in the diagram.

The complex relation thus schematized may be conveniently called the 'discourse-situation'. What I want to maintain is that any discussion about the meaning of language, in the sense of words and sentences, must have regard to the discourse-situation in which that language has arisen. This remark gives point to a criticism that was earlier made in summary fashion, when it was said that the logical positivists tended to treat language as something existing in a vacuum, so to speak, and that they failed to distinguish between language and discourse. Language might be described as the precipitate of the discourse-situation. It has its life in that situation, and indeed is the focus and the bearer of what is going on in the situation, but cut off from it, language is an abstraction which may readily die and become unintelligible.

This point must not be pushed too far. Because languages are public and historical phenomena, they transcend all particular discourse-situations and could be said to have a life of their own. Meanings and connotations are public, not private, and so it may be that when something is said in a given situation, the language might imply something more or something different than was explicitly intended by the speaker. This characteristic of language makes possible misunderstanding and also makes necessary interpretation and the working out of hermeneutic principles.

Yet even when we allow that language does have a certain life of its own, we can still see the need for relating it to its discourse-situation if we are to confront it in its living concreteness. The point is well expressed by Urban who calls language the '*petrifact* of living creative speech'.[1] It follows that a logical analysis of words and sentences that have been abstracted from their discourse-situation cannot conclusively pronounce about the meaning or lack of meaning in this language. It may be that there are some modes of discourse of such a kind that the language can be abstracted from the discourse-situation without suffering any serious distortion of meaning, and that in such cases a logical (syntactical) analysis of language is all that is required. But all discourse-situations are not of the same kind. A poetic or paradoxical utterance, for example, might appear complete nonsense when subjected in abstraction to logical analysis; indeed, a paradox could appear as nothing but nonsense or self-contradiction if we had regard only to the internal

[1] *Op. cit.*, p. 67.

syntax of the language, but such utterances, poetical and para-doxical, might make very good sense in their own discourse-situations. This may remind us of the theological debates mentioned near the beginning of this book.[1] Viewed in abstraction, they looked rather silly, but we thought it likely that at least some of them had dealt with very real issues in their own historical situations. The discourse-situation is the 'home' of language, and we can judge it properly only when we see it in its home.

Probably scientific language is the kind that gets along best in abstraction from any discourse-situation. Such language has a universality that may be traced in turn to its initial abstractness. The failure of the logical positivists to distinguish between language and discourse is just one more evidence of their initial prejudice in favour of the physical, and their tacit acceptance of language about the physical as the norm for all language—the doctrine of 'physicalism', as taught by Carnap and others.

The concept of 'discourse' is wider than that of 'language'. Perhaps the distinction is more clearly maintained among German philosophers. 'Discourse' or 'talk' corresponds to *Rede*, the living speech, which may be distinguished from *Sprache*, words and sentences. 'Discourse' corresponds likewise to the *logos* of the Greeks, and it is noteworthy that they do not seem to have had any word for language as such. Discourse always includes the triadic relation which we have already outlined. Since at least two of the three terms of this relation are persons, namely, the person who speaks and the person (or persons) to whom he addresses himself, it follows that discourse always has a personal dimension. Talk is always somebody's talk, and is addressed to somebody. This personal dimension may be more or less important in different types of discourse, but it is never entirely absent, since discourse takes place only in a community of persons. When we consider the language only, we are leaving out this personal dimension, and so depersonalizing the

[1] See above, p. 12.

discourse. Sometimes it may be desirable to do this, but some-times such a procedure could utterly distort and obscure the meaning of the discourse.

Science, as we shall see in due course, uses a highly deper-sonalized type of discourse. This brings advantages when we have certain tasks in view, but it does not entitle us to suppose that the language of science has a normative status. In any case, even scientific discourse retains in some measure the triadic character of all discourse.

Our study of language then has directed us to the wider phenomenon of discourse, within which language functions as the focal and constitutive element. So far, however, we have before us only a bare schema, showing the minimal structure of a discourse-situation. The next stage in our phenomenological analysis of saying must be to fill in with more detail what is involved when someone (A) says something (L) to someone (B) about something (S).

Let us take our departure from the person who does the saying —from the point A in our diagram. When this person says any-thing, he expresses himself. Discourse is therefore *expression*, and the medium of this kind of expression is language. In recognizing the element of expression in language, we are doing justice to its existential dimension, and also to the idealist insistence on the active and creative character of language, as what gives shape to our world. We do not mean, of course, that some isolated thinking subject objectifies itself or its ideas in a world. Human existence is not adequately conceived as a bare thinking subject that has to relate itself to a world. The existent is already a being-in-the-world; it is always self and world together, and these, though distinguishable, are not separable. So we must say that when someone speaks, what expresses itself is existence in the world, or being-in-the-world.

There would seem to be different modes of expression, and these differ according to the degrees in which existence ex-presses itself. It is interesting to recall that Martin Buber began *I and Thou* by talking about language, and the different extents to which we put *ourselves* into what we say. He observes that there are two primary word-combinations, I-Thou and I-It, and he goes on to remark: 'The primary word "I-Thou" can only be spoken with the whole being; the primary word "I-It" can never be spoken with the whole being.'[1] If we were to revert to our own terminology, as used in this book, we might say that Buber is drawing attention here to the different degrees in which existence may come to expression in discourse. In some forms of discourse, total existence (being-in-the-world) gets expressed; in other forms, some aspects of existence get excluded from expression.

By the expression 'total existence', as used in the last paragraph, I mean the full range of what is implied in being a self-in-the-world. In such 'total existence', there is no sharp objectification of the world. The self and the world are expressed together, as the inclusive situation where the self finds itself in its world. Perhaps this is the primordial kind of discourse from which all other modes are derived.

It is possible, however, to modify the kind of discourse in which total existence gets expressed. This modification takes place by dimming down, as it were, certain aspects of existence in the world, so as to concentrate attention on other aspects. In particular, it is possible to dim down whatever belongs to the side of the self or to personal being, such as feeling, volition, value-judgments, concern and so on, so that the self remains as a mere point, a cognitive subject which stands over against its object. In the course of what we have called the 'dimming down' of some of the dimensions of the original self-world relation, the situation of a participant has been reduced to that of an observer or spectator. The spectator does not express 'total existence'. What finds expression in his utterance is simply a report of the 'objective facts'. These, in turn, are obviously never more than an abstraction from 'total existence', that is to say, from the full range of being-in-the-world. Of course, such

[1] *I and Thou*, trans. R. Gregor Smith (Edinburgh: T. & T. Clark, 2nd edition, 1958), p. 3.

an abstraction will, under many circumstances, be extremely useful. Ability to cut out some aspects of our experience and to concentrate on others is indispensable if we are to organize our knowledge of the world and learn to predict and manage the phenomena that we meet within it.

Damage is only done if people come to suppose that this abstract kind of discourse shows us all that there 'really is'. What we have called 'total existence' is forgotten, or its expression is considered to be a subjective or emotive business, of no cognitive significance. This leads straight into the positivistic view, where the abstract language of science, expressing only what can be objectively observed by the thinking subject, has been made the paradigm. But this abstract discourse cannot be elevated to a paradigmatic or normative status. Such discourse is a highly specialized variety. It is one of the latest kinds of discourse to develop, and, as already mentioned, it is extremely useful. The abstractness of the mode of expression belonging to scientific discourse allows us to understand how this language can be much more readily detached from its discourse-situation than can many other kinds of language. Scientific language therefore enjoys a kind of universality that does not seem to belong to other more concrete ways of talking.

Poetry, theology, history, and much of our everyday talking about the world in terms of our practical concern with it, are instances of modes of discourse in which one approaches, in varying degrees, a fuller expression of existence, understood as self and world together. But since we have claimed that existence is always self and world together (or being-in-the-world), then even in discourse where the mode of expression abstracts most from the self, some element of concern and evaluation cannot be entirely absent. Michael Polanyi has argued that there is a personal factor in all knowing, and that even scientific understanding involves personal participation, without thereby becoming merely subjective.[1] It is surely noteworthy that

[1] See *Personal Knowledge* (New York: Harper & Row, and London: Routledge and Kegan Paul, 1962).

Bertrand Russell could write: 'Mathematics, rightly viewed, possesses not only truth but supreme beauty—a beauty cold and austere, yet sublimely pure.'[1] I may quote too a sentence from Heidegger: 'Mathematics is not more rigorous than historiology, but only narrower, because the existential foundations relevant for it lie within a narrower range.'[2] We maintain therefore that all discourse expresses existence (being-in-the-world), though some modes express it more fully, others more abstractly, almost to the point where the 'personal' factor has been dimmed down to vanishing.

In our discussion of the discourse-situation and what constitutes it, we have set out from the person who does the saying. Now we are going to turn our attention to that about which something is said (S). How does this enter into the discourse situation? There are, I think, two ways in which we commonly describe the relation of talk to that which is talked about. We can say that the talk 'refers' to its subject-matter, or we can say that the subject-matter is 'represented' in the talk. So not only expression, but also *referring* and *representing*, belongs to discourse, and language is again the medium through which such referring and representing can take place. Language, if it conveys any kind of understanding, seems always to point beyond itself and to refer to some person or thing or state of affairs; and this is somehow represented in the language, so that the language stands for that about which something is said.

But how is it possible for language to point beyond itself, or to stand for something? The answer must lie in the form or structure of the language; for language, as distinct from mere noise or sound, has a definite form. Perhaps even the bird cries, to which we alluded earlier, are able to indicate danger because of their distinct formation, and so they might qualify as a kind of primitive language. But human language, in so far as it can represent something and give information about it, goes much further, and of course it has a much more complex structure. Every word has its form, and may even have several forms, such

[1] *Mysticism and Logic* (London: Longmans, Green & Company, 1918), p. 60.
[2] *Op. cit.*, p. 195.

as singular and plural. Moreover, the sentences which are constituted by the words have their own form and structure. In some manner, the form and structure of the language brings before us something of the form and structure of what we are talking about. We have, however, already seen reason to reject the belief that language represents what is talked about by 'picturing' or 'copying' it. Apart from the handful of onomatopoeic words in spoken language and the ideograms of some archaic kinds of written language, words are not pictures or copies of anything. Perhaps indeed we could call them 'signs' or 'symbols', especially those words that 'refer' to entities in the world, but they are not pictures. It would be even harder to believe that sentences can properly be called 'pictures', 'copies', 'maps' or whatever, though indeed the sentence would seem to have a more definite logical shape or configuration than the isolated word. But, to mention just one objection—though it is said to have been the one that eventually turned Wittgenstein away from the 'picture' theory—the number of possible sentence-structures would seem to be much less than the fantastic number of factual structures which we find in the real world and which we might wish to talk about. It would seem then that one grammatical structure may have to do duty in representing widely different factual structures, when we talk about these.

Here we have moved over from talking about logical structures and shapes to grammatical ones, and these two do not coincide. Grammar, logic and fact are not easily correlated, and for this reason language can misrepresent, by leading us to believe that similarity of grammatical structure implies similarity of logical form or perhaps even similarity of factual structure among the things talked about in similar sentences. One of the great merits of modern logical analysis is just that it has taught us that grammatical form is often a deceptive guide to the meaning of what is said. 'He was in his office'; 'He was in a state of grace'; 'He was in the worst of tempers'; 'He was in glory before the world began'—these are all sentences of roughly similar grammatical form, but it would be a task bristling with difficulty to determine the logical status of each and to describe what kind of 'fact' (if any) each of them refers to. It is obvious in any case that we do not have simple 'word-pictures' reproducing facts.

Just as we have seen that there are different modes of expression proper to different kinds of discourse, so now it will be shown that there are different modes of referring and representing. I shall not say too much about referring here, since we shall return to the matter in the next chapter when we consider the question of the function of names, and of the respective roles of denotation and connotation.[1] But I think one may safely claim that some language represents more fully and more concretely, other language represents more abstractly. Furthermore, it is the case that some modes of referring and representing are more direct than others. An analogical statement seems to be at one further remove from the subject-matter which it represents than a simple statement of fact, for the analogical statement represents indirectly the situation which it is desired to talk about, through another situation which is supposed to have features that are in some respects similar. These considerations point us to many difficult problems, such as what can be meant by 'similarity', 'referring', 'symbolizing' and so on. We shall try to come to grips with these problems later in the book. It is sufficient for the moment to concentrate our attention on what our analysis shows us about the essential part played by representation in the discourse-situation. It would seem that language is empty unless it has some content that links it to a reality beyond the language. The link may be indirect, but it ought to be possible to show that there is such a link, even in the case of symbolic and analogical talk. Moreover, we have seen reason to believe that there are different possible modes of representation, ranging from the most abstract 'objective' representation to the modes in which we seek to represent what we are talking about in the most concrete way, including such characteristics as may be at least partly dependent on our own

[1] See below, p. 87ff.

relation to what we are talking about. To give an illustration, the most abstract mode of representation might restrict itself to such universal and objective characteristics as size, mass, shape and the like, whereas more concrete modes might speak of, let us say, beauty. In any case, what we talk about is, through its representation in language, made accessible to the understanding. It is articulated and given shape. It is brought into the light, so that we can relate ourselves to it and find our way about in the world as intelligent beings in an ordered environment.

We have still to look at the discourse-situation from the point of view of the person to whom something is said (B). When we look at it in this way, discourse presents itself as *communication*. This is not to be thought of as the transferring of ideas from one thinking subject to another. That might be propaganda or suggestion, but it would not be genuine communication, for this involves a sharing. Just as the person who expresses himself in language does so as an existent self-in-a-world, so the person who hears and understandingly appropriates the language does so as a self-in-a-world; furthermore, it is in each case the same world, the common or shared world in which they both are. Communication takes place when some aspect of the shared world is lit up and made accessible to both parties in the discourse.

All communication is interpretation. As Josiah Royce, following some suggestions of C. S. Peirce, pointed out, interpretation has the same triadic character that we have come to recognize as basic to the whole discourse situation. As far as interpretation is concerned, one must recognize that there is always an interpreter, the matter that is to be interpreted, and the person to whom the interpretation is offered. Communication, we may say, takes place in a community of interpretation. Such a community presupposes a basis upon which the interpretation can proceed: a shared world, shared interests, a shared 'universe of discourse', to use an expression that is sometimes found in logicians to designate the context of meanings and ideas within which on any given occasion our talking takes place. Because we talk against the background of such a universe of discourse, we rarely talk about anything exhaustively; we generally leave something 'understood', as we say, and it is possible for it to be understood because of the shared universe of discourse.

Discourse is meaningful if it succeeds in lighting up and making accessible to the understanding that which is talked about. Expression, representation and communication would all seem to be essential to meaningful discourse. If nothing is expressed or represented, nothing is brought to light. And even if something is expressed and represented, the discourse breaks down and is unmeaning to the person to whom it is addressed if it fails to communicate. It may fail if shared presuppositions are lacking, that is to say, if there is not a common universe of discourse. For instance, an ancient myth might both express and represent something, yet it would fail to communicate to persons who no longer shared the presuppositions of mythical discourse, and to them the myth would be unmeaning. What would be required in such a case would be a new act of interpretation, if what the myth expressed and represented is to be again communicated.

We have said here that discourse is meaningful if it brings what is talked about into the light, that is, if it *says* something, in what we took to be the original significance of 'saying'. Perhaps the notion of meaning has to do also with 'placing' the language in some frame of reference that we already have, and indeed this seemed to be implied in what was said about communication. In any case, what we understand here by 'meaning' is closely related with the notion of truth as 'unhiddenness'. We could say that truth is the ideal or limiting case, in which that which is talked about has been fully manifested for what it is. In this sense, we could agree with Urban's statement that 'the totality of intelligible discourse *is* the truth.'[1] We could say also that our discourse is true when it *adequately* performs its function

[1] *Op. cit.*, p. 729.

of letting us see, and this notion of 'adequacy' is already central to St Thomas' conception of truth as *adaequatio intellectus et rei*, though presumably in this definition of truth (which St Thomas had taken over from Avicenna) the notion of *adaequatio* (*conformitas, convenientia*) was rather differently understood from the way we are taking it here.[1]

To complete our analysis of the discourse-situation, something further remains to be said. Language has been exhibited as the centre of the situation, and in this position it has a twofold character. On the one hand, it *unites* the speaker both to what he is talking about and to the person to whom his speech is addressed. At the same time, language separates them by standing between. Does this mean that discourse is made possible because there are still more direct and fundamental relations than the mediate one of language between the speaker and the two other terms of the discourse situation? I shall maintain that it does, and the point may have some importance for later discussions. In the case of what we talk about, the underlying relation that makes discourse possible may be called 'intuition', in a sense rather like that of the Kantian *Anschauung*. Without expression in structured language, intuition would remain blind, if we may adapt Kant's expression. It is because man is open in his being-in-the-world that he has anything to talk about at all. I believe, however, that this openness is not restricted to those sensuous intuitions on which depends our perception of objects, and so our developed knowledge of these objects, but that we have intuitions of another kind as well. I allude to affective states, such as anxiety, to which in recent times existentialist philosophers have drawn our attention. These affective states too are intuitions, disclosing existence in the world, and making accessible structures that can be brought to expression in language. These structures are not like the objects intuited through the senses, but we might claim that they are of an even more fundamental kind, since they have to do with what we have called 'total existence', and embrace both subject and object. But for

[1] *De veritate*, I, 1.

this reason, they can never be objectified, and we are aware of them only through participation.

Equally, one may suppose that discourse implies a direct person-to-person relation which makes possible communication and interpretation. Admittedly Buber, with his stress on 'primary words', seems to indicate that person-to-person relations already imply language. I think, however, that there is

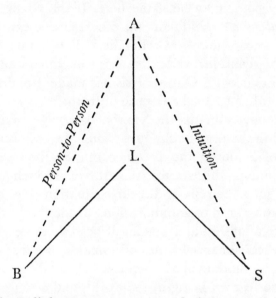

a more primordial person-to-person relation, one that is on the level of an as yet inarticulate feeling, and yet one that is genuinely personal. This point of view would seem to get support from Heidegger. He writes: 'In discourse, Being-with (*Mitsein*) becomes explicitly *shared*; that is to say, it *is* already, but it is unshared as something that has not been taken hold of and appropriated.'[1] Royce makes much the same point in a different way in his theory of interpretation. It may well be significant that this theory is expounded in the second volume of his book, *The Problem of Christianity*, after he has set out Christianity as a religion of loyalty. Interpretation, and with it the whole intellectual enterprise of mankind, always implies the

[1] *Op. cit.*, p. 205.

community of interpretation, and what makes this community possible is the loyalty or fidelity of its members. Thus there is a personal loyalty that precedes interpretation and communication. Thus we can fill in two additional relations on our diagram of the discourse-situation—the direct relation of A and S through intuition, and the direct relation of A and B through a person-to-person relation. These are shown by the broken lines.

Another point may be made here. If the Greeks expressed truth as *alētheia*, 'unhiddenness', the Hebrews expressed it as '*emeth*, 'trustworthiness' or 'reliability'. There is no need to set these up as rival ideas of truth (as is sometimes done in books of biblical theology). Our analysis has made it plain that both conceptions belong to the essence of truth.

Let me now sum up the view of language that has been developed in the present chapter. Language has been shown as the focus of discourse, and discourse, in turn, has been shown as a relation among three terms, at least two of which are persons. Essential to a complete discourse-situation are expression, representation and communication. Underlying this highly complex relationship and making it possible there would seem to be two basic characteristics of human existence, or perhaps only one: its fundamental openness, which shows itself as an openness to its own being-in-the-world, and as an openness to other centres of existence in the same world. With these general considerations about language in mind, we must now turn back to the specific problem of theological language, and see whether we can find a place for this language within the general framework of discourse.

# 4

## *The Theological Vocabulary*

FROM OUR EXPLORATION of some of the problems that are raised by language and discourse in general, we must now return to the specific problem of theological language. We have to show the place of this language within the general pattern of discourse as this was expounded in the preceding chapter. This would mean answering such questions as: 'What does theological language express?' 'How does it refer, or to what does it refer, or how does it represent?' 'How does it communicate?'

In order to answer these questions with even a degree of adequacy, we shall have to consider concrete examples of the many variations that are to be found within theological language itself. But although such detailed investigations will eventually be demanded, it may be worthwhile to begin by giving a sketch of what I take to be the basic logic of theological language, the logic which underlies the many kinds of theological talk and allows them to get off the ground, so to speak, as meaningful forms of discourse.

We have seen that theological language arises out of the wider area of religious language, as a reflective and rather sophisticated kind of God-talk.[1] Theological language has therefore its roots in such experiences or states of mind as faith, grace, creaturely feeling, the sense of the holy, commitment, adoration and so on. These all involve what we have called 'total existence', that is to say the whole range of our being-in-the-world, in its

[1] See above, p. 19.

cognitive, affective and conative dimensions alike. So we find that theological language is related also to those affective states or moods which, it was claimed,[1] constitute along with sensuous intuitions that openness to existence which is fundamentally characteristic of man as a self-in-a-world that is disclosed to itself.

Among these affective states or moods is that basic tension or malaise which is, perhaps somewhat misleadingly, called usually 'anxiety' (*Angst*), the sense of the precariousness of an existence that at any moment may cease to exist. What is disclosed in this mood (as in other moods, and in sensuous intuition) can be brought to expression in words, when we attain explicit awareness of the finite and transient character of the existence of a self-in-a-world. Yet the very attainment of such an awareness is also a transcending of mere transience, and is the awakening of the quest for grace and meaning.[2] This is the starting-point for religious language and, *a fortiori*, for theological language.

No doubt the most intense awareness of the fragmentary character of our human existence and of the deep-seated quest to 'make sense' of it comes in what Karl Jaspers calls the 'limit-situations' of existence—situations such as guilt and death, where, so to speak, we come up against a wall and there is disclosed to us the structure of finite being. This structure is, of course, at the very centre of our existence: finitude and fragmentariness are of the essence of man's being. But ordinarily they escape notice or lie beneath the surface of our everyday awareness, so that it is only in something like a 'limit-situation' that they come explicitly before us and we become a question to ourselves. I mention this because Dietrich Bonhoeffer's criticism of talking of the 'human' boundaries[3] and his insistence that Christian faith must rather touch men at the centre of their

---

[1] See above, p. 76.

[2] See my *Principles of Christian Theology* (New York: Charles Scribner's Sons, 1966, and London: SCM Press, 1967), chapters III and IV, pp. 53ff.

[3] *Letters and Papers from Prison*, revised edition (New York: Macmillan, and London: SCM Press, 1967), p. 154.

lives is sometimes thought to discredit the idea of the 'limit-situation'. Actually, it does nothing of the kind, since the limit-situation remains the 'place' where the essential structures of our everyday living are lit up for us. We should perhaps remember that Bonhoeffer's own most interesting insights came to him in a limit-situation, as he lay in jail with death never far off.

But what are we to say of these insights or intuitions of our own being-in-the-world that may open out to us in some situation where superficial answers will not do any more and the radical question of human existence forces itself upon us? It must first be said that what we intuit in such ways can never be brought to objectified expression, as is possible with what we intuit through the senses. Anxiety and similar moods disclose situations in which we ourselves are involved. If we may continue to use Jaspers' terminology, for his subtle analyses gather together and explain a great many phenomena, the disclosure belongs to the 'comprehensive', by which he means a mode of awareness that is neither purely subjective nor purely objective, but embraces both sides of the subject-object split.[1] It touches on what we have called 'total existence', and it is total existence that theology tries to bring to expression. This 'total existence', where the adjective alludes to the whole range of our being-in-the-world and to the 'comprehensive' character of a situation in which we are ourselves involved, has, of course, nothing to do with the notion of the totality of all existent entities, such as an all-embracing metaphysic might seek to describe. In saying that theology tries to bring 'total existence' to expression, we are certainly not implying that it aims at a metaphysical system.

Since considerable stress has been laid on affective states, we must pause for a moment to face the challenge offered by emotive theories of religious language. There is a tendency among some philosophers to dismiss as merely 'emotive language' whatever goes beyond such factual objective assertions as can be anchored in sensuous intuition, or verified by sense-perception.

[1] *The Perennial Scope of Philosophy*, trans. Ralph Manheim (London: Routledge and Kegan Paul, 1950), pp. 16ff.

Some writers, indeed, divided language into 'informative' and 'emotive', as if all utterances other than tautologies could be assigned to one or other of these classes.

The cruder forms of the emotive theory of religious, moral and aesthetic language are not very widely held nowadays, and perhaps they never were seriously held by anyone, except when he was engaged in philosophical argument. It is hard to believe, for instance, that Russell's remarks on the austere beauty of mathematics or his advocacy of the cause of pacifism were meant to be taken simply as sophisticated cries evincing animal feeling, though this is what some of his own theories would demand us to suppose. The emotive theories arise from initial metaphysical prejudices about the priority of the physical, from a gross over-simplification of the nature of language, and from inadequate and one-sided views on the structure of discourse. Against such prejudgments of the case, it must be maintained that when we consider the kind of affective states or moods that we have talked about, we see that they afford disclosures of existence which, just as much as what is disclosed in sensuous intuition, have some cognitive significance that can be brought to expression; though admittedly the mode of expression will be more complex than what is involved in pointing to the observable but not very exciting fact that 'the cat sits on the mat'.

But let us return to our sketch of the basic logic of theological discourse. The disclosure of finitude and the shock (to use Tillich's word) of possibly ceasing to exist brings Being itself to our notice for the first time. This experience is what Heidegger calls the 'wonder of Being' or even the 'wonder of wonders', and although Wittgenstein seemed to think it inexpressible, the experience was presumably not entirely foreign to him when he could write: 'Not *how* the world is, is the mystical, but *that* it is.'[1] This encounter with Being, the coming alive to the mystery that there is a world and not just nothing, lies very close in its epistemological structure to what the theologian calls 'revelation'.

[1] *Tractatus Logico-Philosophicus*, p. 187.

This too is a coming alive to the presence of Being, but we call it 'revelation' in the theological sense because Being gets experienced as holy, and calls forth the commitment of faith. It is the content of this encounter with holy Being that theological discourse seeks to represent. But such representing can never be simply a matter of indicating some observable fact, for what is here represented belongs once more in the realm of the comprehensive.

To continue the analysis, we may say that theological language communicates by awakening the person to whom it is addressed to the encounter with holy Being. Theological language does not convey subjective impressions from one mind to another, still less does it convey scraps of metaphysical information. Rather, through expression and representation it interprets and lights up a shared existence at the deepest levels.

Thus we see that theological discourse displays the three constitutive moments that were set out in the last chapter as characteristic of discourse in general: expression, representation, communication.

When we call to mind the three theologians whose views on the nature of theological language were sketched out at an early stage of our inquiry,[1] we see that our own sketch does not coincide with any of theirs, but we may hope that as we proceed to develop it, it may overcome some of the deficiencies that we saw in the three examples that we considered. However, we still have much in common with all three cases. We are in agreement with Tillich in assigning an important role to the idea of 'being'—an idea which, admittedly, will call for much more clarification than we have so far offered. Yet clearly too we have maintained links with Bultmann and Barth. Like Bultmann, we have taken our start from the existent who raises the question about his being-in-the-world; but like Barth, we have found the content of theological language to come by way of an experience that we could only call 'revelation'. In any case, our sketch is simply a skeleton outline, a formal logical pattern which, in actual

[1] See above, p. 34ff.

theological discourse, would be filled out with concrete symbolism and imagery.

To carry our investigation further, we may recall that Rudolf Carnap once pointed to a useful way for investigating a language. He suggested that any language may be considered with respect to its vocabulary and with respect to its syntax. The vocabulary is the list of significant words; the syntax embodies the rules whereby these words may be put together in meaningful sentences. Although Carnap's *Logical Syntax of Language* expounds a very different view of these matters from the one which we have seen reason to favour, we may nonetheless adopt the approach which his distinction between vocabulary and syntax suggests, and this would mean that we now proceed to examine the theological vocabulary.

Words appear to be the units—we could almost say, the bricks—out of which language is built. Yet we ought to be quite explicitly aware that in considering individual words, we are abstracting elements from the living texture of language. It is clear that letters and isolated sounds, vowels and consonants, are mere fragments apart from words that they help to constitute; but it can be maintained with almost equal plausibility that words are fragments apart from larger wholes of discourse. The *Gestalt* psychology has provided good evidences for supposing that we first of all grasp the whole before we sort out the elements which constitute that whole. This would suggest that we ought to study the syntactical structure of sentences before we turn to individual words. Just as we have already seen that language is a kind of frozen abstraction when lifted out of the discourse where it belongs, so we could say that words are, if not dead, at least in a state of suspended animation when lifted out of sentences. They come to life only when we set them in motion. In a dictionary, a word may be assigned three or four meanings, but these are only potential meanings, until the word is actually used and takes on one or other of its possible senses.

It has sometimes been argued that in the history of language, sentences came before words. If we took this literally to mean that men uttered more or less complex combinations of words before they uttered single words, then it would not seem to be a very plausible theory. Many writers, especially those of nominalist tendencies, have indeed had much sport at the expense of this theory. Russell, for instance, agrees that it is possible that highly exceptional persons such as Lord Macaulay may have begun to speak in sentences, for the infant Macaulay's first utterance is said to have taken place at a party where some hot tea was spilled over him, and he is reported to have said after a time to his concerned hostess: 'Thank you, madam, the agony is abated.'[1] But Russell points out that the ordinary child begins less ambitiously by uttering single words.

However, I do not believe that Russell's witty argument establishes his point. If we reflect further, we see that when an ordinary child or perhaps a primitive man utters a single word, such as 'Horse!', this is already in every case an elliptical sentence. It may mean, 'That is a horse!' or perhaps 'I want to see the horse,' or something else that may be gathered from the context of the utterance, from what is 'understood', as we say. It would seem to need a real effort of abstraction simply to utter the word 'Horse!', without asserting anything or asking for anything, but simply in order to conjure up the image of a horse or perhaps the bare notion of equine being.

It is plain that single words are not devoid of meaning, and some philosophers have called the kind of meaning that belongs to words their 'signification' (corresponding to the German *Bedeutung*) as distinct from the 'meaning' (*Sinn*) that belongs to sentences. We may find it helpful to observe this distinction. But it is equally clear that the signification of a single word is an abstraction from the wider field of meaning that belongs to the sentence in which the word gets used, and that belongs eventually to the whole field of discourse. Thus, while it is permissible for us to begin as a matter of convenience with the theological vocabulary, the list of significant words belonging to the discipline, we must do so with the reservation that any single

[1] Cf. *An Outline of Philosophy*, p. 54.

theological word can be understood only in the context of
theological discourse.

If we read any page of theology, we shall notice that by far
the most of the words used are shared with other kinds of discourse. Words such as 'if', 'as', 'but' and the like are logical
operators that occur in all our talking. Furthermore, many of
the nouns, verbs and adjectives of the theologian are likewise
words that are shared with other modes of discourse, even if
some of these words are occasionally used in special or technical
senses. The theologian talks about 'history', 'man', 'language'
and so on, and by these words he wants to point to the same
phenomena as they denote in ordinary everyday talk, even if
he may want us to understand some of these matters in special
ways.

This point of a vocabulary that is for the most part shared is
not to be dismissed as a merely trivial circumstance, for it makes
plain that theological discourse claims to be part of the totality
of discourse. Theology is not a mere 'speaking with tongues', if
by that expression we understand some kind of esoteric and
perhaps ecstatic utterance. Theology is not a 'private' language.
Since one of the dimensions of discourse is communication, the
notion of a private language is indeed something of a contradic-
tion in terms. The more private or restricted any language is,
the less cash-value, so to speak, can it have; for anything said in
such a language will not be achieving what an act of saying sets
out to do, that is to say, lighting up what is talked about and
letting it be seen for what it is. So theological talk, in so far as
it makes use of the common stock of words and follows normal
linguistic usage, claims to be an area within the whole realm of
meaningful discourse. It follows that any account of theological
language must pay as much attention to its place within the
general framework of discourse as to its peculiar and distinguishing characteristics.

There is, of course, a distinctive theological vocabulary, and
we find it among those words which we call 'names'. Here I am
using this expression in the widest sense for all words that do not

simply relate other words, but are supposed to stand for something, it may be an object or an activity or a quality or a situation or a person or something else. Within the distinctive theological vocabulary, it is possible to discern various kinds of names  Some of the names stand for physical objects associated with the cult, such as 'cross' and 'altar', or for observable activities carried on within the cult, such as 'baptism' and 'laying on of hands'. Another group of names, and a very important one, stands for experiences or attitudes that belong to the life of religion; examples are 'sin', 'faith', 'grace', 'salvation' and so on. Still other names stand (or appear to stand) for entities which are not observable by the senses—words like 'God', 'angel', 'soul', 'demon', 'spirit'; or for qualities which supposedly characterize some of these entities—'omnipotence', 'immortality' and the like. This list of some of the kinds of theological names makes no pretence to be either systematic or exhaustive. The total number of such theological words must be very great, and this can be easily seen by glancing through any dictionary of theological terms.

Before we inquire further into theological names, we must ask the general question: 'What is a name?' Many answers have been given to this question, and we may begin by considering an extreme answer, the view that a name is simply a label. It is a conventional sign that we use in order to refer or point to an object or an event or a situation. This way of understanding the function of names has a good deal of plausibility so long as we confine our attention to objective ways of talking about observable occurrences. In the sentence, 'At sea-level water boils at 100 degrees Centigrade', the word 'water' is simply a label for a familiar substance. However, the word 'water' has in the course of its history acquired a kind of penumbra of associations. This was almost inevitable, when one considers the many uses and indeed the absolute necessity of water in relation to human existence. In some contexts, one or other of these associations might be specially suggested when the word 'water' is used. For instance, in a treatise on baptism, the writer may be using the word 'water' with an interest in water's cleansing function, while in a poetic context some other association of water may be intended. According to Susan Stebbing, the aim of the scientist in his language is to cut out such variations of meaning in the words he uses. 'His aim,' she writes, 'is to use his verbal symbols so as to achieve uniqueness of reference, and thus to use language in order to communicate information that is exact and precise.'[1] He succeeds in his aim when his words refer simply and un-equivocally to a referend.

Actually, it may be much harder than was formerly supposed to find and employ precise verbal symbols, names that will refer in the precise way that Susan Stebbing demands. Names tend to have what Friedrich Waismann has called an 'open texture',[2] implying that we cannot set precise conceptual boundaries to what these names denote. In order that his names may be precise, we often find that the scientist in a particular discipline will abandon ordinary language altogether, and construct a more precise one of his own. Thus the chemist, instead of using the word 'water' with its 'open texture' and all its associations, may use the symbol $H_2O$. This symbol, as far as possible, seems to refer simply and exactly to the substance formed by the chemical union of hydrogen and oxygen in a certain proportion (ice, water, steam).

The striving for exactness of language is entirely desirable and praiseworthy in any intellectual discipline whatever, and we certainly have no quarrel with the endeavour of the scientist to make his talk as unambiguous and precise as he can. This is most useful, and in different ways the historian, let us say, or the theologian should also aim at a clearcut language. But we must

---

[1] *A Modern Introduction to Logic* (London: Methuen, 6th edition, 1948), pp. 16–17. Is it just an accident that we find almost the same description of 'Newspeak' in George Orwell's frightening *1984*? 'Every concept that can ever be needed will be expressed by exactly *one* word, with its meaning rigidly defined, and all its subsidiary meanings rubbed out and forgotten.' Orwell's point is that 'the whole aim of Newspeak is to narrow the range of thought'. In particular, it abolishes the personal dimension of speech, and Miss Stebbing too thinks of impersonality as a virtue in language. See below, p. 90.

[2] 'Verifiability' in *Logic and Language*, ed. A. N. Flew (Oxford: Blackwell, 1952), vol. I, pp. 138ff.

enter a very strong protest when Miss Stebbing (and others) tell us that when language is not used in the precise denotative way which is the aim of the natural scientist, then this language has become merely emotive, and the question of its truth or falsity does not arise. Writers who take this view often go on to say that for every significant name that we use, it must be possible to point to some object or some observable state of affairs in the empirical world, to which the name refers. And if we find ourselves unable to do this for such names as 'God' or 'soul', then we are told that the imperfection of ordinary language has misled us into supposing that because we use these nouns, there must be 'things' corresponding to them, whereas there are no such 'things'. This very objection, however, is surely confused, at least in the case of God, for not even someone who has an actual material image of God supposes that God is a 'thing' that can be pointed out.

There is, however, some measure of truth in the kind of criticisms of theological language that stem from the position which we have illustrated from Miss Stebbing's writings. Many names are undoubtedly charged with emotional associations, and nowadays we know only too well how the propagandist and the advertiser, by skilful exploitation of these emotional associations, can appear to be describing facts whereas they are really inculcating emotional attitudes, and may even be grossly distorting the facts in the process. Furthermore, we may readily agree that some of the names used by the theologian do not refer in the same kind of way as names used in scientific discourse. The theological vocabulary and indeed theological language as a whole do not fit the pattern that we find in the natural sciences.

But because theological language is different, this does not mean that it is to be lumped in with emotive utterance, or that it is to be denied genuine cognitive insights, though the theologian may reasonably be expected to show on what grounds the claims of his language are based. The fact that theological language is different does not mean either that, for fear of being blinded by the emotions, we must cut out the existential[1] associations of names, and take refuge in the 'impersonal' language of science. The adjective 'impersonal' is quoted directly from Miss Stebbing, and if her account of scientific language is correct, then she rightly calls it 'impersonal'. But the use of the word 'impersonal' reveals the error (not hers alone) of making a simple-minded division of language into informative and emotive. Once again, we meet with the failure to recognize the triadic character of discourse, which always has a personal dimension, in so far as two of the three terms in the discourse relation are persons. Hence, even an adequate account of scientific language would need to recognize some personal dimension in it, as has been done in various ways by philosophers like Royce and Polanyi.

The doctrine of names as mere labels is an abstraction which concentrates exclusively on the relation of words to things and leaves out of account the function of words as vehicles of communication. It is in the dimension of communication and interpretation in the community of discourse that the whole latent background of names comes alive. The associations which belong to the names in the context of the human existence within which they are used come into play. These associations, of course, may vary according to the particular field of discourse and the shared presuppositions of the participants. It may well be the case that in such modes of discourse, names are less sharply denotative than in scientific usages, yet they may be none the less successful in lighting up that which is talked about. Moreover, if we recall our earlier discussion about affective states and the disclosures or intuitions which they yield, we see that the associations that go with words in discourse are not to be dismissed indiscriminately in a mass as 'mere emotion' (an impossible abstraction in any case!) but that they include what we may call 'existential connotations'. By this expression, I

---

[1] The word 'existential' is used here in the continental sense, that is to say, as having to do with human existence, not in the wider British and American sense which may have to do with any kind of existence, as when one speaks of an 'existential proposition'.

mean much the same as Urban and others have called 'intuitive connotations'. These are not to be thought of as accretions that have overlaid and obscured the 'true' or 'precise' significations of the words we use. Rather, it is likely that all names originally had strong existential connotations. Friedrich Max Müller delighted to show how even the most abstract words in our vocabulary can be traced back to simple operations of the human existent in his world. For instance, the various roots that express even such an abstruse notion as 'to be' in the Indo-European languages originally expressed such everyday activities as breathing, growing, dwelling. However sophisticated some of our words may have become, 'they will always disclose behind their faded features clear traces of an original purpose, very definite, very palpable, very sensible.'[1] The names of many common objects are derived from the uses to which man first put these objects. But if this is correct, the impersonal use of names as mere labels is something derivative and highly specialized.[2]

If we reject as inadequate the view that names are mere labels (or that they function best when treated as simple labels), what else are we to say about them? I certainly do not wish to revive the ancient debate between nominalists and realists, and my criticism of the nominalists is not meant to be an espousal of any particular school that has been opposed to them. All I have tried to do so far is to show the inadequacy or even the poverty of a thoroughgoing nominalism.

At the risk of being charged with lapsing into a mystical or even magical attitude toward words, let me now draw attention to another view of names. This one is at the opposite extreme from the one we have considered, and it is just as one-sided. It concentrates not on the reference of the name but on the name

---

[1] *Biographies of Words* (London: Longmans Green, 1888), p. 20.

[2] There are differences of opinion on this point among those philosophers who have written on language. As an illustration, one may contrast Heidegger's view that the spatial sense of the preposition 'in' is derived from the wider existential sense of 'dwelling', with Urban's opinion that the spatial sense of 'in' is the original one, and that it has been expanded by metaphorical transference. My own view is that Heidegger's opinion (and so Max Müller's) is more likely to be the correct one.

itself, perhaps implying that some power or virtue belongs even to a name. Obviously, when we name something, we do indeed acquire a certain power, for the name makes the thing manageable and accessible, so that we can talk about it and relate it to other things. It is not therefore surprising that in ancient times names were supposed to possess an inherent power or virtue. The Egyptian creator-god is said to have brought himself into existence simply by the power of his name. In the Old Testament, the naming process was part of the creation of an ordered world.[1] In the *Didache*, we read that creation was for the sake of the Name,[2] and more generally it was taught that creation took place by the Word or Logos.[3] When God made himself known to Moses, it was by revealing his name.[4] The divine name, as is well known, was regarded with such reverence among the Jews that they would not even pronounce it. The name became hypostatized as the Angel of the Name, the angel of whom God says: 'Give heed to him and hearken to his voice . . . for my name is in him.'[5] In some of the heterodox Jewish sects, the Angel of the Name became almost a second God, 'Little Yahweh', as he was called. In the New Testament, it appears that the name of Jesus soon acquired a power and virtue of its own. When St Peter and St John were questioned about the healing of a lame man, they replied that it had been done 'by the name of Jesus Christ of Nazareth', and they added that 'there is no other name under heaven given among men by which we must be saved'.[6] The Christian Church still observes the Feast of the Holy Name, there are many hymns of devotion to the Name, and it is customary in church, especially in reciting the creeds, to show reverence to the Name by making an inclination when it is mentioned.

Our first reaction may be to dismiss these illustrations as mere examples of magic and superstition, a reverence for names which is on a level with the use of spell words like 'abracadabra'. Admittedly, the lapse into magic is an easy one, and no doubt

---

[1] Gen. 2.19.    [2] 10.3.    [3] John 1.3.    [4] Ex. 3.14.
[5] Ex. 23.21.    [6] Acts 4.10, 12.

it often occurred, not only in the archaic religions but also among Jews and Christians, when certain names were used for the purposes of exorcism and the like. But such lapses have always been criticized and overcome by the best insights of the religious faith itself. To give an instance from right outside the biblical tradition, we may remember that Brahmins practised meditation on the sacred syllable 'Om', and in some quarters this came to be regarded as a magic word, unlocking the secrets of the universe or serving as a spell or incantation. But this unintelligent mechanical attitude is satirized in the Upanishads themselves, where we read of a procession of dogs, marching like priests, each holding the tail of the dog in front and chanting: 'Om! let us eat! Om! let us drink! Om! may the god Varuna bring food here!'[1]

Just as abstraction is the cause of the erroneous view that a name is merely a label, so it is vicious abstraction of another kind that results in magic power getting ascribed to a name. Once again, the name has been removed from its 'home'; it has been wrenched out of the context of living discourse and gets treated as an independent entity, having power inherent in itself. But although such abuses have occurred, we should not allow this to obscure the fact that, within discourse, the connotations of words give them a certain interpretative power. This is no magical power. It is an interpretative power in the sense that it lights up meaning. The interpretative power of a vocabulary is just as basic and essential a function of names as is their capacity to refer to objects. We have seen, of course, that interpretation presupposes a universe of discourse that is shared between persons. The names only operate against this kind of background. The name of Jesus, for instance, would have no connotations for someone ignorant of the Christian story. Such a person might indeed try to use this name as a magic spell, but this is something entirely different from the interpretative power which the name has come to have in Christian devotion.

[1] *The Principal Upanishads*, ed. S. Radhakrishnan (London: Allen & Unwin, 1953), p. 358.

However, shared presuppositions are necessary to all genuine discourse; this is simply to state the obvious fact that one cannot talk a language (much less, intelligently criticize it) without first learning it.

Now, it would appear that in some modes of discourse the denotation of names is of primary importance, whereas in other modes their connotation plays a major part. Generally speaking, scientific language is interested in denotation; as we saw from Miss Stebbing's remarks on the subject, each name must refer as precisely as possible to some referend in the observable world. In other modes of discourse—not only theology, but also history, poetry, and many other subjects and everyday ways of talking—the existential or intuitive connotations of words are of great importance for the understanding of the discourse. Sometimes a contrast is made between the scientific and the dramatic uses of words: in the first, words refer to objects; in the second, we may say, they express situations in which both subject and object participate, situations which belong to what we have called 'total existence'.

The name 'water' can undoubtedly be brought to the point of abstraction at which it simply labels the substance having the chemical formula $H_2O$; though even so, one would perhaps have to say explicitly whether the word was to be used for this chemical substance in all its states (such as steam and ice) or only for the liquid form, commonly called 'water'. However, I am simply making the point that with a word like 'water', something approaching an abstract, impersonal, denotative use is possible, and the rich background of connotations can be dimmed down almost to vanishing-point.[1] But how does it stand with such a name as 'love'? Can this name signify anything apart from its existential connotations? Can it have any significance for a person who has not participated in the experience of loving or of being loved?

Even in a case like this, the exponents of the alternative point

[1] How rich these connotations are may be seen from Paul Tillich's miniature essay, 'Water', reprinted in James L. Adams, *Paul Tillich's Philosophy of Culture, Science and Religion* (New York: Harper & Row, 1965), pp. 62–64.

of view will fight a stubborn rearguard action. They will say that it is unnecessary to appeal to some unverifiable inward experience to know what 'love' signifies, for the word can be understood as standing for a perfectly overt and observable type of behaviour, just as open to empirical observation as water, let us say. We need not suppose such a view to be tied to the old-fashioned mechanistic type of behaviourism, but it does represent a kind of neo-behaviourism. It tries to get away from unobservable experiences known only through participation in the situation, and to acknowledge only what can be seen and described by any neutral observer. Thus we would say that a man loves his wife if we observe in him certain consistent patterns of behaviour towards her.

The attempt to dispense with any appeal to inner experience or existential participation has been strengthened lately by the development of electronic brains and the rise of the accompanying science of cybernetics. These electronic machines are said to 'think' and to 'remember', and, of course, the processes of 'thought' and 'memory' as they occur in such machines are observable processes, entirely amenable to objective investigation. Is not the same true then about apparently similar processes in man? Can his thinking and remembering not be studied also as overt kinds of behaviour, without appeal to such inaccessible mysteries as how it 'feels' to think or to remember?

Lord Samuel has written on this question as follows: 'Surely an electric computer no more thinks than the machinery in an automatic telephone exchange thinks when it is connecting one subscriber's number with another's: or a cash-register in a shop is doing a sum in arithmetic when it is adding the amount of the last customer's money to the cash already in the till: or an alarm clock, set for 7.30, remembers when 7.30 arrives and it duly makes its noise.' He adds: 'Cybernetics has no more connection with the problems of life and mind than has any other form of engineering.'[1]

[1] *A Threefold Cord*, A Discussion between Viscount Samuel and Professor Herbert Dingle (London: Allen & Unwin, 1961), p. 181.

Lord Samuel's common-sense argument is no more logically cogent than was Dr Samuel Johnson's attempt to refute Bishop Berkeley by kicking a stone. For all we know, if we could get 'inside' the machine, so to speak, we might find that it does think, in the sense of having conscious processes similar to ours. Or, more likely, there may be a critical stage of complexity at which conscious thought 'emerges' in a machine. Perhaps there is even a critical stage at which spontaneity and freedom come along, and the machine takes over and proceeds to operate the engineer. But surely the point of Lord Samuel's remarks is that any attempt to explain the signification of words like 'thought', 'memory' or 'love' *purely* in terms of overt behaviour misses precisely what is most characteristically intended by these words, the 'inside' of the behaviour, something that can never be observable but is known only by participation in acts of thinking, remembering, loving and so on. In any case, if a machine did get constructed that was capable of spontaneous acts, so that we had to judge that this machine had acquired the characteristics of a person, including, presumably, a conscious life, then we would have to say that the machine had in fact graduated to personhood and could be no longer understood as just a machine.

In linguistic terms, the issue we have just been considering is sometimes argued as the difference between third-person or other-ascriptive language ('he loves') and first-person or self-ascriptive language ('I love'). The other-ascriptive language seems to refer to overt, observable behaviour while the self-ascriptive language seems to refer to my states of mind. Are we to say then that such a verb as 'to love' completely changes its meaning as we move from the first person to the third person? It would seem to be absurd to assert such a logical gap. Are we then to try to assimilate self-ascriptive language to other-ascriptive language? This would be to cut out an essential part of the meaning, which is constituted by both the first-person and the third-person usages. P. F. Strawson has argued the point very clearly. He maintains that to regard all the meaning as contained in the other-ascriptive use of such words is 'to forget that we have to do with a class of predicates to the meaning of which it is essential that they should be both self-ascribable and other-ascribable to the same individual, where self-ascriptions are not made on the observational basis on which other-ascriptions are made, but on another basis. It is not that these predicates have two kinds of meaning. Rather, it is essential to the single kind of meaning that they do have, that both ways of ascribing them should be perfectly in order.'[1]

If we consider the metaphorical uses of language, the importance of the intuitive or existential connotations of words is even more strongly evidenced. When a word is used metaphorically, it does not label or directly refer to what we are talking about at all, but only indirectly refers through something else. However, certain connotations of the word are carried over to what we are talking about, so as to give us a new insight into it, or to light it up for us in the manner characteristic of discourse. If anyone says either that a metaphor never yields insights but only expresses emotion, or that the metaphor can always be replaced without damaging the insight which it yielded, surely these are statements that will not bear a moment's consideration. The metaphorical transfer of names has an essential place in language and in cognition. Indeed, every language is full of 'dead' metaphors, showing how the language has developed and become more subtle through the transference of intuitive connotations.

The metaphorical uses of names shows us as clearly as anything could the importance both of reference and of connotation in the function of names. These two are equally primordial, and the claims of neither of them should be pushed exclusively at the expense of the other, though admittedly their relative importance may vary in different kinds of discourse. I say that the two aspects of the function of names are made specially clear in metaphorical usage, because, if we take the metaphorical word literally, that is to say, if we attend exclusively to

[1] *Individuals*, pp. 106–7.

its reference, it misrepresents, since it is intended to refer to something other than the referend to which conventional usage has assigned it; on the other hand, if the metaphor is simply a floating centre of connotation, so to speak, it tells us nothing. Metaphor succeeds when we transfer some connotational element of the name from the conventional referend to our intended referend, in such a way that the latter gets illuminated and interpreted as perhaps could not happen otherwise.

Theological language, of course, abounds in metaphors and other kinds of indirect talk. Some of the metaphors are living, as when we talk of the 'flesh', in the Pauline sense. Many others are dead metaphors—words like 'spirit' and 'transcendence', which we are no longer hearing as having anything to do with 'breath' or 'mounting up'. But all the terms in the theological vocabulary are rich in connotations. Some of the words we have in mind could hardly be called 'metaphors', but their wealth of intuitive connotation puts them in the class of symbols, rather than in that of mere signs or labels. If we recall some of the illustrations mentioned earlier: as used in a theological context, such as a discussion of the atonement, the word 'cross' does not simply denote a particular kind of instrument of execution, but rather connotes all that Christ's death has come to mean in the Christian experience of salvation; the word 'salvation', in turn, is not the name for an empirically observable process—though presumably there would be some perceptible accompaniments —but stands rather for the Christian's experience of letting himself be grasped by God.

If we explore the various items in the distinctively theological vocabulary, I think that somewhere among their connotations we are always pointed to the experience of God. This would be true even of names that stand for physical objects used in Christian worship. An 'altar' is not just the name for a structure of stone or wood, but means the place where sacrifices are offered to God; 'sin' is not just a synonym for guilt or wrongdoing, but implies separation from God. The anthropologist or the psychologist or the sociologist might try to account for these words without reference to God, but he could do so only by abstracting from the full signification of the words as used by those who are actually participating in the life of faith. Theology is God-discourse or God-talk, and it is within this particular field of discourse that the theological vocabulary functions, and that its names have their peculiar connotations and interpretative powers.

Thus 'God' is the key-word in the theological vocabulary. Theology without God would indeed be like *Hamlet* without the Prince of Denmark. This was already asserted at the very beginning of this book, when we mentioned the position of Paul van Buren and maintained that his so-called 'reduced' theology could not properly be considered as theology at all. We now see much more clearly the reason for this, namely, that the whole theological vocabulary is tied in with the word 'God'. It is this word that, so to speak, organizes or co-ordinates the others within a framework of significance. If we can show the fundamental signification of this word 'God', then we have the clue to all the other words in the theological vocabulary. What then does the word 'God' signify?

Let us recall what was said at the beginning of this chapter on the basic logic of theological discourse. It was pointed out that in the affective state of anxiety, there is disclosed to man his finitude and transcience, the nothing over which he is poised. But even if the disclosure takes place in a limit-situation, it simply lights up the way we exist all the time. Just as we are never aware of the air we breathe unless maybe there is a threat to cut it off, so it takes the shock of the encounter with the nullity of his own existence to open up to man for the first time the wonder of Being. We only notice this wonder when it is placed over against nothing. But then we see that overcoming nothing and standing out from it is Being, not as something else that exists, but in the sense of that wider Being within which all particular beings have their being. Since Being is not another being but the *transcendens*, the incomparable and wholly other source and unity of all beings, it normally escapes our notice. Just so, as John Cobb has recently expressed it, 'the constancy of God's presence militates against our consciousness of him'.[1] In either case, it takes something like a revelatory experience in order that the disclosure may take place.

Man is the ontological entity, because he not only has being, like any other entity, but has his being disclosed to him, so that he has the potentiality to become the being to which Being as such manifests itself, gives itself and entrusts itself. 'God' is the religious name for Being as experienced in a faith-awakening revelation. Of course, in any actual religion, the encounter with Being, here expressed schematically, gets clothed in concrete symbolism. In the Christian religion, this symbolism centres in a God who becomes incarnate and gives himself in self-sacrificing love for men. Such symbolism is possible because every particular being has its participation in Being and so to some extent manifests and illuminates Being. But some symbols illuminate Being more adequately than others. We have already seen that the essence of truth is adequacy (*adaequatio*). A religious symbol is true to the extent that it illuminates Being adequately, and clearly the illumination will be the more adequate, the higher the symbolizing entity stands in the hierarchy of beings. Yet even the most adequate symbol, since it is a symbol, does not directly disclose what is symbolized but only indirectly through the transference of connotations, and so even the most illuminating symbol preserves the otherness and mystery of Being.

The ontological dimension of the word 'God' is indispensable to it. God is the one who is before all beings, nothing less than Being that lets them be. Hence, as St Thomas wrote, 'Since the being of God is his very essence (which can be said of no other being) it is clear that among other names this one (Being, *esse*) most properly names God; for everything is named according to its essence'.[2]

But so far we seem to be talking about the God of the philosophers rather than the God of the Christian or any other faith. We cannot indeed leave aside the fundamental *esse* of God, but

---

[1] *A Christian Natural Theology* (Philadelphia: Westminster Press, 1965), p. 232.
[2] *Summa Theologiae*, I, q. 13, art. 11.

The Theological Vocabulary

as the word is used in religion, it implies an existential just as much as an ontological dimension. Indeed, this cold word 'being' expresses much less than the word 'God'. 'Being' is an ontological term, lacking the connotations that belong to the religious word 'God', and to find an equivalent expression for 'God', we would need to say something like 'Holy Being', where the adjective introduces the dimension of our own relation to Being. It will be remembered that the encounter with Being, as described above, always belongs to the comprehensive. The Being encountered is not an object of which we can talk in a disinterested way, but the Being in which we live and move and have our being. So too, religious discourse is always of God in his relation to us. When we talk of God, we talk at the same time of ourselves. The word 'God' does not just signify Being, but also implies an evaluation of Being, a commitment to Being as Holy Being, Being that is gracious and judging. This existential or evaluating dimension of the word 'God' is clear enough in such common expressions as 'He makes a god of money', which simply means that someone is devoting his life to money. The name of 'God' is not a disinterested label for Being or Reality or any other remote abstraction, but connotes our existential concern with Being. In Tillich's language, God is both Being itself and ultimate concern. The complex signification of the word 'God' is what we might expect, when we recall that the language in which this is the keyword arises from 'total existence', from the whole being of man in his world; thus discourse about God (God-talk, theology) moves in the sphere of total existence, alike in its expressing, representing and communicating.

As the key-name in the theological vocabulary, the word God supplies the clue for understanding the significations of the other items in the vocabulary. We shall not go further into this for the present. But surely we have seen enough to show us that these theological names are not exhaustively accounted for in emotive or even in conative terms. They genuinely illuminate structures of existence and Being, as these are disclosed to the whole man.

# 5

## *Theology and Logical Empiricism*

THIS CHAPTER WILL be something of a digression. After we had seen the divergences of opinion among theologians concerning what they have to say about the language they use, we decided that we would have to go to the philosophers and see what we could learn from them about language in general. In the interval, we have surely come a considerable way towards forming a clearer conception of what language is and what it does, and also toward making progress with our specific problem, the language of theology. But it may seem that in these discussions we have drawn very little upon the writings of what is, after all, the school of contemporary philosophy that has concerned itself most with language—the school of logical analysis. We have indeed frequently alluded to philosophers who, in a broad way, could be taken to belong to this school, but the views we have developed seem to lie nearer to the theories about language found in such philosophers as Royce, Urban and Heidegger. It is desirable that we should now consider in a more detailed way what some of the logical analysts have said on the theme of theology or of God-talk in general, and ask how what they have been saying is related to what we ourselves have said in the two preceding chapters. Although the adherents of the type of philosophy which we are to consider have often seemed hostile to the claims of theology, I shall draw attention to those developments in the school which have tended toward a more affirmative attitude to theology, and show that the

movement has been away from the abstractness of logical positivism toward a more concrete consideration of language that
is not too far from the existential account of the matter, as we
have expounded it above.

Although the current linguistic philosophy has important
roots in continental European philosophy, England has been
the scene of its greatest achievements and also of its widest
popularity. It is well-known that the philosophical climate of
England underwent an almost complete change during the first
half of the present century. Indeed, it has become customary to
speak of the 'revolution in philosophy'. At the beginning of the
century, the idealist school, associated with such great names as
Caird, Bradley, Bosanquet, McTaggart and many others,
dominated the scene, and some of its members spoke with
almost an air of finality. Today, in England at least, the idealist
school has almost vanished away. A new kind of philosophy has
taken its place. Of course, this new philosophy has been very in-
fluential elsewhere than in England, and it is very strong in the
United States. However, in American universities and colleges,
alternative types of philosophy are still very much in evidence—
phenomenology, existentialism, process philosophies, and so on.
In England, on the other hand, the new philosophy has assumed
quite a commanding position in the universities. It has progressed
from being the protest of a minority to becoming the outlook of
the majority, from being a heterodoxy to becoming a new orthodoxy. Many people seem to assume that this is the only kind of
philosophy worth doing—though admittedly adherents of other
schools have in the past shown the same kind of exclusivism!

When a political party ceases to be in opposition and is called
to assume the reins of government, it almost invariably curbs
some of its former excesses and assumes a more constructive—
even more conservative—attitude to the problems of the day,
for which it now has a new responsibility. A similar change of
attitude has come over the philosophical movement of which
we are speaking. In its beginnings, it assailed many traditional
beliefs with an almost iconoclastic fervour. As it has won

recognition and become more and more established, it has relinquished polemics for more constructive attitudes, and has sought ways to rehabilitate some of the beliefs which, at an earlier stage, were being ruthlessly swept away. The changed attitude is to be seen even in the designation of the movement itself. It used to be known as 'logical positivism', but few philosophers seem willing to accept that label today. Most of the adherents of the movement prefer such non-committal and flexible appellations as 'logical analysis', 'logical empiricism', 'linguistic philosophy'. Of course, perhaps this very non-committal attitude is itself a kind of reflection of positivism.

While it is our purpose to consider some of the changes that have taken place or are taking place in the way in which logical empiricism looks at the question of God-talk, we shall take a moment to recall the basic characteristics of this way of doing philosophy.

What then is this new philosophy that has come to occupy so dominant a place in contemporary thought, at least in the English-speaking countries? It is possible to distinguish three major strands that are woven into it. The first strand is a strong empiricism. In this respect, the new philosophy is no innovation but rather a return to the British empirical tradition, which was for a time interrupted by the ascendancy of idealism. But the new philosophy stands in the indigenous line of Hobbes, Locke, Berkeley and Hume. A second strand derives from modern developments in logic. These have led to a much wider understanding of the subject than was possible while it was still dominated by the traditional Aristotelian conceptions. As far as this second strand is concerned, Bertrand Russell has been a major influence, together with many others such as Whitehead and Frege. A third strand, which is possibly the most typical of the movement, is to be found in its interest in language. It is in words and sentences that our thinking about the world expresses itself and becomes accessible. But language is full of pitfalls, and it is the conviction of many members of the school that some of the most stubborn traditional problems of philosophy have arisen from confusions of language. So we are directed to the analysis of language as a fundamental philosophical task, and here perhaps we might mention the name of Moore as a philosopher who did much to establish the habit of careful linguistic analysis.

It is not, however, our business to probe into the origins of logical empiricism. Like every other philosophical movement, this one has had its precursors and has been prepared for in the past. But we may say that the contemporary development opened with the appearance in 1922 of Ludwig Wittgenstein's *Tractatus Logico-Philosophicus*. By any standards, this is a difficult book, even for persons with a philosophical training. It already shows the three strands I have mentioned, for it is marked by a strong interest in logic and mathematics, by an investigation of language and its limits, and by an underlying empiricism. The somewhat cryptic concluding proposition of the book was one fraught with meaning not only for philosophers but for a much wider circle: 'Whereof one cannot speak, thereon one must be silent.'[1] In other words, there are limits to language, and there are some themes on which nothing meaningful can be said. What are these themes (if it is even permissible to use this word)?

Although the answer was already there in Wittgenstein's book, it was spelled out in a more popular and percussive form in Alfred J. Ayer's brilliantly provocative *Language, Truth and Logic*. In spite of its brevity and the youthfulness of the author when it first appeared in 1935, this book has been one of the landmarks in twentieth-century English philosophy, and it really put the new philosophy on the map. It became the classic statement of logical positivism.

According to Ayer, there are two kinds of propositions that may be meaningfully asserted. The first kind includes analytic propositions, especially the propositions of logic and mathematics. These are tautologies. They assert nothing about reality and are not, as used to be supposed, synthetic propositions. They get their meanings from our agreement to use certain

[1] *Op. cit.*, p. 189.

symbols in certain ways, and they simply draw out the implications of our definitions. 'A being whose intellect was infinitely powerful would take no interest in logic and mathematics. For he would be able to see at a glance everything that his definitions implied, and, accordingly, could never learn anything from logical inference which he was not fully conscious of already.'[1] The second kind of meaningful propositions are the genuinely synthetic ones. These do make assertions about the real world. They get their meaning from the fact that, at least in principle, they can be verified with reference to some sense-experience.

Thus if I say, 'Twice two are four', or, 'There is a cat on the doorstep', I am making meaningful assertions; and the truth or falsity of these assertions can be determined, in the first case with regard to the definitions of the terms used, in the second case by going and looking. But suppose I say with Browning, 'God's in his heaven', this is not obviously a tautology, but neither can I verify it by any relevant sense-experience. Such a sentence is therefore, according to Ayer, meaningless, incapable of being either true or false. Such, on his view, are all the 'pseudo-propositions' of metaphysics, ethics and theology. Since they fall into neither of the two categories of meaningful propositions, they are, strictly speaking, nonsense. At most, they may be reckoned as emotive utterances. So if a man says, 'God's in his heaven', he is not making any meaningful assertion, though the words may evince a feeling of optimism or well-being on his part.

Of course, an emotive theory, whether of ethical or theological language, has its own difficulties. I have argued above[2] that the feeling which undoubtedly does find expression in religious utterances is not a mere subjective emotion, but carries with it an awareness of the situation in which the person who has the feeling participates. So to point to the element of feeling that finds expression in religious utterances (and likewise moral judgments) is not to show that these are meaningless, but to raise the question about their meaning in a new way. The value

[1] *Language, Truth and Logic* (London: Victor Gollancz, 2nd edition, 1946), pp. 85-86.
[2] See above, p. 76.

of Ayer's critique of ethics and theology[1] lay principally in the fact that it showed that the statements of ethics and theology are of different kinds from the propositions of science and every-day experience.

The new philosophy therefore eventually came to recognize that it is unsatisfactory just to say that some utterances are meaningful propositions and the rest nonsensical pseudo-propositions, or to think that one can make a neat division between informative and emotive utterances. Instead of laying down in advance what kinds of statements are to be regarded as meaningful, linguistic philosophy took as its task the investigation of different kinds of language, seeing how they get used and what meaning can be assigned to them. Notable work was done in the area of ethics, and the interest spread to religious and theological language.

What then can be said about religious and theological statements? It may be worthwhile recalling some of the ways in which logical analysts have talked about their meaning.

The first move would be to ask whether they are not amenable to some kind of empirical verification. But since such verification is usually limited to sense-experience, then, as I have already pointed out,[2] the notion that religious assertions could be proved by some sense-experience went out with mythology, and with its belief that the divine sensibly manifests itself as a phenomenon in space and time. The fact that no direct empirical tests are nowadays considered relevant to the verification of religious beliefs is the starting-point of John Wisdom's essay, 'Gods'. But he claims also that the difference between the theist and the atheist is more than just a difference of emotional attitudes in the face of the world. Each of them tries to trace patterns of structures in the world that tend to support his point of view, and this is an empirical procedure, though presumably it is never conclusive.[3] The believer often does appeal to experience, though not sense-experience; for instance, Joseph pointed

---

[1] *Op. cit.*, pp. 102ff.  [2] See above, p. 21.
[3] Cf. *Philosophy and Psychoanalysis*, p. 159.

to the way his past experiences had turned out for good as indicating that the providence of God had shown itself in them.[1] But such appeals could never be conclusive, and it would be open to any sceptic to say that the events in question had been merely coincidental.

In any case, it would be difficult to find any standard method of verification comparable to those used in the empirical sciences. Almost anything can be pressed into service as 'verification' for a belief so wide in its scope as, let us say, the belief in divine providence.

Thus the demand may become one for a principle of falsification, rather than of verification. What evidence would count decisively *against* the belief in question? This principle of falsifiability has been developed chiefly by Karl Popper, and what caused him to pay attention to it was his dissatisfaction with Marxism and Freudianism. These are both theories so wide in their scope that they can account for just about everything that happens, and are almost irrefutable. But Popper saw that irrefutability is really a vice, and that a theory that is compatible with any and every state of affairs has very little to tell us. One may recall the jest about the patient visiting his psychiatrist. If he arrived early, this was taken to show that he was anxious; if he arrived on time, this meant he was compulsive; and if he came late, he was resentful. Whatever he might do, the theory would account for it. Is there any way of testing the truth of the theory if there is no state of affairs that would be taken to falsify it?

The principle of falsifiability is easily applied to religious assertions, and looks like causing them trouble. A man is crossing the street and gets narrowly missed by a bus. He says, 'God loves me, for the bus did not hit me'. On another occasion he is struck by a bus and injured. This time he says, 'God loves me, for the bus did not kill me'. Finally he is actually killed by the bus. But now his friends say, 'God loves him, for he has called him out of this unhappy and sinful world'. The ground of verification shifts each time, and it seems that nothing that might

[1] Gen. 45.4–8.

happen would be taken as falsifying the religious belief. But it would seem that such an irrefutable belief has been voided of any worthwhile content. In Antony Flew's expression, it has undergone 'the death by a thousand qualifications'.[1]

The failure to point to a standard way of verifying (or falsifying) religious assertions has been taken to count heavily against the claim of such assertions to have any cognitive content. In any case, statements about God look like metaphysical statements, and even logical analysts who have been willing to reconsider the rehabilitation of ethical and religious language have usually been still quite definitely against the reinstatement of metaphysics. Anything like the old-style natural theology is ruled out. The point has been clearly put by Ronald Hepburn: 'If we are convinced that Hume and Kant and their successors have once and for all refuted the arguments of rational apologetics, we are faced with a choice between agnosticism (or atheism) and the discovery of an alternative method of justifying belief'.[2] What could an 'alternative method' be except one that presented religion independently of any metaphysical view of the world? This would not necessarily be an emotive account of religious language, but it might well attribute to it a 'meaning' that had nothing to do with any supposed knowledge of God or the supersensible.

There have in fact been various accounts of religious language that have tried to screen out from it any 'transcendent' reference. These accounts include: a 'religious atheism' which recognizes the value in personal and social life of the religious attitude, while rejecting any theistic view of the cosmos; the assimilation of religious language to moral language, so that statements about God can be understood as assertions of moral intentions; the understanding of religious language as a kind of poetry which is helpful in the forming of life and character but which may have nothing to tell us about the nature of the universe in which we live. I do not propose to discuss these various points of

[1] *New Essays in Philosophical Theology*, ed. A. Flew and A. MacIntyre (London: SCM Press, 1955), p. 97.

[2] *Metaphysical Beliefs*, ed. A. MacIntyre (London: SCM Press, 1957), p. 89.

view, though many of the points raised by their protagonists are of great interest. But much has been written about them already, and in any case, my own conviction is that any satisfactory account of religious language (and still more, of theological language) must ascribe to it a definitely cognitive dimension and take seriously its claim to deal with the knowledge of God. On the other hand, I do not think that this implies that one must accept the possibility of metaphysics, if this is understood as a rational investigation into reality.

When I was writing on these themes about ten years ago, I ventured to express the opinion that the attempts of logical analysts to give somewhat more affirmative accounts of the meaning of religious language than had been done in the earlier period when all God-talk was dismissed as nonsense, could be interpreted as 'constructive contributions to the philosophy of religion' and represented a changed and more hospitable attitude toward theology on the part of these philosophers.[1] This remark drew a reply from Ronald Hepburn, one of the philosophers to whom I had alluded. He took me to task for having been too ready to conclude that the new attitude was a 'constructive' one. Probably his rebuke was justified. Soon after, he published *Christianity and Paradox*, in which he stated explicitly that the book did not make a 'constructive contribution', though on the other hand he also said that it was not 'negative polemic' of the kind that the earlier positivists had written.[2] This book does, I believe, show a genuine understanding of religion and a wide knowledge of contemporary theology. But it also contains, I should say, some very damaging criticisms of some commonly held positions in current or recent theology. For instance, no self-respecting theologian should now talk glibly of a 'self-authenticating encounter' until he has read Hepburn's acute analysis of this conception, and found some answers to his strictures.

Actually, Hepburn's careful style of analysis raises more

[1] 'Changing Attitudes to Religion in Contemporary English Philosophy' in *The Expository Times*, vol. LXVIII, pp. 298ff.
[2] *Christianity and Paradox* (London: Watts, 1958), p. 1.

serious problems for the theologian than did the brash and often superficial attacks of the positivists. These attacks were usually directed on some abstract beliefs regarded as 'religion' by men who had obviously no sympathy or even acquaintance with the concrete realities of the life of faith. But Hepburn's critique is on quite another level. Thus we should not delude ourselves into thinking that the retreat from an iconoclastic positivism leads automatically to a situation in which analysis makes a constructive contribution to the problems of theology or of the philosophy of religion.

Analysis, as a methodology, remains neutral. Nevertheless, the fact that linguistic philosophers no longer rule out religious language as senseless from the outset has created quite a different situation from that which prevailed in the heyday of logical positivism. I wish now to mention five specific points on which this particular school of philosophy has come to findings that point the way to a more favourable and affirmative account of religion and theology than would have been at all possible in the earlier stages of the movement. Though I shall mention five points, it will be seen that some of these tend to overlap.

The first point is the recognition that there is a *multiplicity of languages*. In the earlier days, as we have seen, it was generally held that, aside from the tautologies of mathematics and the like, there is only one kind of meaningful language—the kind which is made up of empirically verifiable assertions; and all other kinds were lumped together as 'emotive utterance'. Ludwig Wittgenstein came near to such a view in his *Tractatus Logico-Philosophicus*; but it was he himself who later pointed to the multiplicity of 'language-games', as he called them, and in the posthumous *Philosophical Investigations* he made one of the frankest and most charming retractions in modern philosophy: 'It is interesting to compare the multiplicity of kinds of word and sentence with what logicians have said about the structure of language—including the author of the *Tractatus Logico-Philosophicus*'.[1]

---

[1] *Op. cit.*, p. 12e.

Recognition of the plurality of languages has meant that the old verification principle, even in its weak or modified form, has come to be considered as too narrow. Following the later Wittgenstein, analysts tell us that the meaning of language is to be sought in the way in which it gets used. This new attitude finds an extreme expression in the slogan: 'Every language has its logic'. Of course, it may be that when a particular kind of language is investigated, it will be found that its logic is defective and incoherent. Or again, it may be that a language commonly supposed to have been in some way informative will be found to be used in ways that can be differently accounted for. We have already seen that the first moves of logical analysts toward the rehabilitation of religious language shied away from attempts to show that this language does—as it has always been supposed to do—give us some insight into the ultimate nature of things. But at least we can say that there is no prejudging of the case. Every language, including that which is used by the religious believer, is to be given a hearing and allowed an opportunity to make clear what its logic is.

A second point, closely related to the first, is the apparent reluctance nowadays to move in the direction of levelling down all language to one single kind of talk, and we may call this the *distrust of reductionism*. In the early positivist writings, such as Rudolf Carnap's *Logical Syntax of Language*, the ideal universal language was held to be that of physics. The goal was the unity of science, and this meant expressing all scientific knowledge in a single language. Even our talk about persons, say in psychology or sociology, ought to be reducible to the universal language of physics; and the possibility of making such a reduction could be taken as a measure of the extent to which these studies of man qualified as sciences. This doctrine which assigned a basic place to the language of physics was called 'physicalism', but it seems to have been involved in metaphysical presuppositions scarcely distinguishable from materialism.

In any case, the contemporary mood seems to have moved away from the desire to reduce all our meaningful talk to the language of physics. In other words, the multiplicity of languages is accepted as a genuine multiplicity. It is worth noting that Gilbert Ryle, though his teaching in *The Concept of Mind* has sometimes been called a 'neo-behaviourism', explicitly disclaims that to deny man is a ghost in a machine is the same as to assert that he is just a machine.[1]

Perhaps this distrust of reductionism seems strange at a time when the new science of cybernetics seems to have opened up fresh possibilities of translating at least some personal language into an impersonal physical language that is appropriate to electronic machines. But we took note that there would seem to be a critical point where impersonal language becomes inadequate, and where personal (participating) language is demanded, either for the psychophysical entities that we ourselves are or for supermachines (if any ever got built) that became capable of free spontaneous acts and thoughts.[2] When these matters were mentioned, an allusion was made to P. F. Strawson's book, *Individuals*. We may now point to another aspect of that book, which reinforces the move away from reductionism. In the course of his 'descriptive metaphysic', Strawson urges the 'logically primitive' character of person-language. Of course, he is not writing 'revisionary metaphysics', and so one cannot interpret him to mean that person-language *cannot* be reduced to thing-language. But there is a *prima facie* case for the irreducibility of person-language in the fact that it is a basic mode of discourse, and Strawson does show some of the difficulties besetting those who might try to make the reduction.

These matters are surely of interest for the problem of religious and theological language. Since this kind of talk is so frequently immersed in personal language, the tendency away from reductionism is an important step towards making possible a nonreductive account of such talk.

A third point is the recognition of *diversity of meaning*, though this is very close to the two points already made and may seem

[1] *The Concept of Mind* (London: Hutchinson, 1949), p. 328.
[2] See above, p. 96.

to overlap them. Back in the days when C. K. Ogden and I. A. Richards wrote *The Meaning of Meaning* (it was published in 1923), nominalism, behaviourism and the general division of language into 'descriptive' and 'emotive' were widely acceptable and so a particular meaning of 'meaning' gained ascendancy.

But nowadays it is recognized that the problem of meaning is much more complex and that the varieties of meaning are much more numerous than was once supposed. 'There are many different ways of conceiving meaning, and what is true of a meaning in one conception is often false in another'.[1] One rather obvious consequence of this recognition of the complexity of the notion of meaning is a change in the style of debate. When 'meaning' was rather narrowly conceived, it was considered rather clever to tell someone that his remarks were meaningless. But now this is not considered clever any more. Rather, it is a confession of failure to understand. So if anyone is told that his remarks are meaningless, he may very well reply that his opponent should try a little harder to find the meaning.

The first three points I have made are perhaps just different aspects of a single point—the recognition of the openness and plurality of the possibilities for meaningful discourse. In itself, this simply clears the way for the kind of thing we are trying to do in this book, namely, to show the logic and the meaning of theological discourse. So these three points may not seem to amount to much. Yet the openness of this situation sharply contrasts with the closed situation of an earlier time.

I come now to a fourth point which is somewhat different. It has to do with the use of *indirect language*. It seems now to be widely acknowledged that important things can be said in 'odd' or 'oblique' language, as well as in straightforward language. The earlier view was that whatever can be said meaningfully can be said clearly, that is to say, in unambiguously descriptive language which refers directly to its referend. We have seen how

[1] L. Jonathan Cohen, *The Diversity of Meaning* (New York: Herder & Herder 1963), p. 169.

this ideal was upheld both by the early Wittgenstein and by the logician Susan Stebbing.[1] But now there is an increasing interest in what may be called the more indirect kinds of language, where the ultimate referend of the talk is hinted at through the mediation of something else. Since religion makes wide use of such indirect kinds of language—myth, symbol, analogy, parable and so on—this new willingness to use or to listen to such kinds of language may lead to interesting results.

As an illustration of what I have in mind, I might mention the ingenious and sometimes vivid stories or parables which linguistic philosophers have themselves employed to elucidate the character of religious discourse, to point to possible meanings for it and ways of testing its truth or falsity. We have already had occasion to refer to John Wisdom's well-known parable[2] of the two men who argue as to whether or not a gardener comes to tend a certain plot of ground, and the way in which each of them defends his point of view. This parable throws light on what the theist and the atheist are arguing about, as each tries to trace patterns in the world that may escape the other. The parable may be said to illustrate the ambiguity of the world, and the impossibility of conclusively deciding for theism or atheism on empirical data. But it also shows that the empirical data are not irrelevant. Both men have, apparently, formed their convictions before they begin their argument, but they are willing to expose their convictions to a confrontation with whatever facts might seem relevant. It seems to me, however, that Wisdom achieves a further point in his parable by indicating that the empirical data relevant to such an argument are not simple 'facts' but rather *Gestalten* or configurations of facts.[3]

Let me add some further illustrations. Basil Mitchell made telling use of the parable[4] of the resistance fighter who meets a stranger, claiming to be the head of the resistance movement,

---

[1] See above, pp. 17, 88.    [2] *Philosophy and Psychoanalysis*, pp. 154ff.
[3] It is unfortunate that many readers seem to be acquainted with Wisdom's parable only in the version given by Antony Flew in *New Essays in Philosophical Theology*, p. 96. Wisdom's own version carries much more constructive suggestions.
[4] *New Essays in Philosophical Theology*, pp. 103ff.

and the fighter is so impressed by the stranger that he remains loyal to him despite all appearances. This parable helps us to understand what is meant by a 'self-authenticating encounter'. Admittedly, one would then have to face all the objections to such an idea, such as those of Hepburn, mentioned above; but something has been done to light up the meaning of our talk about God. Again, there is John Hick's parable[1] of the two travellers, one of whom believes that the road leads to the Celestial City, while the other does not. The point of the story is that although no kind of verification is available at the present, the truth will be revealed at the end of the journey (eschatological verification). As a last illustration, I might mention Gilbert Ryle's story[2] of how an undergraduate is permitted to look at the college accounts. The auditor explains that everything that goes on in the college is covered in his accounting, but the undergraduate feels that the most important things have somehow been left out. The story is meant to call in question such reductionist doctrines as physicalism; when the physicist has exhaustively described the world, are there not very many and very important 'intangibles' that have been left out?

These parables have been mentioned here not so much for their contents (though these are surely important enough) as just to show that analytic philosophers seem willing to turn to oblique language when they come to discuss the questions of religion. Even God elusively appears in these stories as 'gardener' or 'stranger', images that are new, yet not so utterly different from the images of 'shepherd' or 'king' in terms of which men once talked of him. It seems to be recognized not only that concepts have an 'open texture' but that there is a place too for evocative images that can perhaps speak to us of those intangibles that interest the 'undergraduate', even if they can never be subjected to the formalization and schematization proper to those matters with which the 'auditor' deals. In other words, the study of these parables seems to indicate an acknow-

---

[1] *Philosophy of Religion* (Englewood Cliffs, N.J.: Prentice-Hall, 1963), pp. 101–2.
[2] *Dilemmas* (London: Cambridge University Press, 1960), pp. 75ff.

ledgement on the part of analytic philosophers that there is a language (let us call it 'symbolic' language) that is not merely emotive but has the power of opening up and illuminating levels of experience in a way that cannot be done through the use of propositions having a straightforward empirical reference. This by no means rules out the possibility that even our most oblique 'symbolic' language has some relation to our everyday experience, and perhaps the 'justification' for such language would consist in showing how it is in fact ultimately anchored in our everyday existing.

The fifth and last point that I want to make—and it seems to me to be the most important one—is the current tendency to place language in the *context of the situation* out of which it arises. This is the point where, I believe, we see something like a convergence between the consideration of language in the analytic school and those more existential accounts of the matter on which our own treatment in this book has for the most part been based.

Formerly, the analyst tended to treat words and sentences as entities that could be considered in isolation. The analysis was concerned with the internal syntax of the language. But the new emphasis on use implies that the meaning of words and sentences may sometimes be properly understood only if we set these verbalizations in the context of the concrete human situation in which they have arisen; and, after all, it is true of all talking whatsoever that it arises in some concrete human situation. We have already seen how, with some kinds of talk, it is necessary to take the situation into account; for instance, the kind of talk that we call 'paradox' is bound to look like self-contradictory nonsense if the language is analysed in isolation from the situation in which it was spoken, that is to say, if a merely syntactical analysis takes place. But if the language is set in the human context in which it was intended to express some insight that had been noticed, then it may very well make sense. In our own terminology, the language has to be related to the discourse-situation. Now religious language in all its forms is bound up very closely with the situations in which it arises, and an exploration of this language must have regard to these situations if it is to arrive at worthwhile results.

One analytic philosopher of religion who has been very much aware of the necessity to relate religious language to the situations where it belongs is Ian Ramsey, now Bishop of Durham. His book *Religious Language*, published in 1957, bore as its subtitle: 'An Empirical Placing of Theological Phrases'. He has consistently tried to set religious language in religious situations, which he has very well characterized as situations of discernment and commitment. This double characterization is, I think, very important. With the new stress on use, many analytic philosophers might be willing to place religious language in situations that might be called 'religious', but perhaps most of them would stress 'commitment' rather than 'discernment', that is to say, they would tend to see the meaning of the religious assertion in moral or social terms and would be reluctant to acknowledge a cognitive dimension of 'discernment', especially if this was supposed to have to do with the discernment or disclosure of some transhuman reality. It seems to me that Ramsey is completely correct in refusing to short-change religious language and in recognizing that it has a twofold character, represented in his terminology by the words 'discernment' and 'commitment'. It will be remembered that our own earlier investigations led us to a similar point of view, which we found exemplified in the use of the key-word, 'God'.[1] As a result of a kind of positivist hangover, the logical empiricist is inclined to confine the meaning of religious language to the immanent context of the social setting. Ramsey's stress on 'discernment' indicates that, like ourselves, he is prepared to set this language ultimately in its ontological context. He has in fact explicitly declared the inadequacy of any merely social account of religious language and upheld the need for our interpretation of such language to be of a kind that will 'preserve a faithful understanding of its own mysterious topic'.[2]

[1] See above, pp. 99ff.
[2] *Models and Mystery* (London: Oxford University Press, 1964), p. 44.

In any case, let me repeat that the tendency among analysts to place language in its 'home', that is to say, in the concrete human discourse-situation, firmly relates language analysis to existential analysis. This was clearly seen back in the days when logical positivism was on the crest of the wave by W. M. Urban, for in his neglected book, *Language and Reality*, he repeatedly stresses that language needs to be viewed within the living human context where alone it functions. The existentialists too had approached the problem of language as one that concerns a basic phenomenon of human existence. It is a basic conviction of this book that any adequate analysis of religious (and theological) language must be correlated with existential analysis.

The five points outlined above make it clear that whatever may have been the case in the earlier days, exchanges of more than a polemical kind are now possible between theologians and analytic philosophers. It is a pity that so many of our theologians seem to be either indifferent or impatient toward this type of philosophy; while a few of those who have been attracted by it seem to have been swept away by the tendency toward positivism. Fortunately there are men, such as Ian Ramsey, Frederick Ferré and John Hick, who are not only prepared to have discussions with the analysts in their own idiom but have also shown the relevance and usefulness of analytic techniques for the work of theology itself. It seems to me that there are at least three areas in which the theologian might profitably consider whether he can get some help for his tasks from contemporary linguistic philosophers.

The first of these areas is the self-criticism of theology itself. Woolly language seems to be an endemic disease in theology, and perhaps there is a good deal of such language too in existentialism, and in the theologies that have drawn upon existentialist philosophy. Every theologian—and every preacher as well—could do worse than just sometimes confront himself with his own sentences and ask: 'What do I really mean when I say this?' Logical analysis can be of great assistance in such criticism. It has, as we have seen, limits to its application, but we can welcome its legitimate uses. It can, among other things, enable the theologian to distinguish grammatical and logical form; it can teach him to recognize category mistakes; it can be useful in helping to discover where the boundaries lie between theology and other disciplines. Theology always needs criticisms of this kind, and logical analysis offers the possibility of really stringent criticism. To appropriate some of its techniques for self-criticism could not fail to result in clearer and better theology.

I wonder whether a second area in which logical analysis might have some contributions to make is the field of biblical theology. This is perhaps the area where, in recent times, theologians have been most intensely preoccupied with language. Especially they have been preoccupied with the biblical vocabulary, and Kittel's *Wörterbuch* is the great monument to the amount of interest and energy that has been invested in such researches. For the most part, however, the investigations have been directed to the history of the meanings of words. The question about the logical functions of words and the kind of discourse in which they operate has been neglected. For a more balanced account, attention would need to be paid to the logic of biblical language, always remembering that the grammar may supply very misleading clues to the logic. These remarks are obviously related to some of the things James Barr has said in his criticisms of certain aspects of biblical theology. The burden of his complaint has been that too much attention is paid to single words, too little to the connected discourse within which these words get their significations. In stressing the sentence as the minimal unit of discourse, Barr is saying precisely what Wittgenstein had said. Barr explicitly declares that his own inquiry is linguistic rather than logical, but he also remarks that in such an inquiry 'important questions of logic and of general philosophy are involved'.[1] If biblical theologians follow up some of Barr's clues, they are bound to come to the question of the logical patterns in theological discourse and to the problem of how the same word may have different semantic func-

[1] *The Semantics of Biblical Language*, p. 1.

tions in different types of discourse. This would also have the effect of integrating biblical theology more closely with systematic theology, to the benefit of both.

I pass to a third area, and this is the most important. The work of logical analysis, together with insights from other schools of philosophy, can make its contribution toward the construction of a new philosophical theology. The old natural theology, which has been declining since the time of Hume and Kant, has suffered further blows from the attacks which analytical philosophy has made upon metaphysics in general. Some theologians have decided that they can get along very well without any natural theology or its equivalent, and they appeal to revelation alone. But this is a desperate and unwise expedient. If Christianity rests solely on an alleged once-for-all revelation and has no support in reason or common experience, then it is doubtful whether it can survive or whether it deserves to survive. What is needed is a new philosophical theology that will take over the essential functions of the old natural theology. It will not set out to prove the existence of God or the immortality of the soul or anything of the sort, but it will show the basic structure of religious faith, what kind of situation gives rise to our talk about God, how this talk is meaningful in the context of that situation, and what kind of validity can be claimed for it. Obviously logical analysis is relevant to this task, especially in its present mood of recognizing that it is important to examine language in the concrete situation that gives rise to it. It is precisely in this connection, however, as was pointed out above, that logical analysis impinges on existential analysis, and it is to both of these together that we must look for the foundations of an adequate and contemporary philosophical theology.

The present book, devoted to the elucidation of the problem of theological language or God-talk, is itself a contribution to the kind of philosophical theology of which I have just written. We must therefore be open to hear what the analytic philosophers are saying, both in their criticisms of theology and in whatever constructive contributions they may be found to offer.

Perhaps Ian Ramsey has gone a little too far in his claim that this type of philosophy 'may even yet revitalize "theological thinking" as it has revolutionized philosophy'.[1] In this book, as already indicated, we shall be turning, even on questions of language, to thinkers of schools other than the analytic one. But it has seemed worthwhile in the present chapter to make it clear that we are not indifferent to what the analysts are saying and that, contrary to what many people believe, there are areas where logical analysis and existential analysis converge and where each of these can get help from the other.[2]

[1] 'Contemporary Empiricism: Its Development and Theological Implications', in *The Christian Scholar*, vol. XLIII, p. 184.

[2] Only after this book was written did I see James Alfred Martin's study, *The New Dialogue between Philosophy and Theology* (New York: Seabury Press, 1966). As well as giving an instructive critical account of the relation between Christian thought and analytical philosophy, this writer hopes for 'a convergence of interests and activity' between analysts and existentialists (p. 203).

# 6

## Types of Theological Discourse
## Case Study: The Language of Saint
## Athanasius

AT THE BEGINNING of the last chapter, it was said that it would be something of a digression. Up to a point, this prediction turned out to be true. We paused to take stock of the analytic philosophy to which allusion had been made from time to time, and to pay closer attention to what adherents of this school have said about theological language. Yet the digression was well worth while, and has brought us back into the mainstream of our argument, for we have seen that contemporary analysts stress the larger contexts within which isolated instances of language have to be set, and stress also the multiplicity of kinds of language that are appropriate in different contexts.

This, as I have said, returns us to the mainstream of our argument, which we had left at the end of our examination of the theological vocabulary. Even in undertaking that examination, we were aware that we were following an abstract procedure that could be justified only on the ground that it happened to be convenient. Not isolated words, but sentences or even chains of sentences are the units of discourse, and it is in the living context of discourse that words and sentences must themselves be studied. We have had further confirmation of this point from our study of the logical empiricists, and now we must move on from the theological vocabulary to the syntax of theology—the way it is put together. What concerns us, of course, is not the grammatical syntax, which is the same for theology as for any other kind of discourse, but the logical syntax, if we are willing to think of 'logic' in a sufficiently wide sense, to include not just the words and sentences in themselves, but their 'place' or 'home' in the community of discourse. We are going to inquire about the way in which theological sentences and arguments get constructed, so that they successfully bring to light those matters about which the theologian intends to speak.

In the earlier parts of this book, we have allowed ourselves to speak blithely of 'theological language', as if this were a language of a homogeneous kind. It is true that we have sketched out what was called a 'basic logic' of theological discourse, and this might seem to involve the claim that it underlies all theological talk; but it was also said that in any actual theology, the basic logic might well be covered up in the concrete expression of the discourse. The mention in the last chapter of Wittgenstein's teaching of the multiplicity of 'language-games' might lead us to expect that theological language itself is very complex and includes, if not several languages, at least several very distinct types of language or discourse.

Everyone knows that there are different styles of theologizing. What a difference separates, let us say, the theological discourse of a Hegelian writer of the nineteenth century (Isaak Dorner would be an example) from that of a dialectical theologian (such as Karl Barth) in the twentieth century! Even in the same theologian, we find different styles of theological discourse alternating in the course of his writings. Yet we group them all within the 'family', as it were, of 'theological discourse'. Does this imply that we think they might all be interpreted or translated in terms of some basic type of theological discourse, such as the 'basic logic' of which we have spoken? Such interpretation or translation would not be a reduction, but rather the reciprocal illumination of two or more kinds of discourse by setting them side by side and tracing their correspondences.

Actually, we do find that theologians who employ several kinds of theological discourse sometimes express much the same insight in more than one kind of discourse, and this is surely significant, as indicating the possibility of the kind of interpretation or translation mentioned above.

We must then try to distinguish and characterize some of the main types of theological discourse. This would also be a first step toward confirming what was said in an earlier chapter about the basic logic of theological discourse, for it ought to be possible to show that this basic logic is applicable to the manifold forms in which theological discourse actually appears.

We have already had occasion to notice some of the divergent forms which theological language takes, as when we took note of the different routes of the *via negationis* and the *via eminentiae*, and when we observed the fondness of theologians for ways of speaking that are indirect, sometimes symbolic, sometimes analogical, sometimes paradoxical. But these observations were of a provisional and almost casual kind, and now a more systematic analysis is required.

But how are we to go about this task? The most promising method, and the one which is most likely to keep us in touch with actual theological usage, as distinct from what we may think *ought* to be theological usage, would be to select some 'standard' theological text, and use it as a case study. We would work through it with a view to discovering what kinds of discourse the writer employs in the course of expressing himself, and whether he shows us the interconnections of these types of discourse, for instance, by interpreting what he has said in one way by going on to say it in another way.

But where could we find the kind of 'standard' text that could serve for our case study? Obviously, no 'standard' text exists, and if it did, it would probably be intolerably dull. But I think we might find something that would start us off on the empirical approach that we have in mind. Our purpose would best be served by a text that has become something of a theological classic, one that has stood the test of time and is recognized by theologians of different schools as having been successful in lighting up the question which it took for its theme. Furthermore, it would need to be a text sufficiently subtle and sophisticated to exhibit a wide range of types of discourse; yet, at the same time, we would not want a text dominated by some explicit theory about theological language and method, such as might inhibit the writer from employing unselfconsciously whatever mode of expression seemed best to suit his purpose at the different stages of his argument. Simply to go to such a text, examine and analyse it, and discover what patterns of discourse are employed in it, would be a big step forward in coming to grips with the syntax of theological discourse.

The text actually chosen for this case study is St Athanasius' famous treatise *De Incarnatione*. It seems to fulfil most of the requirements mentioned and to offer a good introduction to the whole range of theological language. Accordingly, we shall proceed to analyse the various types of theological discourse that St Athanasius employs in this writing, in the reasonable hope that by so doing we shall get a view of some of the major types of theological discourse in general.

We notice first that some parts of the *De Incarnatione* are unmistakably cast in the form of what we call 'mythical' discourse. Since myth, like theology, brings a religious faith to verbal expression, it must be closely related to theology. However, we commonly reserve the name 'theology' for a kind of expression that has a more definitely reflective and conceptual character than myth, though on the other hand we have seen that the language of theology still retains something of the imaginative and evocative character of myth. Perhaps even in theologies that deliberately seek to 'demythologize', the lines of connection with myth remain. At any rate, while the *De Incarnatione* as a whole is theology rather than mythology, some sections of it move in an almost completely mythological context of ideas.

Let us consider as an example the following passage, in which St Athanasius argues that it was fitting for Christ to die on a cross, rather than by any other death: 'If the devil, the enemy of our race, having fallen from heaven, wanders about our lower atmosphere, and there bearing rule over his fellow-spirits, as his peers in disobedience, not only works illusions by their means in them that are deceived, but tries to hinder them that are going up; while the Lord came to cast down the devil, and clear the air and prepare the way for us up into heaven—well, by what other kind of death could this have come to pass, than by one which took place in the air, I mean, the cross? For only he that is perfected on the cross dies in the air. Whence it was quite fitting that the Lord suffered this death. For thus being lifted up, he cleared the air of the malignity both of the devil and of demons of all kinds.'[1]

We have not yet attempted anything like a strict delineation of what is meant by 'myth', though this will be offered in due course;[2] but we have nevertheless touched on the topic of myth more than once, and have already criticized mythical language as one which, in the course of time, has ceased to be meaningful. The reason we gave for this decay of meaning was that even if the myth genuinely expresses, refers to and represents something, it breaks down nowadays on the level of communication, which is an equally essential constitutive item in discourse. The discourse breaks down at the level of communication because there is a lack of the shared presuppositions or shared universe of discourse that makes interpretation possible. The passage quoted above bristles with presuppositions that are completely foreign to us and that belonged to the mythical mentality of a former time.

Let us try to set out some of the presuppositions that must have been in St Athanasius' mind when he wrote the passage cited above. Among these presuppositions may be mentioned first a region called 'heaven', situated somewhere above the surface of the earth; next, a desire or even a kind of tendency

---

[1] xxv, 5–6. I have used the Greek text in the edition of Frank Leslie Cross (London: S.P.C.K., 1957); except for some words which I have wished to translate otherwise, I have used the English translation of Archibald Robertson (London: D. Nutt, 1891).
[2] See below, Chapter 8, pp. 171ff.

on the part of human souls to 'go up' to heaven; further, there
is the story of how Lucifer and his associates moved in the
reverse direction, by 'falling down' from heaven after their
primeval revolt against God; and, as a consequence, there is the
belief that the lower atmosphere is now the dwelling place of
the demonic crew, the air being so filled and dominated by
evil spirits that the way up to heaven is blocked to the souls
desiring to ascend. But since none of these presuppositions are
shared by the modern man, he cannot make sense of St Athanasius' argument. The modern person may indeed have heard, in
the course of his literary or religious education, of the story of the
fallen angels, but it is not likely to form any part of his serious
presuppositions about the world. Certainly, he would not think
of this story as supplying a clue to the topography of the outer
envelopes of our planet. The atmosphere for him is not the
abode of demons, but a mixture of nitrogen, oxygen, carbon
dioxide, water vapour and other gases, and such layers or
regions as there may be in it depend on density, radiation and
other purely physical factors. He would not be conscious either
of any desire to 'go up', though he might readily interpret this
as simply the desire for a better kind of existence.

Of course, it is important that we should not read St Athanasius' words in a crudely literal and matter-of-fact way. If sophisticated cosmological theories were far from his mind, so was the
stark literalness that characterizes so much of our modern
thinking. In mythical discourse, what we recognize as 'literal'
and 'symbolic', objective reference and existential or ontological
interpretation, have not yet been separated out. They are interwoven inextricably in an as yet undifferentiated matrix. It is
likely enough that from this matrix, in course of time, many
differentiated modes of discourse began to sort themselves out.
St Athanasius himself only rarely employs mythical language,
and just precisely what it meant to him would be very hard to
say. There is no doubt that such language is heavily laden with
connotation and interpretative imagery. 'Heaven' certainly does
not just refer to the upper regions as a location, but implies

everything that belongs to the abode of God and the blessed spirits; the 'atmosphere' is not just the environing element as it might be described by a scientist, but is an actual domain, a place of power and influence where personal existences have to fulfil or lose themselves. It is the realm of him whom the New Testament, moving obviously in the same circle of ideas, calls 'the prince of the power of the air'.[1] Thus, while our first reaction on reading St Athanasius' mythological passages may be one of bewilderment or amusement, a little reflection must make us more sympathetic. There is more here than we might at first suppose. But this means that we are asking for a reinterpretation. If, as is likely enough, the mythical ideas did once genuinely express and represent something, though they now break down on the level of communication, is it possible that the content of the myth could be reformulated in a fresh act of interpretation, so that communication can take place once more?

Here we must remember that language—and still more, discourse—is not static. We have continually stressed its living character as something that belongs within the context of human existence, and, as living, it must be also moving and developing. Wittgenstein has remarked: 'Our language can be seen as an ancient city: a maze of little streets and squares, of old and new houses, and of houses with additions from various periods; and this surrounded by a multitude of new boroughs with straight regular streets and uniform houses.'[2] From the point of view of our own inquiry, the obvious way of interpreting Wittgenstein's description is to see the archaic language of myth as belonging to the picturesque but unplanned city-centre. Some people would probably regard all religious language as belonging to the tortuous old town, and would suppose that the airy well-planned boroughs are inhabited exclusively by the sciences. But even in ancient Christian writers such as St Athanasius, myth was only one form of their discourse, and not even the dominant one. Theological language too has developed in new forms, even if it often retains mythical elements. Theology has not indeed

[1] Eph. 2.2.  [2] *Philosophical Investigations*, p. 8e.

migrated to the suburbs, for by its very nature it could not become like one of the natural sciences, but it has certainly expanded from its original home in 'Myth Alley', so to speak. Perhaps we should count it among the 'houses with additions from various periods', mentioned by Wittgenstein. In any case, it shows all styles from myth to demythologizing.

But let us come back to St Athanasius' language, which is our chief concern at the moment. We freely concede that he uses myth as one of his modes of discourse. As well as the illustration given above, one could point to many others in the *De Incarnatione*. I shall mention one, as we shall have occasion to allude to it later. This is the belief, taken from the Old Testament, that death is to be understood as the punishment for sin, consequent on the disobedience of Adam. But although St Athanasius speaks in these mythological ways, he has other modes of discourse at his disposal. Long before his time, God-talk had expanded beyond its original home. As we continue to study the language of the *De Incarnatione*, we shall find specially interesting those cases in which the author re-expresses the very themes of his myths in non-mythical forms, thus pointing the way to new interpretations and new possibilities of communication. Further, as I shall try to make clear, these alternative and more sophisticated kinds of theological discourse tend to move in the direction of what we have already called the 'basic logic' of theology —a logic which must be already present, though not, of course, explicitly, in the undifferentiated and seemingly alogical language of myth.

Let us turn now to a second mode of discourse. In a provisional and very general way, we may call it 'symbolic'. We have already considered a passage in which St Athanasius speaks of the fittingness of death upon a cross, and spells out this fittingness in mythological terms. Standing directly alongside this passage is another, which runs as follows: 'It is only on the cross that a man dies with his hands spread out. Whence it was fitting for the Lord to bear this also, and to spread out his hands, that with the one he might draw the ancient people, and with the other those from the Gentiles, and unite both in himself.'[1] This passage, though like the other it deals with the 'fittingness' of death upon a cross, could not be called 'mythical'. Yet it certainly involves symbolism, and a very impressive symbolism too. The crucified figure with hands outstretched symbolizes the fact that in the Christian community which the crucified and risen Lord had founded, the ancient factions of mankind were being drawn together in a new unity.

How does this kind of symbolic discourse differ from myth? In our discussion of the mythical passage, it was said that myth is an undifferentiated kind of discourse, in which the literal and symbolic meanings of words and stories have not yet been sorted out, and there is as yet no attempt to distinguish the symbol from what is symbolized—at least, in any clear, conscious, consistent manner. Different from the undifferentiated language of myth is the conscious use of imagery. This conscious use of imagery does differentiate between the symbol and what is symbolized, and we may say that the appropriate use of good imagery is a highly skilled and sophisticated kind of language, even if it perhaps has no more 'power' than a myth that has come out of the unconscious depths. In the passage about Christ's dying with hands outstretched, St Athanasius is employing a conscious symbolism, and the symbol is clearly distinguished from what it symbolizes. He is quite explicitly taking one situation, namely, the figure fastened to the cross, to light up quite a different situation, the coming together of Jews and Gentiles in the Church. Yet although these two situations are different, they are also related, otherwise one could not symbolize the other. The relation is expressed by St Athanasius in terms of the outstretched hands, yet obviously it is a deeper, more intrinsic relation than this circumstance of Christ's death, taken in and by itself; somehow, it is the very life of the Lord at work in his disciples. In all this, we are moving in quite a different realm of ideas from the kind that confronted us in the thought that the crucified one had purged the atmosphere.

[1] xxv, 3.

Furthermore, the symbolism of Christ's outstretched hands is not involved in the presuppositions of myth, such as constitute a barrier to communication. In this second passage, the only presuppositions seem to be some understanding of human life, feeling and suffering, and these presuppositions have a universality that separate them from the historically and culturally conditioned assumptions of a mythology. Hence this second passage on the fittingness of death on the cross is one that probably still communicates very effectively with modern man, or could do so with a minimum of interpretation.

One of the major differences between myth and the kind of symbolism we are now considering is that in the latter case, the symbols are recognized as symbols and so distinguished from what they symbolize. It may well be the case that the first consciously used religious symbols were derived from the unconscious symbolism of myth. This would happen when the myth began to be recognized as myth, and when religious thinking advanced to a more reflective and analytical level. The work of Plato shows us both the criticism of myth and the conscious, sophisticated use of myth to express philosophical truths. But this sophisticated use of myth that has been recognized as myth is better called 'symbolizing', for the symbols have become detached from the undifferentiated mythical matrix and are now used explicitly as symbols and recognized as distinct from what they symbolize, as well as somehow akin to it. In a later chapter,[1] we shall consider in detail the symbol of light, from its beginnings in mythology where God and light are scarcely distinguished, through its development as an explicit symbol, to its eventual decline. In this whole area of symbolism, it becomes possible to use images and pictures in the explicit awareness that their reference is to be sought beyond themselves or beyond their immediate and obvious reference.

I have suggested that perhaps the first religious symbols to be used consciously as symbols were taken from the archaic mythical material. But once the use of symbols, consciously recognized

[1] See below, pp. 202ff.

as such, had become established, then there were no limits to the selection of symbolic material. It was possible for the sensitive or poetic person to introduce many images that had never been used in the traditional mythology. Along with all the traditional symbols, the whole figurative use of language (something which we may suppose to be very ancient) could be pressed into service. So far I have been using the expression 'symbolism' in a very general way, to cover many different indirect kinds of language. Later, we shall want to distinguish more carefully between symbolism and analogy.[1] For the time being, however, let us simply notice how St Athanasius—and in this he is typical of most theologians—employs a wide variety of images in an indirect style of discourse where one situation is used to throw light on another. This is now quite different from mythology, for the person who uses such symbols is quite aware that they are nothing but symbols, and that they have perhaps never before been used in the way he uses them.

A favourite kind of indirect language with St Athanasius is the extended simile, and one could cite a great number of examples. As a monarch, by taking up residence within a city, makes it secure, so the Logos, by taking a body, has checked the enemies of mankind; as a portrait on a wooden panel becomes stained and disfigured with the passage of time, so that the subject must return for the portrait to be renewed, so the divine image in man has been progressively defaced by the fall, and must be restored by the return of the Logos, of which man had been given a reflection; as the light of the sun is not defiled or extinguished by touching bodies upon the earth, but rather cleanses and illuminates them, so the glory of the eternal Logos was not diminished by the incarnation but much rather worked for the transforming of creaturely being; and so on in many other passages.[2] The interpretative power of such imagery cannot be denied; these imaginative situations give us some inkling of that mysterious situation which it is the whole aim of the *De*

---

[1] See below, p. 215.
[2] The examples cited are in ix, 3–4; xiv, 1–2; xvii, 7.

*Incarnatione* to explicate for us. Moreover, the controlled and conscious use of symbolism marks a great advance on mythology.

But the crucial question in all language of this sort is that of how the images presented in the familiar situation of the analogues or symbols can succeed in illuminating or representing the much more obscure situation to which this indirect language is intended ultimately to refer. Just how wide a gulf can this symbolism bridge? One can see that an analogy, for instance, may very well be illuminative for another situation of the same order—for instance, one legal situation may help toward understanding another analogous one. But how could any everyday situation be illuminative for another one of a quite different order—or, to make the point quite concrete, how could things we can say about kings, portraits or the sun be illuminating for something so remote from these relatively intelligible matters as the incarnation? Yet it is this mystery that St Athanasius wants to talk about and bring to light.

Indirect language, including symbolism, analogy and whatever other kinds it may be useful to distinguish, is undoubtedly a great step forward from mythology, because the language now operates more reflectively and distinguishes between the symbol or image and that for which it stands. But still other forms of theological discourse are required if this indirect language itself is to be interpreted and vindicated, and if we are to see what steps lie between the imagery and that which it is supposed to represent.

But we are still only at the beginning of unfolding the manifold types of discourse employed in the *De Incarnatione*. We must now turn to a third type, and one which is very central to St Athanasius' whole discussion. We may call this 'existential' discourse, the kind of talk which expresses man's own existence in the world, its structure, possibilities and limitations. St Athanasius was one of the least speculative of the Alexandrian theologians, and his argument is much more closely concerned with the human situation than with cosmic or metaphysical matters. I think our analysis will show us that there was good reason for

Emil Brunner's judgment that the Athanasian teaching has 'a non-speculative existential character'.[1] His use of the language of human existence may also indicate the centrality of existential interpretation in theology generally.

The existential interest emerges very early in the treatise, and in rather a striking way. The matter under discussion is the doctrine of creation out of nothing, but it soon becomes clear that this is to be treated not as a speculation about the origin of the universe but as a clue to man's own creaturely being-in-the-world. Creation out of nothing is interpreted in terms of the finititude and transience of human existence. Man's 'natural state' (*to kata physin*) is said to be the nothing out of which he has come, and just as he has had his being out of nothing, so there is for him the possibility of lapsing back into nothing. It is asserted that 'man is by nature mortal, inasmuch as he is made out of what is not.'[2] If man orients his life by created transient things and sets his heart on the mastery and possession of these, as his highest good, he falls back progressively into the nothing out of which he has come, for he is more and more conformed to the transient being of the creation. But to set one's heart on something as the highest good and to orient one's life by it is, as we have seen, to make it 'god', in that sense of the word which can be expressed as 'ultimate concern'. It is in fact idolatry, and in biblical teaching idolatry is a practice which leads to the distortion and diminution of the existence of those who engage in it.[3]

It is at this point that we find a connection between St Athanasius' existential discourse and his mythology. Indeed, the existential discourse is nothing less than a reinterpretation of the mythology, a restatement of its content in another mode of discourse.

When he is speaking mythologically, St Athanasius attributes the origin of evil to the malignancy and deception of these demonic powers which, as we have seen, have made their abode

[1] *The Mediator* (London: Lutterworth Press, 1934), p. 229, n. 1.
[2] iv, 4–6.           [3] Cf. Ps. 115.

in the lower atmosphere and prevent the souls from going up to heaven. But he can also say quite explicitly that 'men devised and contrived evil for themselves.'[1] The root evil that they did, in St Athanasius' view, was to make idols: 'they transferred the honour of God to stocks and stones and to every material object and to men.'[2] St Paul is quoted: 'They worshipped and served the creature rather than the Creator.'[3]

Now, of course, for the ancient Christian writers, including St Athanasius, an idol was not just nothing; it was a demon, the abode or personification of one of those fallen angels of Satan's host. So the mythological idea that the origin of evil is to be found in the malignancy and deceits of those demonic powers that have descended upon the world is basically equivalent to the quite unmythological and existential idea that when man idolizes that which is creaturely and transient, or when, to use Tillich's language, he makes an ultimate concern of something that is not really ultimate, then the finitude and nullity of that which is thus idolized is reflected in the diminution and perversion of the idolater's own self; and, as a consequence, he slips back into the nothing out of which he was created.

The term used by St Athanasius to describe man's tendency to slip back into the nothing out of which he has come is *phthora*. It is unfortunate that this word has usually been translated into English as 'corruption', for in modern English usage, 'corruption' may mean simply a deterioration in quality, and is often used to mean moral deterioration. But *phthora* (and presumably also *corruptio*) meant something more radical, something like a fundamental break-up or loss of being. The word *phthora* was regularly used in Greek philosophy to signify 'ceasing to be' or 'passing out of existence'. A classic instance is Aristotle's treatise, *De Generatione et Corruptione*, on 'coming into being' (*genesis*) and 'passing out of being' (*pthora*).

When we bear in mind this existential-ontological sense that is given to the word *phthora* in St Athanasius, then light is thrown on another aspect of his mythological teaching. It will be

[1] iv, 4.  [2] xi, 4.  [3] Rom. 1.25.

remembered that we mentioned that among the mythological elements in the *De Incarnatione* we find the ancient belief that death was imposed as a punishment for the sin of Adam. But when the author talks in existential rather than in mythological terms (and these two modes of discourse are never far apart in this text) it becomes clear that by 'death' is not meant just the observable phenomenon of coming to the termination of life, but rather, as it is called, an 'abiding in *phthora*', a kind of reduced and diminished state of existence, a loss of being which is not some arbitrary punishment imposed for sin but is rather sin itself in its consequences for man, that is to say, in the break-up of the human person which it effects.

But while the *De Incarnatione* stresses the finitude and transience of man's being and directs attention to the nullity which permeates human existence, as it does the being of all finite entities that may cease to be, this is not the whole of the Athanasian anthropology. Ceasing to be can be experienced *as a threat* only because man has some positive potentiality (*dynamis*) for fuller being; or, to put it in another way, only because man does not have a fixed nature but is in the openness of existence, an openness which is open upward toward fuller being as well as downward toward the nothing whence man has come. In the language available to him, St Athanasius was saying pretty much what we mean when we call man the 'existent', the one in whom being has become transparent to itself, so that he can either lay hold on his being, and 'exist' in the fullest sense, or let slip his possibilities for being and lapse into that loss of being which the ancient author called an 'abiding in *phthora*'.

The terminology which St Athanasius uses to express the positive potentiality for fuller being in man centres on the word *logos*. Man is said to be 'rational' (*logikos*), though this expression should not be understood in too narrowly intellectualist a sense. It is explained to mean that man somehow participates in the divine *Logos*. The language of the *De Incarnatione* is very guarded. Man is given 'a portion of the power or potentiality (*dynamis*) of the *Logos*' so that he may be said to have a 'reflection (*skia*) of the *Logos*.'[1] In the *De Incarnatione* this share in the *Logos* is said to be an extra endowment, and does not belong to man in virtue of his 'nature'—so far as one can talk of his 'nature'.[2] This is indeed the 'extra' which differentiates man from all other known finite entities and in respect of which we can say that he 'exsists' or stands out. This extra, moreover, is given not as a permanent possession, but as *dynamis*, the possibility or potentiality for being, which may be either gained or lost in responsible existence. The loss of being is *phthora*; the opposite of this, in St Athanasius' terminology, is *aphtharsia*, etymologically a negative term, and yet, since it is the negation of loss, a strongly affirmative idea, namely, the fullness of being opened up to man by his participation in the *Logos*.

St Athanasius' existential discourse merges imperceptibly into what we may recognize as a fourth type, and which we may call 'ontological' discourse. This discourse employs the language of 'being' and 'nothing'. It lies so close to the existential discourse that perhaps it would be better to recognize just one type rather than two, and call it 'existential-ontological' discourse. This would have the further advantage of preventing confusion between ontological and metaphysical discourse. This kind of ontological discourse has nothing to do with the attempt to construct a rational science of being, even if one were to deem it possible to undertake such a task. The kind of ontology found in St Athanasius is existentially rooted; it talks of being and non-being not as possible objects which could be investigated by a disinterested philosophical inquiry, but of the being and nothing that are really encountered in existence itself.

St Athanasius does not explicitly equate Being with God. But what else can be implied in his famous doctrine that deification (*theopoiēsis*) is the end of humanity?[3] The obscurity of this doctrine and its allegedly pantheistic tendency are removed when

[1] iii, 3.
[2] On the other hand, in the *Contra Gentes*, the earlier companion piece to the *De Incarnatione*, St Athanasius teaches that *by nature* man is rational and immortal. The view of the *De Incarnatione* surely represents a great advance toward a more personal and existential understanding of these matters.
[3] Cf. liv, 4.

it is understood that 'to be God' is simply 'to be' in the fullest sense. To say that man is to be made God simply means that he is to realize the fullness of his being. In the *De Incarnatione*, human existence is, in different passages, represented as standing between limits, toward either of which it may be tending, and we may think of these pairs of limits as correlated. There are at least four ways of expressing these limits. Man is between *aphtharsia* and *phthora*, between, let us say, the gain and the loss of himself; he is between the good and the evil; he is between the divine and the demonic; he is between being and nothing. So *aphtharsia*, good, God, Being are correlated on the one side, and *phthora*, evil, the demons and nothing on the other side. These pairs of terms provide alternative ways of lighting up the same fundamental human situation.

A variety of expressions is employed because each one brings to our notice some special aspect of the situation. We have seen in an earlier discussion that the word 'God' is not a simple equivalent of 'Being', for this can be used in a neutral sense. The word 'God' speaks of Being as ultimate concern, Being which is at the same time *summum bonum*, uniting highest reality and highest value. In other words, God is holy Being, at once gracious toward man and demanding on him. 'God' is Being as it gives and entrusts itself to man, who is called, elected and enabled to enter into his potentiality for being, and experiences this as the gift of Being. This explains the reason for St Athanasius' claim that man's potentiality for fuller being is an added endowment; and although in this paragraph we have used the somewhat arid language of ontology, we are saying nothing else than what St Athanasius makes the main theme of his whole treatise on the incarnation, and which he expresses in the concrete symbolism of the Word's becoming flesh.

One further point may be noted in connection with St Athanasius' ontological discourse. We have already seen his ability to discourse about the nature of evil in two ways—the mythological way and the existential way. Now we find that this theme gets expressed in a third way, in the language of being and nothing. He writes: 'What is evil is not, but what is good is.'[1] Like many other Christian theologians, he is claiming that evil is to be understood in terms of negativity. This quotation about the nature of evil affords a further corroboration—if indeed any is still required—of the correlation in St Athanasius of the terms 'God', 'good' and 'Being'.

This examination of the existential and ontological elements in St Athanasius' theological language makes it clear to us that underlying his whole treatise is something like what we have called the 'basic logic' of theology. This is an existential-ontological mode of discoursing which proceeds from 'total existence' through the awareness of the existential question to the confrontation with Being, and, as we have tried to show, it is a manner of discoursing that expresses both cognitive and evaluative elements.

If we were to try to relate our analysis of St Athanasius' language to the sketches given in an earlier chapter of the language-styles of three contemporary theologians, I think St Athanasius shows most affinity with Tillich. One might even say that the structure of the early Athanasian writings is an example of what Tillich calls the method of 'correlation'—a method which is essentially existential-ontological. The *De Incarnatione*, as is well-known, is the companion piece to a slightly earlier writing, the *Contra Gentes*. In the earlier treatise, St Athanasius analyses the human situation as it was known to him, in terms of man's finitude, fall, sin, idolatry, and the concomitant dissipation of human existence in the old pagan world. That is to say, this treatise posed the existential question arising out of the situation of that time. The *De Incarnatione* tries to answer this question in terms of holy Being's approach to man, here presented in the Christian symbolism, whether mythological or analogical, of revelation through the incarnation of the divine word. But one could argue further that this existential-ontological method, seen as exemplifying the basic logic of theology, has its roots in the New Testament itself. St Paul's Epistle to the Romans,

[1] iv, 5.

beginning from man's idolatry of the creation, his enslavement to it and his sense of impotence, and then his experience of grace, had set the pattern long before St Athanasius, and, of course, much longer still before Tillich.

We are, however, not yet at the end of our analysis of the types of theological discourse to be found in the *De Incarnatione*. In addition to the four (or thereabouts) types already considered, there are several other subsidiary types, and these too demand some consideration.

Some passages in the *De Incarnatione* are distinctly metaphysical in character. For instance, arguing against the Epicurean view that all things have come into being by chance transformations of matter, St Athanasius appeals to something like the familiar argument from design, or, at any rate, from a discernible order to an Orderer. More precisely, he argues that the differentiated and structured order of the universe points to some intelligent creative Power. 'We see', he writes, 'a distinction of sun, moon and earth; and again, in the case of human bodies, of foot, hand and head. Now, such separate arrangement as this tells us not of their having come into being of themselves, but shows that a cause preceded them; from which cause it is possible to apprehend God also as the Maker and Orderer of all.'[1]

If this were intended to be a rational demonstration of God, then it would be open to all the objections that modern criticism has directed against the argument from design. But it might be possible to defend the language here by saying that it is not intended to be a rational demonstration, though it might indeed have a kind of negative value in showing that the Epicurean view is not a particularly reasonable one. But one might claim that St Athanasius here is looking for an alternative way of expressing the awareness of creatureliness in the face of Being, as it gives itself to man. In this case, one could say that the metaphysical language is also anchored, though more obscurely, in the basic logic of theology. One often does hear it contended nowadays that the traditional proofs for the existence of God

[1] ii, 2.

were never meant to be taken cold, as it were, as if by strict logic they could draw irrefutable conclusions from premises that all reasonable people would accept; they were intended rather to be reflections and clarifications directed to convictions already held by the believer, and of the reasonableness of which he desired to satisfy either himself or other people. One might make such claims about St Athanasius' argument, especially as his remarks on the creation are simply a preface to what he has to say about the constitution of human existence.

But I have no wish to make such a claim, and think it more likely that the ancient author did intend to put forward a metaphysical argument that would counter the arguments of his opponents. In any case, even if we allowed that the metaphysical language were to be interpreted as something other than a proof, we would then have to complain that this language suffers the defect of being highly deceptive, for it certainly has the appearance of a proof and most readers would think that it was intended to be a proof. Like mythology, the metaphysical element in theology, where it occurs, needs to be interpreted anew in an idiom nearer to the basic logic of theology; and metaphysics shares with mythology, though in a different way, the serious fault of appearing to talk of God and other theological themes as if these could be made objects for our inspection.

Occasionally St Athanasius uses the language of authority, though whether this should be reckoned a distinct kind of discourse I do not know. Still, the contrast between appeal to authority and rational argument is sufficiently striking to call for notice. While he opposes the Epicurean view about the origin of things with a metaphysical argument, he takes a different line when opposing the view of certain sects, presumably Gnostic, who maintained that the created world, as essentially evil, could not have originated from God. St Athanasius brings no arguments against them at all, but simply quotes some passages from the Bible, such as: 'All things were made through him, and without him was not anything made that was made.'[1]

[1] John 1.3.

No doubt the sects in question accepted the authority of the Bible, so that he needed to say no more.

We did take note that Frederick Ferré had characterized the theological discourse of Karl Barth and his followers as the 'logic of obedience'.[1] Of course, any body of theological teaching is usually governed by some authority. This may be clearly defined or it may be more flexible, but any theology claiming to be Christian would move within certain limits, determined by scripture and tradition, as received in some particular Christian community. We even have a special name for an authoritative theological pronouncement—we call it a 'dogma'. However, the authority of a dogma is derived from something beyond itself—it may be the Bible or the Church. These too can be questioned about their credentials, and eventually we come back to the source of authority in the revelation of God on which the community of faith has been founded. For God makes his absolute claim upon anyone whom he addresses. Thus the most fundamental and authoritative dogmas of any theology must find their final justification in the basic logic of theology. But when we call to mind the character of this logic, then we can draw the conclusion that a dogma is not a statement of objective fact, but, like all other theological language, combines cognitive insight with existential concern.

In the later parts of the *De Incarnatione*, considerable use is made of empirical arguments in order to support the truth of Christianity. Such arguments have a special interest, in view of the prevalence of empirical attitudes in our time.

These empirical arguments are of various kinds. One is the familiar argument from prophecy—an argument that was still being used by empiricist John Locke in *The Reasonableness of Christianity* many centuries later. The argument was very common in patristic writers, but in the light of modern biblical scholarship, it is almost worthless. In retrospect, we see that passages from the Old Testament were read in the early Church with reference to what these early Christians believed about

[1] See above, p. 49.

Jesus Christ, and appropriate passages were taken to be predictions although in many cases it is most improbable that they were ever intended to be anything of the sort. In some cases, it even seems likely that incidents in the life of Christ were invented simply to fulfil what were taken to be messianic prophecies. At most, one could only say in a general way that Christianity fulfilled some of the aspirations of ancient piety. Another argument is of a more pragmatic sort. St Athanasius points to the decline of paganism. The old temples, he claims, are being deserted and people are turning to the Christian Church. It may be recalled that our author had himself lived as a boy through the last great persecution of the Church, when his own bishop in Alexandria was among the martyrs. Then he had seen toleration granted under the Edict of Milan, and these events had made a profound impression on him. They seemed to give empirical evidence of the superiority of the Christian faith. Here indeed we are dealing with verifiable events, but the argument itself proves nothing of importance. The fact that one religion ousts another does not prove that the successful one is 'superior' to its vanquished rival, still less that it is 'true'. If it did, then the same argument could be used to show that Islam is superior to Christianity because it ousted its rival in the lost African provinces of the Church; or that Marxism is better than Christianity because it has largely ousted the traditional faith of the Russian people. A third kind of argument merits more serious attention. The *De Incarnatione* claims that with the rise of Christianity, morals have improved and society has been cleansed and pacified.[1] This is not purely an empirical argument since it obviously implies a judgment of value. We have seen, however, that all religious language has its evaluative side and expresses an existential attitude. If any confirmation of the 'truth' of Christianity or any other religion is to be obtained—that is to say, any confirmation that the man of faith has indeed been addressed by God and is not just the victim of an illusion—then perhaps it

---

[1] These empirical arguments are found in xxxiii-xxxviii (prophecy), xlvi-1 (decay of paganism), li–liii (reform of society).

can be only of the kind to which St Athanasius draws attention in his argument: the emergence of new and fuller life in the community of faith, a new wholeness and integrity of being, in contrast to that dissipation of being that is experienced in the condition of *phthora*. Thus the language which takes its rise in 'total existence' comes back to existence for its eventual confirmation.

Mention must be made finally of paradoxical language, though there is little of this in the *De Incarnatione*. One might say of course that the whole theme of the treatise, that of the Word becoming flesh, is itself the greatest paradox of all. Already, however, we have had occasion to notice one rather striking example of paradox—the expression *en tē phthorā diamenein*, which might be translated into English as 'enduring in transience' or 'continuing in ceasing to be'.[1] If we do not have regard to the context of the discourse, paradoxes are contradictions and defeat the purpose of the discourse. But after all that has been said about how we are to understand 'death', 'ceasing to be' and all the other items in the Athanasian context of ideas, we see that this particular paradox is not nonsense. As soon as theology begins to clothe its basic logic in a concrete symbolism—and in practice it always does so—then since symbols are compounded of truth and fiction, they must be at once affirmed and denied. Thus the element of paradox inevitably arises, but in this kind of discourse it is so far from defeating the purpose of what is said that rather it can shock us into seeing what is meant.

Our analysis of the *De Incarnatione* has shown us the manifold nature of theological discourse—we have seen at least six and at most nine different modes of theological talk. There is no pretence that the list is exhaustive, and there are also mixed and intermediate types. What, for instance, would we say of the sentence, 'The Word ... takes to himself a body capable of death'?[2] Is this mythology or metaphysics or a mixture of both with perhaps some empirical and existential elements thrown in? But nevertheless, our inquiry has shown us some of the main

[1] See above, p. 137.    [2] ix, 1.

types of discourse. Theological language combines these types in different proportions, and the different theological styles are constituted by the preponderance in each of them of a certain type of discourse. Obviously, not all of these types are of equal importance, and we have tried to argue further for the claim made earlier in the book that there is a 'basic logic' for theology.

Here I have presented the types only in outline, as we have discovered them in our study of a 'standard' text. Most of the remainder of this book will be devoted to a fuller investigation of each of the major types of theological discourse. But before we do this, we must investigate another phenomenon that we have seen in our study of the *De Incarnatione*, namely the possibility of expressing the same ideas in two or more modes of discourse, and so of providing a fresh interpretation. So our next chapter will deal with the problems of interpretation and hermeneutics.

# 7

## Language and Interpretation
## Case Study: Heidegger on Hermeneutics

IN THE LAST chapter, we saw something of the manifold types of theological discourse, and we tried not simply to enumerate them but to show, to some extent, how they are interconnected and how themes expressed in one type may be expressed anew and differently in another type. This means that we were already engaged in the task of interpretation, for interpretation is the exploration and elucidation of meaning, and this seems to imply the possibility of expressing anew and in a different way that which is to be interpreted. But our involvement in the tasks of interpretation goes back to the earlier chapters of the book, and one might even say that the whole inquiry into the meaning of theological language is an exercise in interpretation. Furthermore, when we showed that an essential element in discourse is communication, we took note that any communication implies some kind of interpretation.[1] So now that we have taken a first look at the basic types of theological discourse, it would seem that our next appropriate task would be to examine more closely this work of interpretation, whereby we relate together the different types of discourse and draw out their meanings.

There is, of course, a science of interpretation—the science of hermeneutics. Its history from Aristotle down to Schleiermacher and Dilthey has been briefly traced by Bultmann,[2]

[1] See above, p. 74.
[2] *Essays—Philosophical and Theological*, trans. J. C. G. Greig (London: SCM Press, 1955), pp. 234ff.

whose own method of demythologizing is perhaps the most notable contribution to theological hermeneutics in recent times. But Bultmann's contribution has in turn been taken up and reshaped by such writers as Ott, Ebeling, Fuchs and others, and the debate over the so-called 'new hermeneutic' has become one of the major theological issues of our time.

New departures in any subject run the risk of becoming exaggerated, and I think that this is a genuine risk for the upholders of the new hermeneutic. There is a danger of so overstretching the term that it ceases to be useful. We are sometimes told that 'Theology is hermeneutic', but this simple identification is not very helpful. If indeed theology is (reflective) God-talk, then it must be involved in a process of interpretation. But is this not true of any science, in so far as it is some kind of talk (discourse, *logos*)? So we could say that history is the hermeneutic of historical existence, or even that physics (especially contemporary physics) is the hermeneutic of nature. So we do not seem to be saying anything distinctive when we say that theology is hermeneutic. We might as well say that theology is language, or an intellectual discipline, or describe it in some other way that would be applicable to many other studies besides. But what we really want to know is the *differentia*—what special kind of hermeneutic, language, intellectual discipline and so on, is theology?

Nevertheless, it may well be the case that in the current situation the stress on hermeneutics is justified, and this accords very well with what we said in an earlier chapter about the key-position occupied by the problem of language in contemporary theological debate.[1] Those who are interested in the hermeneutical problem likewise see the centrality of the problem of language, 'in which', says Gerhard Ebeling, 'all the questions about the world and man and history are increasingly concentrated'.[2]

I have already indicated that interpretation demands the exploration and elucidation of meaning, and that this in turn would seem to demand the relating together of different modes

[1] See above, p. 54.
[2] *The Nature of Faith*, trans. R. G. Smith (London: Collins, 1961), p. 182.

148

of expression. As far as our own specific task is concerned, interpretation would demand the relating both of the various modes of theological discourse among themselves and of theology or God-talk as a whole to the entire realm of discourse. As a first step, let me set out some characteristics that would seem to belong to any kind of interpretation whatsoever.

The first point is that all interpretation would seem to proceed on the condition that the interpreter already has some understanding, however vague and marginal, of that which he has to interpret. This understanding that he already has is sometimes called the 'preunderstanding'. Without such a preunderstanding, surely we could make no progress in interpretation at all. If what confronted us were utterly strange, we could only gaze upon it without even the possibility of beginning to understand it. We must be able to relate it to some frame of reference that we already bring to it. We have already touched on this point when we noted that language rarely speaks exhaustively of anything, since so much is tacitly 'understood'; or again, when we noted that the condition for successful communication is the sharing of a universe of discourse. It follows then that interpretation is never without some presuppositions and that we do not come with a mind that is a *tabula rasa*. We come to any text or any phenomenon with some idea of what it is about and where it belongs in a 'world', and if we did not do so, it is hard to see how we could have any point of entry into understanding the matter.

A second characteristic of interpretation is the circularity that is involved in the process. We already bring to the work a preunderstanding; yet the whole point of interpretation is that a new understanding should be gained. There is a reciprocity here. The preunderstanding that we bring allows us to penetrate into the meaning of what is to be interpreted; yet as this meaning becomes clearer, it reacts upon our preunderstanding so that this is enlarged, modified and, if need be, corrected. One might also say that interpretation of a text becomes at the same time interpretation of oneself. The text has to be interpreted in the light of what one already understands, but what one already understands is itself interpreted in the light of a significant text. A true reciprocity has to be maintained in the work of interpretation. This demands on the one hand an explicit awareness and analysis of one's own presuppositions, and the holding of them in a tentative way; but on the other hand, a questioning of the text that relates it to the interpreter's situation. If this reciprocity is upset, then one may simply impose one's presuppositions on the text, or at the opposite extreme one may simply hear the words without appropriating them.

In the third place, there might be mentioned the need for more than one mode of expression. A person living in an entirely mythical world, let us say, could not interpret his myths for us. Interpretation becomes possible only when another mode of expression is available. A simple case is translation from one language to another. I must know both German and English to transpose meaning from the one language into the other. The modes of expression are not always verbal. The movement of the dance may be said to interpret the music, while the music in turn interprets the movement. Sometimes one mode of expression is verbal, while the other is not. In no case must it be assumed that the one language or mode of expression can say all that the other says, that is to say, that the interpretation can be complete. More likely, we shall once again have a reciprocal process. Each language or mode of expression sheds light upon the other, and at the same time receives light from the other. Some languages and modes of expression are, of course, more widely used and understood than others, so that the general direction of interpretation will be from the less familiar to the more familiar.

A fourth point that seems to be called for in interpretation is a measure of sympathy or affinity of interest between the interpreter and what he is interpreting; and a corresponding appropriateness in the language or mode of expression that he uses for his interpretation. What we have in mind here is very difficult to pin down precisely. Once again, we are thinking of the presuppositions that the interpreter inevitably brings to his task, but the affinity of interest which is now our concern seems to be different from that preunderstanding which was mentioned earlier. The affinity of interest has to do rather with the manner of approach to the subject-matter, and it includes evaluation as well as understanding. An illustration will make this clearer. Let us suppose that a mystic writes a diary of his experiences. Apart from any preunderstanding required—and obviously one would need to have some acquaintance with, and ability to recognize, certain mental states—an interpretation would be very much influenced by one's sympathy or lack of sympathy for the way the mystic evaluates his experiences. An interpretation that accepts that the mystic is having commerce with a transhuman reality would be very different from the interpretation of a sceptical psychologist who might possibly regard the whole business as pathological. Both interpretations might claim to be capturing the meaning, or something of the meaning. The first might claim to come closer, on the grounds that it really did participate in the mystic's attitudes. But it could be argued on the other hand that a critical interpretation, doing violence to the mystic's own account of his experiences, really comes closer to the 'true' meaning. But here we strike on the difficult question of what constitutes a 'true' interpretation. Perhaps there are many interpretations, and no one of them is the 'true' one, or any more true than another one. Yet it hardly seems satisfactory to say this, for we do think that there are misinterpretations, and the very fact that one can talk about a 'science' of hermeneutics and of 'rules' for interpretation seems to set some bounds to what may be accepted as 'true' interpretation. It may be the case that there will be more than one valid interpretation of a given text or phenomenon, but it may also be the case that some interpretations capture more of the meaning than others, or again that others are more abstract and ignore more of the content of what is to be interpreted. If so, a good interpretation would demand at least some affinity of interest and some appropriateness in the language of the interpreter.

These remarks are already pushing us in the direction of our fifth point—the recognition of a scientific element in interpretation. This is very clear in the case of the interpretation of a text. One has first to establish, by textual criticism, what the actual text is. Then one can bring the full battery of philological science to bear upon it. Questions of grammar, of accidence and syntax, of usage and idiom, of the meanings of words and of variations of meaning in the course of time or from one area to another—these matters all call for close consideration. Philological questions merge into historical ones, for the language and its usages has to be understood in the context of the culture where that language was used and where the allusions of the text had their home. Most of these questions can be settled in a more or less 'scientific' way, and so there are provided certain 'objective' criteria that rule out wildly subjective interpretations.

However, our sixth point must be that, just like history itself, interpretation must be reckoned an art as well as a science, and it draws on the imagination and experience of the interpreter in ways that seem to evade any attempt to formulate them in rules. R. R. Niebuhr has written about Schleiermacher that 'the act of interpreting appeared to him to be something personal and creative as well as scientific, an imaginative reconstruction of the selfhood of the speaker or writer'.[1] Concerning St Paul's idea of interpretation (*hermeneia*), James M. Robinson writes: 'The interpretation itself has revelatory character, and consequently ranks as itself a charismatic gift.'[2] Let us just notice some of the adjectives used in these two quotations: 'personal', 'creative', 'imaginative', 'revelatory', 'charismatic'. When all the scientific conditions have been observed, it seems that there is still a creative act on the part of the interpreter, and that this depends on his being a 'good' interpreter. Perhaps one should not speak of 'true' interpretation but of 'responsible' interpretation, where

[1] *Schleiermacher on Christ and Religion* (New York: Scribners, and London: SCM Press, 1964), p. 79.
[2] *The New Hermeneutic*, ed. J. M. Robinson and J. B. Cobb (New York: Harper & Row, 1964), p. 2.

the word 'responsible' points to this constructive answering of the text by the interpreter.

I propose now to focus the discussion on a concrete case study —the treatment of hermeneutics in the writings of Martin Heidegger. Even within his work, we shall concentrate attention more on the way that he himself actually carries out the task of interpretation than on what he says about interpretation in general; and in order to do this, we shall study his interpretations of three poems. These interpretations belong respectively to the earlier, middle and later stages of his philosophy.

Before turning to the first of these examples of interpretation, let me say something about Heidegger's interest in hermeneutics and his importance for the current problems. He mentions himself that he first came across the term 'hermeneutic' when he was studying theology in a Jesuit seminary.[1] At that time, he was concerned with the problem of the relation between the word of Holy Scripture and the thinking of systematic theology. For Heidegger, the problem widened into that of the relation between language and Being, but he sees this problem as continuous with the other and acknowledges that without the stimulus he had received from theology, he would not have pursued his philosophical investigation.

The notion of hermeneutics is introduced at an early stage in *Being and Time*, where the phenomenology of *Dasein*, the kind of being that belongs to man, is called a 'hermeneutic' and is assigned a fundamental role in any inquiry not only into man and the phenomena of man's life but into entities other than *Dasein*, and into the question of Being in general.[2] At an early stage too Heidegger makes clear the circular character of interpretation. In this case, we are inquiring into *Dasein's* being in order to find a way into the question of Being as such; yet in order to ask about the *being* of *Dasein*, we must already have some understanding of Being as such.

It is worth noting that throughout *Being and Time* Heidegger

---

[1] *Unterwegs zur Sprache* (Pfullingen: Neske, 1959), p. 96.
[2] *Op. cit.*, p. 62.

uses two words that would both be translated into English as 'interpretation', but that he is very careful to distinguish between them. One of these words is *Auslegung*, and by this Heidegger seems to mean an informal kind of interpretation that accompanies every act of understanding. When we understand anything, we relate it to a frame of reference (*Vorstruktur*) that we have already brought with us into the situation where this thing encounters us; and furthermore, in relating it to this frame, we understand it 'as' something (*Alsstruktur*), and this 'as' already implies an interpretation. For instance, when one hears a sound, it is immediately interpreted as, let us say, the wind and incorporated into our total understanding. As well as this informal kind of interpretation, there is another kind which Heidegger designates by the word *Interpretation*. This is explicit, thematic interpretation, as, for instance, the interpretation of a text. In such a case too there will be presuppositions that we bring to the task, and the totality of these presuppositions constitute what Heidegger calls the 'hermeneutical situation'.[1] In *Being and Time*, the stress is laid upon the need to clarify and make secure the presuppositions that are brought to the work of interpretation, and the interpretation itself has a strongly existential character. In other words, Heidegger's view of interpretation, as expounded in *Being and Time*, is very close to the kind of hermeneutic worked out by Bultmann, largely on the basis of Heidegger's work.

To illustrate these points, we now turn to the first example of an actual piece of interpretation offered by Heidegger—his treatment of a classical fable taken from Hyginus. I quote first the Latin, then an English translation by Edward Robinson and myself described as a compromise between the German translation quoted by Heidegger and the original Latin:[2]

*Cura cum fluvium transiret, vidit cretosum lutum*
*sustulitque cogitabunda atque coepit fingere.*

[1] *Op. cit.*, p. 275.
[2] See *Being and Time*, p. 242, also n. 1 on pp. 242–3 and n. v on p. 492.

*dum deliberat quid iam fecisset, Jovis intervenit.*
*rogat eum Cura ut det illi spiritum, et facile impetrat.*
*cui cum vellet Cura nomen ex sese ipsa imponere,*
*Jovis prohibuit suumque nomen ei dandum esse dictitat.*
*dum Cura et Jovis disceptant, Tellus surrexit simul*
*suumque nomen esse volt cui corpus praebuerit suum.*
*sumpserunt Saturnum iudicem, is sic aecus iudicat:*
*'tu Jovis quia spiritum dedisti, in morte spiritum,*
*tuque Tellus, quia dedisti corpus, corpus recipito,*
*Cura eum quia prima finxit, teneat quamdiu vixerit.*
*sed quae nunc de nomine eius vobis controversia est,*
*homo vocetur, quia videtur esse factus ex humo.'*

Once when 'Care' was crossing a river, she saw some clay; she thoughtfully took up a piece and began to shape it. While she was meditating on what she had made, Jupiter came by. 'Care' asked him to give it spirit, and this he gladly granted. But when she wanted her name to be bestowed upon it, he forbade this, and demanded that it be given his name instead. While 'Care' and Jupiter were disputing, Earth arose and desired that her own name be conferred on the creature, since she had furnished it with part of her body. They asked Saturn to be their arbiter, and he made the following decision, which seemed a just one: 'Since you, Jupiter, have given its spirit, you shall receive that spirit at its death; and since you, Earth, have given its body, you shall receive its body. But since 'Care' first shaped this creature, she shall possess it as long as it lives. And because there is now a dispute among you as to its name, let it be called 'man' (*homo*) because it is made out of earth (*humus*).

Like Bultmann in his demythologizing, Heidegger interprets this myth as an expression of man's self-understanding, that is to say, the interpretation is in existential terms. Admittedly, in this particular case an existential interpretation is peculiarly appropriate, since the myth deals specifically with the origins of man, the existent. Nevertheless, we shall see from a later example

that in his more mature period, Heidegger perceives an ontological dimension even in a passage explicitly devoted to unfolding the character of human existence. In the myth now before
us, there would arise the question of how we are to understand
such cosmic or ontological symbols as Jupiter and Earth, but
Heidegger does not deal with this question. The story is seen
primarily as a pre-ontological, pre-philosophical statement on
man's part as to how he understands himself. This pre-ontological, mythological language is brought into relation with the
existential language developed by Heidegger in his analysis of
*Dasein*, and these two languages are allowed to illuminate one
another.

Thus the 'spirit' and 'body' which together form the primordial endowment of man and have been traditionally interpreted as two 'substances' out of which he is constituted are here
seen as united in 'care', and are re-interpreted in non-substantial
terms and non-mythical terms as the 'possibility' and 'facticity'
which are the basic constitutive factors in human existence, and
the tension between which sets up 'care' as the being of the
*Dasein*, so long as it lives. This 'care', moreover, which in its
possibility and its facticity looks before and after, is made possible by the temporal character of existence. So we find Heidegger pointing out that it is 'time', personified in the myth as
Saturn, that decides about the creature and hands it over to
care.

Although *Being and Time* does stress the importance of our
presuppositions in interpretation and although it lies close to the
Bultmannian emphasis on the existential dimension in interpretation, these points should not be exaggerated. In some places,
Heidegger already speaks of clearing away obstacles that prevent us from hearing what the text is saying. His interest in
etymologies and in restoring the primordial meanings of words,
and his closely parallel interest in the pre-Socratic philosophers,
together with his doctrine of repetition and his respect for history, are pointers toward a further stage in his thinking about
hermeneutics. In this next stage, there is a shift in emphasis from

our presuppositions to the text that confronts us, in its very words and language. Moreover, Heidegger's ontological interest, present indeed in *Being and Time* which is 'fundamental ontology' and not 'philosophical anthropology', emerges from its relatively background role to play a leading part.

This second phase in Heidegger's hermeneutic, already thoroughly prepared for in the first, may be studied in his treatment of a chorus from the *Antigone* of Sophocles.[1] Again the theme of the poem is man, but this time we shall find that the interpretation is not just existential but ontological as well, or, better expressed, that it is existential-ontological. What we have is a concrete illustration of what Heidegger calls 'repetitive thinking', the kind of thinking that takes place when we go back into the past and there think with and through the thoughts of some historical figure, so that his thinking comes alive again in our historical situation. But to do this, says Heidegger, we must play down our presuppositions. In particular, we must try to come without ready-made ideas of who man is, already there in our minds. 'We must attempt to hear only what is said.' But he warns us that 'we are inexperienced at such hearing' and 'our ears are full of things that prevent us from hearing properly'.

Let me now quote the chorus from Sophocles. I shall use Ralph Manheim's translation, which in turn is based on Heidegger's German translation of the Greek original, and the reader should bear in mind that Heidegger's translations are also (as perhaps all translations are) interpretations, and made with considerable freedom. Thus he may want to consult another English translation, such as that of R. C. Jebb.[2]

> There is much that is strange, but nothing
> that surpasses man in strangeness.
> He sets sail on the frothing waters
> amid the south winds of winter,

[1] *An Introduction to Metaphysics*, trans. R. Manheim (New Haven: Yale University Press, 1959), pp. 146–65.

[2] *Plays* (Sophocles), (Cambridge: University Press, 1904) pp. 138–9. See also *The Complete Greek Drama*, ed. W. J. Oates and Eugene O'Neill (New York: Random House, 1938), vol. I, p. 432.

tacking through the mountains
and furious chasms of the waves.
He wearies even the noblest
of the gods, the Earth,
indestructible and untiring,
overturning her from year to year,
driving the ploughs this way and that
with horses.

And man, pondering and plotting,
snares the light-gliding birds
and hunts the beasts of the wilderness
and the native creatures of the sea.
With guile he overpowers the beast
that roams the mountains by night as by day,
he yokes the hirsute neck of the stallion
and the undaunted bull.

And he has found his way
to the resonance of the word,
and to wind-swift all-understanding,
and to the courage of rule over cities.
He has considered also how to flee
from exposure to the arrows
of unpropitious weather and frost.

Everywhere journeying, inexperienced and without
  issue,
He comes to nothing.
Through no flight can he resist
the one assault of death,
even if he has succeeded in cleverly evading
painful sickness.

Clever indeed, mastering
the ways of skill beyond all hope,
he sometimes accomplishes evil,
sometimes achieves brave deeds.

He wends his way between the laws of the earth
and the adjured justice of the gods.
Rising high above his place
he who for the sake of adventure takes
the nonentity for entity loses
his place in the end.

May such a man never frequent my hearth;
May my mind never share the presumption
of him who does this.

How then does Heidegger go about the task of interpreting this chorus? He acknowledges first of all that his interpretation could not be adequate unless it took into account the whole tragedy, or even the entire work of Sophocles, and here once again we meet the contemporary recognition of the need to place language in context if its meaning is to be properly grasped. No doubt any interpretation—and likewise our ability to judge any proffered interpretation—depends on a whole unspoken background of knowledge and experience.

However, to come to the explicit subject-matter of the interpretation, we notice that Heidegger proposes to construct his exegesis in three phases. The first aims at setting forth 'the intrinsic meaning of the poem, that which sustains the edifice of words and rises above it'. In the second phase, we shall pass through the successive parts of the chorus and mark out the boundaries of the whole area that the poem opens up. The third phase is 'to take our stand in the centre of the poem', and to judge how it answers for us the question about who man is.[1]

Although this outline does indeed suggest an orderly approach to the problem of interpretation, it must already seem doubtful to us whether one could formulate the kind of thing Heidegger is trying to do as a 'method' or whether one could derive from his procedures any 'hermeneutic rules'. At the stage of existential interpretation, as exemplified in *Being and Time* and in the work

[1] *An Introduction to Metaphysics*, p. 148.

of Bultmann, one could at least seek to clarify one's presuppositions and to formulate one's questions in accordance with some fairly definite principles. But now that the interpretation leans more toward the text than to our presuppositions and the stress is more on listening than on asking questions, the whole procedure of interpretation seems to have become much more personal, more dependent on individual sensitivity and on *ad hoc* approaches. Yet, as I shall try to show in the following comments on Heidegger's interpretative work, I do not think that he falls into merely subjective and fanciful exegesis.

The first phase, as I understand it, has to do with the inner structure and form that binds the words together in a meaningful whole. Heidegger sees this structure as itself a threefold one, and it is significant that the three elements in it upon which he directs attention are three paradoxes, so that right away we are introduced to the notion of 'violence' in interpretation—a violence which we would misunderstand if we thought that it had to do with the wrenching and distorting of meaning, for it has to do rather with what we have earlier called the 'stretching' of language,[1] the driving of words and constructions beyond their everyday usages so that they become creative and illuminating for new and hitherto hidden areas, thereby achieving that kind of unconcealment which is the coming to be of truth (*alētheia*). If we are correct in saying this, then Heidegger's interest in points of conflict and paradox is intelligible.

The first of the three paradoxes is contained in the double meaning of the Greek word *deinos*, 'strange':

> There is much that is strange, but nothing
> that surpasses man in strangeness.

As Heidegger interprets it, the word *deinos* can mean 'strange' in the sense of 'terrible' or 'awe-inspiring'; as he understands this sense of the word, it seems not too far away from Otto's 'numinous'. Also, *deinos* means 'powerful', even 'violent'. In the interpretation, these notions are applied both to man and to the

[1] See above, p. 27.

wider realm of beings within which he has his being, that is to say, the interpretation has an ontological as well as an existential dimension. Everything that is has the character of strangeness, reminding us perhaps of the ontological question from which this particular book of Heidegger takes its beginning—'Why is there anything at all and not just nothing?' This is the wonder of being. But of all the beings, man is the strangest, and he is so as the 'violent' one, the being that goes beyond the limits of the familiar and the routine into the uncanniness of being; this is just to say that he is the existent, the one that has no fixed nature but pushes forward into new ways of being. He is himself the strange and the overpowering, and he breaks into the strange and overpowering realm of beings around him.

The second paradox is in the words: 'Everywhere journeying, inexperienced and without issue, he comes to nothing.' In the Greek, this reads: '*Pantoporos aporos ep'ouden erchetai*', which makes clear that the point of the paradox lies in the sharply contrasted words *pantoporos aporos*. Immediately, we must expect an argument over Heidegger's translation, which Marjorie Grene has called 'a beautifully simple mistranslation'.[1] She takes exception primarily to Heidegger's rendering of the passage as meaning that man must eventually 'come to nothing', presumably in the ceasing-to-be of death. Certainly, one could translate the Greek quite differently. If we take *pantoporos* and *aporos* to mean 'with all resources' and 'with no resource', then the sentence could simply mean that man is never caught unprepared: that having all resources, he never comes to anything resourceless. Yet one could say that Heidegger's own ironical translation here is precisely an example of the 'violence' which he (and Sophocles) have just been imputing to man. It is violence in the realm of interpretation, but a creative violence, so to speak, that breaks open a new level of meaning. It would probably be beside the point to debate about what Sophocles himself intended by the words. They are, after all, ambiguous. The fact that Sophocles goes on almost at once to speak explicitly

[1] *Martin Heidegger* (London: Bowes and Bowes, 1957), p. 118.

of death lends some support to Heidegger's interpretation. But what is important is surely this, that language, which is never private but always belongs to a historical community, means more than we may be aware of expressing at any given time. Whatever Sophocles may have intended, Heidegger's interpretation is legitimate, for it is there in the language and (this is equally important) it is consonant with the rest of the poem. We have the whole paradox of human existence in this sentence about the one who, having all resources, must come to nothing.

The third paradox concerns the one who 'rising high above his place . . . loses his place in the end'. The Greek words contrasted here are *hypsipolis apolis* and I think we could get the contrast between these better by translating them respectively as 'citizen of a proud city'[1] and 'one having no city'. The *polis* or city is where the overpowering gets humanized, yet man remains lonely and alien among the beings, surpassing them all in strangeness.

The second phase of Heidegger's interpretation conducts us through the strophes and antistrophes of the chorus where we hear how the being of man unfolds. But Heidegger is insistent that as we do so, we bear in mind what has already been said about the strange in the first phase of the interpretation. As we read how man sets out on the sea in his frail ships or how he turns up the land with his plows and cultivates it or how he hunts the animals and domesticates some of them to serve his needs, we would, thinks Heidegger, altogether misinterpret what is being said if we reduced it to some commonplace story of human development. He claims here about human existence as a whole what he claims elsewhere for Western philosophy in particular—that 'the beginning is the strangest and mightiest'.[2] No doubt here, as in similar things that he says elsewhere about language and philosophy, Heidegger exaggerates and tends to represent the whole history of these matters as a decline, or, to use the expression he employs in the present context, a 'flatten-

[1] So Liddell—Scott—Jones, *Greek-English Lexicon* (Oxford: Clarendon Press, 1953), p. 1910.
[2] *Op. cit.*, p. 155.

ing'. Yet he is pointing to a truth, namely, that the appearance of the distinctively human (that is to say, the rational and responsible), is a greater happening than any subsequent developments based upon it, and that we should not be too easily misled by the notion of 'progress' as understood in the natural sciences. One may contrast with the progress of these sciences the state of affairs in art, or philosophy itself, where what was achieved at the beginning is worthy to stand alongside the achievements of later times, and certainly one cannot trace some progression from one to the other.

But let us pass on to what is mentioned next as the poem unfolds the character of man. After what is said about the sea, the earth and the animals, the chorus proceeds to speak of the world of man himself—language, understanding, the building of cities. Here again Heidegger's interpretation may surprise us. So far is he from taking these human activities in a purely existential way that he goes out of his way to stress their ontological dimension and their roots in a wider being than man's own. These human phenomena are no less 'a part of the overpowering power than sea, earth and animal ... The pervading force becomes no less overpowering because man takes it into his power, which he uses as such'. Heidegger asks: 'How could man ever have invented the power which pervades him, which alone enables him to *be* a man? We shall be wholly forgetting that this song speaks of the powerful (*deinon*), the strange and uncanny, if we suppose that the poet makes man invent such things as building and language'.[1] Here Heidegger's interpretation is claiming what in other places he has expressed in other ways— that man can speak only when he has been addressed, that his language is the home of Being, that man himself is the particular being where the unveiling and naming of Being take place. Yet this being, man, shatters against death. He remains paradoxical in his being, so that he can never rest in the familiar but is always in the strange, between *technē*, 'art' or 'skill' (which Heidegger identifies with the violent, power-exercising side of

[1] *Op. cit.*, p. 156.

*deinos*) and *dikē*, the 'law' or 'norm' of Being (identified with the overpowering, numinous aspect of *deinos*).

The third and last phase of the interpretation tries to gather up the truth of the poem in what it says about the identity of man. The closing lines of the chorus look like a pronouncement against the *hybris* or arrogance of the man who has taken such powers to himself. But Heidegger rejects such a tame and conventional exegesis. He takes the words to mean that the 'strangest of all' has no place amid the secure and familiar. Man by his very existence is ontological. Being itself drives him to venture out beyond the everyday, to be violent and creative in breaking open the beings and in assuming responsibility.

I have said enough to make clear the difference between the kind of interpretation based on repetitive thinking and the earlier kind which was determined by existential questioning. We have seen how the move has been from questioning to listening; from our presuppositions to the language that confronts us; from predominantly existential thought-forms to ontological ones. But as this has happened, there seems also to have been a move away from any definite method of interpretation, in spite of the threefold pattern that Heidegger has mapped out. Certainly, there are no rules that can be mechanically applied. And what are we to say of the 'violence' that the interpreter employs, or of the assertion that 'the actual interpretation must show what does *not* stand in the words, and is nevertheless said'?[1] Does this not lead us into a purely subjective and imaginative activity of interpretation? Not quite, for the language itself acts as a norm and sets limits to the exegesis; yet these limits are wide ones, and clearly much depends on the sensitivity and perceptiveness of the exegete.

However, we go on now to consider a third illustration from Heidegger's writings. Again he takes a poem and discusses its meaning, but this time we seem to have moved to the furthest extreme from allowing to the interpreter an active or questioning role. Perhaps I should say, from allowing any such role to

[1] *Op. cit.*, p. 162.

the poet himself, rather than the interpreter of the poem, and yet it is not easy to distinguish their roles. The poet is the interpreter of life, of experience—even the interpreter of Being. He has a kind of direct *rapport* with his theme, so that his poetic thinking (like the 'primordial' thinking, of which Heidegger sometimes speaks) is not mediated through some historical figure, as was the case in the repetitive thinking, exemplified in the interpretation of Sophocles' chorus.

But let me quote the poem, which is by Stefan George and is entitled *Das Wort* ('The Word'):

> *Wunder von ferne oder traum*
> *Bracht' ich an meines landes saum*
> *Und harrte bis die graue norn*
> *Den namen fand in ihrem born—*
> *Drauf konnt ichs greifen dicht und stark*
> *Nun blüht und glänzt es durch die mark . . .*
>
> *Einst langt ich an nach guter fahrt*
> *Mit einem kleinod reich und zart.*
> *Sie suchte lang und gab mir kund:*
> *'So schläft hier nichts auf tiefem grund.'*
> *Worauf es meiner hand entrann*
> *Und nie mein land den schatz gewann . . .*
>
> *So lernt ich traurig den verzicht:*
> *Kein ding sei wo das wort gebricht.*

If I were to venture a translation, it would run something like this: 'Many a wonder and dream I brought from afar to my country's border, and waited till the grey Norn found the name for it in her well. Thereupon I could grasp it tightly and strongly, now it blossoms and gleams through the border-land . . . Once I arrived after a good journey with a rich and precious treasure. She searched for a long time and then told me: "Nothing like this lies sleeping in these depths." Whereupon it slipped through my fingers, and my country never gained that treasure. So I sadly learned to be resigned to this, that nothing can be where the word breaks off.'

Heidegger's discussion of this poem occurs in an essay on 'The Essence of Language'.[1] The point of the concluding lines of the poem, that there cannot *be* anything unless it is included in language, is a matter that has already come to our notice in various ways, as when we talked about the creative character of language and how it shapes a world. But in his late work, Heidegger comes near to identifying Being and language, and many of the things that he earlier said about Being now get said about language. In the essay under consideration, there is something like a recurring refrain: 'The essence of language is the language of essence'—and the word *Wesen*, which I am here translating by its usual equivalent 'essence', has almost certainly a much more verbal and dynamic sense in the way Heidegger uses it. The essence of language is Being's self-expression to us in language. In the poem of Stefan George and in Heidegger's remarks based upon it, man has become almost completely passive and language is seen as an ontological rather than an existential phenomenon. This is expressed mythologically in the poem, for the word is not chosen by the poet, but is chosen for him and communicated to him by the Norn, the Germanic goddess of fate. Language is a gift, almost a revelation. The poet, as the interpreter of life and Being, has his interpretation as a gift; and the interpreter of the poem receives its meaning as a gift in turn. Whether indeed all interpretation has this gift-like character, there can be little doubt that Heidegger in this late writing is claiming that the interpretation of the poet and perhaps likewise of the philosopher is, like the interpretation of which St Paul speaks, charismatic.

Though he is not writing specifically about this passage, a remark of Laszlo Versényi may be appropriately quoted here: 'The quasi-biblical tone of Heidegger's pronouncements is quite appropriate to what he is trying to say. For in his conception of thought—as thought by Being, for Being and of Being—the

[1] 'Das Wesen der Sprache' in *Unterwegs zur Sprache*, pp. 157ff.

importance of the thinker as a self-certain subject is as much reduced as it is in the biblical conception of revelation—of God, by God and for the greater glory of God. At the same time, just as in and through biblical revelation, man obtains a new dignity as the preserver of the truth of Being, called by Being into the preservation of its truth.'[1] Certainly Heidegger's reading of George's mythological reference here lays all the stress on what is done to man and for man by the transhuman, and may be sharply contrasted with his reading of the mythology in the ancient Latin fable from which our case study set out.

I think, however, it would be a mistake to suppose that Heidegger's final word on language and interpretation is that the interpreter can only be passive and listen for the voice of Being. Much depends here on how one views the relation between his earlier and his later work. If one is prepared to accept Heidegger's own claim—as I do—that these constitute a unity so that neither is intelligible apart from the other, then his doctrine of interpretation too has to be considered as a whole. Language has to be understood as both an existential and an ontological phenomenon; interpretation demands both questioning and listening, a sense of direction and a willingness to be directed.

If anyone goes to Heidegger looking for a ready-made 'hermeneutic method' that can be applied generally, he is going to be disappointed. But if he goes to Heidegger to find out something of what interpretation involves, in all its complexity as both science and art, then I think he can learn a great deal. It is in the hope that we might learn something about interpretation that would be useful for our own purposes in this book that we have spent this time over a consideration of Heidegger's hermeneutics.

[1] *Heidegger, Being and Truth* (New Haven: Yale University Press, 1965), p. 112.

# 8

## Mythology

IN THE EARLY chapters of this book, we moved from the problem of theological language into a discussion of language and discourse in general. We came back to the special problem of theological language, and through an analysis of the *De Incarnatione* we set out some of the major types of theological discourse. Using Heidegger's work as an illustration, we next looked at the problems of interpretation, the elucidation of meanings and the possibility of bringing different types of discourse together so as to throw light upon each of them. Following upon all this, we shall devote the remaining chapters to studying the specific kinds of language and discourse that enter into the texture of theology. We shall try to expound the principal characteristics of each type, and to deal with the question of how its meaning is to be interpreted, and how it is to be related to other types of theological discourse. We shall try also to show how all of these types are related to what we have called the 'basic logic' of theology.

We begin with the language of myth. In view of what we have seen in our study of the *De Incarnatione*, where we found mythology, analogy, metaphysical arguments, empirical assertions and other types of discourse besides all interwoven, we shall have no hesitation in recognizing that it is quite wrong to say (though one frequently hears it said) that myth and God-talk are one and the same, or that the language of religion can be simply equated with myth. This may have been true of primitive religion, but it is obviously not true of any religion that has developed beyond a primitive stage. Indeed, if we think of theology as reflective God-talk, then any religion that has developed a theology has passed beyond a purely mythological stage. In such a religion, myth will probably still appear as one form of discourse among others, though in some cases it hardly appears at all. Whatever was originally expressed in the myths has been translated into alternative kinds of discourse.

Yet while it is wrong simply to identify the language of religion with myth, it would be true to see in myth the matrix out of which the refinements of religious language, including theological language itself, have arisen. In the Bible, for instance, while many different kinds of discourse are employed and one could not dream of lumping everything together as 'myth', we do find substantial sections that are either themselves mythical in form, or that allude to myths lying further back in the history of religion, or that proceed on presuppositions drawn from mythology. Thus even the contemporary Christian theologian, however abstruse, rationalistic and sophisticated his thought may become, will, in all probability, still carry some residual elements of myth into his theological constructions; he is almost bound to do so, in so far as he turns to the Bible for the sources of his theology. As W. M. Urban has expressed it: 'The mythical origin of most of the primary symbols of religious expression is historically beyond question. Even the most spiritual symbols of the most moralized religions have their source in the womb of the unconscious out of which the myth and its symbols have been born. The most exalted idiom of theology no less than the language of purest devotion makes use of this treasury of the ages.'[1]

Thus even if we reject—as Urban also does—any simple identification of the language of religion with myth, we are still bound to return to the question of myth as the matrix out of which the various forms of religious language, and perhaps of other kinds of language besides, have arisen. What is the

[1] *Humanity and Deity* (London: Allen & Unwin, 1951), p. 89.

structure of myth, and how do we recognize a myth? What possibilities are there for the translation of mythical talk into alternative kinds of discourse, such as might be more intelligible to people of modern times? What principles should govern the translation of myth, and how can we be sure that they follow a sound hermeneutic procedure? Can myth be wholly translated into other forms of discourse, or is there an intractable residue that must persist as myth?

These questions are by no means new. The question of interpreting myth and sacred legends has been known to theologians and then to historians of religion for a very long time. Already in the early Church the allegorizing of biblical narratives was a recognition of the problem which they present, but the modern question of myth has developed mainly since the eighteenth century. The earliest investigators, in accordance with the rationalistic spirit of their times, tried to reconstruct matter-of-fact accounts of what they supposed had actually happened, and had then been elaborated as myth and legend. Some of these reconstructions may strike us as rather amusing. According to the German scholar Eichhorn, 'The flame and smoke which ascended from Mount Sinai, at the giving of the law, was merely a fire which Moses kindled in order to make a deeper impression on the imagination of the people, together with an accidental thunderstorm which arose at that particular moment. The shining of his countenance was the natural effect of being overheated; but it was supposed to be a divine manifestation, not only by the people but by Moses himself, he being ignorant of the true cause.'[1] The 'rational' explanations of the myths and legends often make greater demands upon credulity than the original stories themselves. David Friedrich Strauss took a great step forward in seeing myth as primarily a construct of the believing community, whereby its faith found expression, and in extending the question of myth in the Bible in a radical way to the whole of the New Testament. The question of myth and

---

[1] As reported by David Friedrich Strauss, *The Life of Jesus*, trans. George Eliot (London: Swan Sonnenschein, 5th edition, 1906), p. 48.

its meaning tended to be pushed aside by the Ritschlians in their attempt to recapture the 'facts' about the historical Jesus, but the question was revived by the history of religions school and, as we have had occasion to note in earlier parts of this book, has been impressively handled by Bultmann in his project for demythologizing.

But before we attempt to answer any of the questions that we have raised in connection with myth, we must try to tie down in a much more precise way just what we mean when we talk about 'myth'. The formal definitions of the term offered by theologians, philosophers of religion, anthropologists and others are not too helpful. Generally speaking, we may say that these definitions suffer from defects similar to those that have attended the many attempts to define religion itself. Such definitions usually seize upon certain aspects of the phenomenon to be defined and by paying excessive attention to these aspects and neglecting others, end up with one-sided and misleading formulations. I have tried to show elsewhere[1] that Bultmann's way of defining 'myth' is unsatisfactory, though I also believe that he does not abide by the definition. It seems to me that our purpose in this chapter would not be served by attempting yet another definition of 'myth', but that we would do better if we tried simply to set out certain basic and perhaps minimal characteristics that would have to be present if we wished to call any particular discourse 'mythical'.

First among these basic characteristics of myth, let us notice that the language of the myth is *dramatic*. It is the language of action, and the action is that of persons, whether they are gods or angels or men, or, in the more primitive mythologies, quasi-personal beings, such as spirits or demons or forces of nature conceived in an animistic way. Although mythical ideas can become detached from a narrative setting—as indeed happens in the Bible, and also in the illustration which we took from St Athanasius' writings—they can be traced back to some concrete story of action, and in that story they have their 'home'.

[1] *The Scope of Demythologizing* (London: SCM Press, 1960), pp. 199ff.

Because some story is either told or implied, myth has often been described as 'stories of the gods'. This, incidentally, is the formula commonly employed by Tillich to describe myth. As far as it goes, the description is true, but it remains imprecise.

Nevertheless, the narrative or dramatic form is basic to myth. A story is concrete and particular, so that myth stands in this regard at the opposite extreme from the abstract generalizing language of science. Concerning this particularity of mythical talk, Ernst Cassirer writes: 'The focusing of all forces on a single point is the prerequisite for all mythical thinking and mythical formulation.'[1] In those periods of history or prehistory in which the myths arose, there was in any case, we may presume, a dearth of abstract and sophisticated terms, so that whatever was to be expressed had to be expressed in a concrete way. Yet this does not mean that the myth simply sets before us some isolated incident or situation, having no reference beyond itself. On the contrary, it can only properly be called a 'myth' if it does point beyond itself and becomes interpretative for a whole series of incidents and situations. If the particularizing language of myth lacks the horizontal spread of the abstract generalizing language of science, it may make up for this by its presentation in depth of the particular situation on which it has concentrated attention. Perhaps too this is an appropriate way of talking about personal situations, just as the generalizing language of science is appropriate to the impersonal. In the same way that a particular historical event or the situation presented in a play or a novel may be illuminating for a great many other situations, so the particular story of the myth can become a kind of paradigm which gets used for the interpretation of a more or less wide range of experiences.

This leads us to a second characteristic of myth, namely, that its language is *evocative*. It is a language with several levels, as it were, and its meaning is not to be read on the surface. We can put this in another way by saying that in myth, the connotations of words bulk more largely than their denotations, and we

[1] *Language and Myth*, trans. Susanne K. Langer (New York: Dover, 1946), p. 33.

have already seen that this holds for religious and theological language in general.[1] Words like 'sun' and 'water', which in the modern world we understand in a matter-of-fact way as denoting well-known objects or substances, carry with them in the language of myth the wealth of associations which had gathered round these things in the life of the peoples who produced the myths. They were mysterious entities. The sun, for instance, illuminating the land, warming men's bodies, promoting the growth of plants, regulating the rhythm of life by its rising and setting, was understood in terms of all these ways in which it impinged on man's life in the world, long before he could even begin to think of it 'objectively' as a celestial body. Thus the sun appears as a personal or quasi-personal agent among the *dramatis personae* of myth long before it could appear as a natural phenomenon in even the simplest factual account of the world.

Thus the language of myth is like the language of poetry—the words used in it are suffused with feeling and are rich in all kinds of evocative connotations. These words are images rather than concepts. They have blurred edges, their content and reference cannot be clearly delimited. This evocative character of mythical language is, of course, a source of its richness and gives it the possibility of yielding interpretations and of providing a matrix from which new kinds of discourse can arise. But for the modern mind, this evocative character has become a major barrier in the way of understanding or appreciating myth. In a post-mythical world that has grown accustomed to matter-of-fact ways of talking, not only myth but poetry too has come to be despised by many and is but little valued. Those who still retain a feeling for poetry—George Santayana would be a good example—may subsume myth under poetry and continue to find some value in it for its aesthetic and subjective satisfactions, but without allowing that it could disclose to us anything about our world.

A third characteristic of myth is its *immediacy*. I think this point is often overlooked in discussions of myth, especially by

[1] See above, p. 94.

those who tell us that we cannot dispense with myth. What they really mean is that we cannot dispense with the symbolism of myth; but the very fact that we have words like 'myth' and 'symbol' at all proves that we have emerged from a strictly mythical mentality. By 'immediacy', I mean the inner attitude to myth, which was quite different among those who really thought mythically from what it is among us who can recognize myth as myth, even if we go on to say that this recognition is appreciative of some truth in the myth.

When we remember the immediacy of the mythically-minded man's relation to his myth, we see that it is senseless to ask whether people who habitually thought in mythical terms took their myths literally or symbolically. The question is senseless because the distinction between the literal and symbolic cannot arise so long as the relation to the myth is still an immediate one. Pure uncritical myth has a wholeness that is not yet broken by the distinctions of analytical thinking. Perhaps we might think of it as something like that wholeness of feeling that lies below the level of discursive thinking. For us, it is hard indeed to imagine what this immediate relation to the myth could be like, for even to have become aware of the relation is to have shattered its immediacy. In this state of immediacy, the symbol and what it symbolizes have not yet been separated from each other. We might say that the mythical man lived as one immersed in his myth; he had not yet, as it were, taken a step back from it to survey it questioningly and critically. He was still in the middle of his dreaming, and had not yet wakened up to reflect about his dream and ask what it might mean. No doubt the mythical man did indeed believe that the incident narrated in the myth was an event that had actually happened in the manner described; but because he still lived in the myth, he was equally aware of what we would call the 'symbolic' meaning that was concealed in the evocative language. He did not, of course, distinguish the 'symbolic' and the 'literal', but both were there for him in undifferentiated union. In the Bible, the stage of unbroken myth has for the most part been already left behind, and the criticism and reinterpretation of myth is already going forward. Yet some elements of myth still survive in something like their primordial immediacy, and in some cases these survivals have maintained themselves through the patristic and medieval periods down into modern times, not only in popular belief but even in some works of theology.

A further characteristic of myth is its *alogicality*—or perhaps it would be more accurate to say that the logic and categories of myth are different from those of common sense and everyday experience. Myth tends to become fantastic, so that in ordinary usage the very word 'myth' has come to be used nowadays in a bad sense for an absurd and incredible story. Because of its pejorative associations, some writers even question the propriety of using the word 'myth' in connection with the stories of the Bible. However, it seems to me that no other word is quite satisfactory for describing the particular kind of discourse designated by the word 'myth'—terms like 'parable' and 'saga' are much too specialized. It seems to me better to use the word 'myth' as Bultmann and many others have done, but to try to make clear the meaning of this word as technically used by the theologian or historian of religion—the very task of clarification on which we are presently engaged. The point we must make here is that alogicality is not to be equated with absurdity.

Psychoanalysts have seen in myth the prelogical processes of the unconscious mind, and have drawn attention to the resemblance between the contents of myth and the contents of dreams. In the myth as in the dream, conventions of space and time, of cause and effect, are set aside—or rather, are simply absent— and we are introduced into a world of wonder and miracle. But does this simply mean that the myth is to be dismissed as an inferior and outmoded way of thinking that was quite misleading and illusory? Or may it be the case that at least some of the discontinuities, wonders and miracles of myth represent the way —perhaps the only way available to them—by which it was possible for those who thought in mythical terms to give expression to certain dimensions of experience of which they had become aware? Does the myth, by the strangeness of what it tells, open the understanding to new dimensions of experience? And while indeed it is impossible for us to employ the same modes of expression, should we not remain open to discovering in the myths some insights that would be missed if we confined ourselves to a sophisticated matter-of-fact view of things?

These considerations draw our attention to a fifth characteristic of myth—the part which is played in the mythical dramas by *supernatural* agencies. These may be good or bad; they may be gods or angels from above, or demons from below. Now this aspect of myth is open to criticism from both the theological and the scientific points of view. A more advanced theology protests against the idea that the divine can be objectified, so as to manifest itself in sensible phenomena; and further, it protests against the idea, as one that is destructive of human responsibility, that men's actions and their history are determined and then given effect by superhuman powers, whether good or bad, that can 'possess' men or 'instigate' their actions, or that can work in the background to bring success or frustration to human policies. This seems to make everything that we do unreal. Besides these theological objections, there are the scientific ones. We have learned to think of our world as a self-regulating cosmos, so that we look for the explanation of one set of events in terms of other events within the same series. We no longer look to supernatural agencies that occasionally supervene to produce special effects. Indeed, from the scientists' point of view, myth is often regarded simply as primitive man's attempt to explain events of which he did not understand the cause, as, for instance, when he attributed disease to demonic agency. Moreover, it will be pointed out that myths presupposed a cosmology which scientific investigation has long since led us to abandon. It might be the Babylonian cosmology, apparent in the Old Testament; or some form of the Ptolemaic cosmology, of which we have hints in the New Testament; or some other cosmology, according to whatever myths might be under consideration. In connection with this criticism, however, we should remember that the cosmology of myths (or perhaps we should say the cosmography underlying the myths) was not a theory of the universe in the sense that a modern cosmology is. To think of the ancient cosmologies in this way would once again be to attribute to them thought distinctions that had not yet emerged, and would miss the evocative character of the language. No doubt mythology did have its world-picture, and no doubt there was included in this such scientific or quasi-scientific elements as were available at different times and in different cultures. Yet one has to say that the heavens and the underworlds of mythology were numinous rather than physical regions. They were not to be taken too literally. Within the as yet undifferentiated matrix of myth, we must be cautious not to draw hard and fast distinctions that belong only to later ways of thinking.

When we bear these points in mind, we do indeed see that the mythological way of representing the supernatural conflicts with both theology and science, as we understand them today. Yet we also see that the conception of the supernatural, even as we find it in myth, cannot just be swept aside. Unsatisfactory though it may have been, it pointed to aspects of man's being-in-the-world which we must either find ways to reinterpret or else frankly acknowledge that we have lapsed into a positivism in which any kind of religious faith and, in particular, any recognizable form of Christianity have become impossible.

Still another characteristic of myth to be noted is that the action of the myth is usually characterized by *remoteness* in time and space. Myths do not tell of events that happened last year or will take place next week. The events narrated in the myth are represented as having taken place long ago, often in the beginning of time; though sometimes the event is represented as one that is to take place in the future, at the end of time. In any case, these events lie outside of the familiar historical time. Similarly, the events are frequently located in a distant or fictitious country, or perhaps 'in heaven'. They are remote from the here and now of actual existence. These events differ from what we can recognize as 'historical' events, for there is no means of verification.

Perhaps this placing of the story in a remote mythical time and space gives to it a timelessness and generality which compensate for the particularity of the story itself. We did indeed notice that although a myth is particularized, it becomes a paradigm for the interpretation of many situations. The indefiniteness of its time and place liberates the story from its particularity, so that, while it has the advantage of remaining dramatic and concrete, and so the advantage of depth, it can be illuminating for a wide range of actual human experiences.

A seventh and final characteristic of myth has to do with its relation to a *community*. I doubt if it is true that myths are produced only by communities. It seems to be the case that sometimes a myth is devised by an individual, and anthropologists have shown that the supposedly 'ancient' myths current among primitive tribes may have originated in some cases with individuals who lived only a generation or so ago. But apart from the question of whether the myth always has its origin in a community, I think that one could claim that it does not become a myth until, so to speak, it has been adopted by the community. A private story might circulate as a legend, but when we talk of a myth, we surely mean a story that has become formative in the history of a community and which helps to constitute the identity of that community.

It would be a mistake to exaggerate this particular aspect of myth, and perhaps there is a tendency to exaggerate it among sociologists. Nevertheless, a myth properly so-called has its social or communal dimension. It serves not only as a cohesive force in the community—perhaps by telling a story of its origin such as will give it standing and significance—but also as a kind of basic ideology, in relation to which the various events that happen in the community's history can be referred and explained. Even modern and progressive nations have some core of stories or ideas that perform a function similar to that of the old tribal mythologies.

All of these points we have made about myth can be illustrated from the Bible itself. The concrete dramatic form of myth is in evidence from the creation stories of the Old Testament down to the basic New Testament drama of the divine being who becomes incarnate and who, after atoning for the sins of men, returns to the heavenly places whence he came. The evocative character of the language is obvious in such expressions in the creation stories as 'the dust of the ground' and 'the breath of life', concrete terms that symbolically express the polarity of man's existence; or in a New Testament incident like the transfiguration, where the shining of light vividly suggests a divine manifestation. The degree of immediacy varies, and, as we have noted, the Bible is far from being restricted to a language of pure myth; yet it would be true to say that some elements of myth persist unbroken through the Bible, even if sometimes they appear only mixed with or as a background to non-mythical ways of talking. The supernatural is there, for miracles and wonders are common in both the Old Testament and the New, and so are sensible manifestations of the divine, ranging from the direct appearances of God in the most ancient parts of the Old Testament to the voices from heaven which, in the New Testament, attest the divine provenance of Christ at his baptism and transfiguration. The mythical cosmology too forms the background to the dramas of the Bible; heaven and earth are the contrasting scenes in the drama of Job, while in the New Testament we have Christ's descent into Hades and his ascension into the heavenly places. I pass over the penultimate item in the list of characteristics, and will return to it in a moment. The last item, the communal character of the myth, is of course a central one, for it is above all their faith in God and in the mighty acts that he is asserted to have performed that constitutes the communities both of Israel and of the Church.

I passed over the last item but one, and I must now come back to it, for here we seem to strike against a significant exception when we try to show that the basic characteristics of myth (as they have been expounded above) can be illustrated from the Bible. The particular item which does not seem to fit is that characteristic of myth which we called 'remoteness in time and space'. The Old Testament creation stories still conform to the pattern—they speak of events 'in the beginning' and mention a vaguely indicated land of Eden, somewhere 'in the east'. But the central events of the Old Testament, though we might have difficulty in dating them and though we might question the veracity of some of the details, belong to history—the delivery from Egypt and the giving of the law. Even more, when we come to the New Testament drama of the Word made flesh, we do not have a myth about a saviour god of the usual kind, but assertions concerning an event that had a perfectly definite location in Palestine and that occurred at a perfectly definite time, under Pontius Pilate, only a generation or so before the New Testament accounts of these happenings were being written. In the Bible, myth seems to be bursting into history, so to speak. The question about the significance of this must be deferred for the present.

Even if our attitude to myth is not entirely negative, and we are not prepared simply to dismiss it as the outworn and mostly illusory thinking of a bygone age, it must still be acknowledged that myth stands in need of drastic reinterpretation if such meanings and insights as it may have contained are to be made available to people in modern times. Whatever superstitions and baseless ideologies may flourish nowadays—and there are plenty of them—they are not myths, in the sense of 'myth' that has been delimited in the earlier part of this chapter. We live in a post-mythical age. Yet I would say that the task of making a reinterpretation of myth, that is to say, of translating the mythical language into some post-mythical language, is not merely an academic problem but one that deeply concerns the future of our Western civilization. We have seen that the biblical faith itself, the faith that has in the past been so intimately bound up with our Western culture, is saturated in mythical ideas, and so in varying degrees are the theologies that have the Bible as their source, or as one of their major sources. Thus, with the decline of myth as an intelligible form of discourse, religious faith too has tended to decline and Christianity has become less and less intelligible. On an ability to reformulate the insights of biblical faith in an intelligible non-mythical way that will none-theless avoid the reductionist error of van Buren and others, may well depend the question of whether our Western culture will continue to hold to its Christian heritage in any lively way, or whether it will turn increasingly in the direction of a pure secularism. I certainly think that the latter course would bring about a severe impoverishment of personal life. Moreover, secularism offers its own dangerous quasi-myths, such as belief in progress, nationalism, scientism. These are not myths in the sense explained earlier in this chapter (Bultmann would call them 'ideologies') but they perform something like the function of myths, and shape men's minds, often in dubious fashion. But however that may be, the question about the future of Christian faith in the Western world is certainly one of momentous practi-cal importance, and lends an urgency and significance for life to what might otherwise seem the entirely theoretical question about the reinterpretation of myth.

Myth just does not communicate any more, and this became very clear to us when we considered a concrete illustration of myth from St Athanasius' *De Incarnatione*.[1] The reason for the lack of communication is certainly not that man has at last become wholly rational and scientific. We know only too well from our own bitter experience that our contemporary irra-tionalities are probably no less than those of earlier times, and can be much more damaging. The failure of myth to communi-cate arises from something else. We have seen that communica-tion belongs to the personal dimension of discourse, as something that goes on among human beings. The condition that there should be communication is that among the participants in the discourse there must be a considerable area of sharing—a sharing of interests, attitudes and presuppositions. In the case of myth, the sharing has been reduced to the point where com-munication breaks down. Myth constitutes for us a strange and almost impenetrable world, the interests and presuppositions

[1] See above, p. 128.

of which we do not share; and in the absence of such sharing, communication has ceased.

We have already in this book alluded more than once to Rudolf Bultmann's programme of 'demythologizing' as the most sustained and successful attempt in recent times to reinterpret the mythical language of biblical faith, yet we have also become aware of difficulties and ambiguities in his work. Broadly speaking, Bultmann urges that the new language into which myth is to be translated should be the language of human existence. In modern times the existentialist philosophers have carried through a remapping of this area, and have provided us with a terminology which is perhaps more extensive and more exact than we have ever had before for describing the structures of our own existence—the terminology of 'possibility', 'facticity', 'anxiety', 'finitude', 'authentic existence', 'limit-situations' and so on. Bultmann has employed this terminology as a hermeneutic key for the decipherment of myth. He has, as it were, looked for a new area of sharing, where communication can take place. The men who thought or spoke or wrote in a mythical language were, after all, still *men* like ourselves, sharing the same basic structures of a personal human existence. Thus human existence itself offers the possibility of a common ground on which communication can be restored. If the mythical language can be translated into existential language, then such insights as it may have contained can be made intelligible and accessible once more.

On Bultmann's view, the essential content of a myth is a self-understanding, and perhaps this is the really crucial issue when it comes to assessing what Bultmann has to say about myth. The earlier investigators of myth classified the stories in various ways. They spoke of myths of theogony, cosmogony and anthropology; and again of ætiological, soteriological and eschatological myths. There were other classifications besides, but the point is that considerable diversity was recognized. Bultmann seems to assume that all myth is at bottom anthropological, and he would probably argue that even myths which are not obviously anthropological really do convey a self-understanding, though this is concealed rather than expressed in the mythical form of the language. A hermeneutic is required whereby the self-understanding can be disengaged from its mythical setting and restated in the language of existence. The myth gets broken, its symbols are recognized as symbols and are elucidated by existential interpretation. This does not necessarily imply that the symbols are to be discarded. It may be that their evocative power is such as to make them worth retaining, and that they may even be able to illuminate the existential terminology, in accordance with that circular or reciprocal movement that we have seen to be characteristic of all interpretation. However, the symbols would be no longer embedded in the dead language of myth but recognized in their symbolic character and explored in their existential connotations.

An obvious consequence of this kind of interpretation is that the essential content of the myth is brought out of the remoteness of mythical space and time into the here and now of the actual historical present. The creation story, for instance, is brought from the beginning of time and the land of Eden into the present, as a self-understanding by which I grasp the finite, contingent and creaturely character of my own existence; the talk of God's making man is understood in terms of the giftlike character of my existence; while the language of the 'dust of the ground' and the 'breath of life' are understood as the polarity of my existence, or of any human existence in the world, as compounded of the possibility and facticity which together constitute the peculiar and precarious being of man. From this point one can go on to interpret existentially the myth of the fall of man, and the whole salvation drama of the Old and New Testaments, exhibiting its content as a pattern of human existence which can be relived in our present human existence and which, so the Christian maintains, is experienced as the transition from a disordered to an authentic existence, from alienation to reconciliation.

Bultmann himself applies the method rigorously and with considerable success through the whole range of such mythical or semi-mythical ideas as atonement, resurrection, the last things, the domination of the world by demonic powers, and so on. The very fact that he has advanced so far in opening up and bringing to light the insights that were in danger of being lost in the remote world of myth is surely a testimony to some fundamental soundness in his approach. Yet we saw that Bultmann himself runs into problems and difficulties.[1] There are many questions that have to be asked. Allowing that myth conceals a content that can be translated into another mode of discourse and that it may sometimes be worth translating, and allowing further that Bultmann has provided a fruitful method of making such a translation, we have still to ask about the adequacy of these hermeneutic principles. Do they really hit the meaning that the mythical language was trying to convey? Do they perhaps by a *tour de force* salvage the myths by imposing on them an interpretation which they cannot really bear? More importantly, perhaps, do they exhaust the content of the myth, or is there some residue that is resistant to existential interpretation? In connection with this last question, what is the significance of Bultmann's appeal to analogy, and of Heidegger's move beyond the existential interpretation offered in *Being and Time* to the hermeneutic procedures of his later writings?

To answer such questions, the first step will be to return to the consideration of myth itself. As a beginning, we could look for confirmation of Bultmann's thesis that myth is to be interpreted existentially by asking whether we can discover in the language of myth itself, and especially of course in the myths and elements of myth that occur in the Bible, a tendency to move in the direction of existential language; or, to put the matter differently, if myth has to do with self-understanding, do we find a tendency for myth to pass into an explicit language of self-understanding? If such a tendency is discoverable, then the existential interpretation of myth will receive support not only from its own persuasiveness but also as fulfilling a goal toward which there is an intrinsic tendency in myth itself.

[1] See above, p. 38.

Here we may recall our earlier analysis of discourse in general, when it was considered from the point of view of the person who talks, then with respect to what he talks about, and finally in relation to the person or persons to whom the talk is addressed.[1] Applying this threefold analysis to the question of mythical language, we shall consider it in these several aspects.

First, then, we ask about the person who talks, and about the mode of expression employed in mythical discourse; and this part of the discussion need not detain us long, for we have already met the answer in our earlier listing of some of the basic characteristics of myth. We may say that the mode of expression employed in mythical discourse is the dramatic mode. In contrast to the scientific mode, the dramatic mode is concrete. It is concrete not only in the sense that it deals with some particular situation, as opposed to the generalizing statements of science, but it is concrete also in its mode of expression, and this is the important point for the argument here. This is no abstract expression, but rather it expresses in its full depth and range the speaker's relation to the theme of his discourse. We have seen from earlier discussions that when someone expresses himself scientifically, his language is the impersonal denotative language appropriate to objective, matter-of-fact observation. But when he expresses himself dramatically, his language expresses his total reaction, affective and evaluative as well as cognitive; and such a language has all kinds of overtones and connotations. It may fairly be called an 'existential' language, if by 'existential' we mean here that which concerns human existence in all its dimensions—'total existence', as we have called it earlier. So the first probe of our investigation does support the claim that myth calls for an existential interpretation.

When we turn to the second factor in mythical discourse, the factor constituted by that which is talked about, the matter becomes more problematical. It may well be the case that there are many kinds of myth, with different subject-matters, and we may recall classifications of myth into theogonic,

[1] See above, p. 68.

cosmogonic, anthropological and so on; or it may be the case that myth is the matrix for many kinds of language, perhaps for scientific and philosophical language as well as religious language. We must be prepared to find that Bultmann has too narrowly existentialist an approach to myth, and that its meaning cannot be compressed within the scope of self-understanding. The criticism has been well put by Barth: 'I cannot admit that myth can be interpreted entirely and exclusively, in a totalitarian fashion, so to speak, as the expression of a particular self-understanding of man. No one would deny that it is in part such a self-understanding. But there have always been an immense variety of myths . . . so that we can hardly believe that myth is only an expression of man's self-understanding and nothing more.'[1]

Still, as Barth says, 'no one would deny that it (myth) is in part such a self-understanding'. Even cosmogonic and theogonic myths talk of the world and the gods only in relation to man, and so they are in part anthropological myths. Perhaps the anthropological interest is the dominant one, and to this extent an existential approach would be justifiable.

Actually, if we confine our attention to religious mythology (perhaps this expression is pleonastic) and especially to such elements of it as we find in the Bible, we do find pointers that support the view that what is chiefly talked about in the myth is human existence, man's understanding of himself in his world. Sometimes it happens that we can compare successive stages in the development of myth. Everyone knows that in the opening chapters of the Old Testament we have two distinct stories of the creation of the world. The second of these stories is much the older of the two, and, significantly enough, it centres attention on man: the creation of man takes place first, and then the natural world is built around him. This suggests strongly that the primordial interest of the myth lay in the question of human existence, the question 'What is man?' or

[1] 'Rudolf Bultmann—an Attempt to Understand him' in *Kerygma and Myth*, ed. H.-W. Bartsch, trans. R. H. Fuller (London: S.P.C.K., 1962), vol. II, pp. 115-16.

'Who am I?' rather than in any curiosity about the beginning of the world. The first story, which comes from several centuries later, is much more sophisticated. God no longer acts directly, in the manner typical of mythology, but mediately through the *fiat* of his word. Man is no longer the first to be created, but comes at the end of an ordered sequence, beginning from the most elemental forces and building up to the more complex forms of existence. There is almost something like a modern philosophical interest in this story, and one gets the impression that it could well have become the matrix for speculative as well as for religious developments. Yet even these characteristics of the story do not turn the scales against its preponderantly human interest, for man, though he now appears at the end of the work of creation, is presented as its climax, and the story remains basically an answer to the question, 'What is man?'

When we pursue the question of biblical mythology further, we find that one type of myth tends to get displaced by another. The older myths—the creation story, the descent of the sons of God, the flood, the tower of Babel—were myths of origins, belonging to 'the beginning', prehistorical mythical time. They belong to the class of archetypal myths, so well described and analysed by Mircea Eliade.[1] They are myths that do not yet reckon with the irreversibility of history, still less with man's responsibility in the face of the future, but think rather in terms of periodic destruction and renewal, as in the myth of the flood, which may well have been originally a myth of the seasons. Then we find a new kind of myth appearing, or at any rate acquiring emphasis and eventually predominance. This happens first in some parts of the Old Testament, then it develops in the inter-Testamental period, and finally the new type of myth colours the whole of the New Testament. This new type is the eschatological myth, the myth which tells of events not at the beginning but at the end of time. It is the myth of the end of the age, of judgment and of the consummation of the

[1] In *Cosmos and History*: The Myth of the Eternal Return, trans. Willard R. Trask (New York: Harper & Row, 1959).

divine purpose. Unquestionably, we still have to do with a myth, for the events are placed in the indefinite future, and are conceived as supernatural irruptions from above.

Yet we might say that in producing the eschatological myth, mythical thinking had itself thrown up the myth that would end all myth. For now that men's attention is directed forward rather than backward, history becomes a reality to them in its irreversibility and its decisiveness, and they learn their own responsibility in the face of the future. It is not surprising that one noted New Testament scholar, Oscar Cullmann, has seen in the eschatological conception of time and history the most distinctive thing in the Bible.[1] Of course, a similar eschatology was current in Persian religion and its later offshoots.

It must be acknowledged that many difficult questions of history and exegesis arise at this point. Old Testament scholars differ among themselves about the answers to these questions, and certainly I do not feel competent to pass a judgment. I seem to have been saying that myths of the beginning were eventually superseded by myths of the end, and that this procedure drove men out of a myth-world into history. This, however, is a much oversimplified account of the matter. The development was not nearly so neat, and just what its exact course may have been, I would not presume to say. Almost certainly, the awareness of history and responsibility was there in Israel before the rise of a definite eschatology. It may have been the disappointments of the course of historical events that led to the rise of the strongly mythological expectations of Jewish apocalyptic. But of course some kind of eschatology was there long before the rise of apocalyptic. Where this eschatological hope came from, whether from myths that were current in the Near East or from nationalistic expectations or from convictions about God's sovereignty peculiar to Israel, is a matter of debate among Old Testament scholars.[2]

[1] In *Christ and Time*, trans. Floyd V. Filson (London: SCM Press, and Philadelphia: Westminster Press, 1951).
[2] Cf. W. Eichrodt, *Theology of the Old Testament*, trans. J. A. Baker (London: SCM Press, and Philadelphia: Westminster Press, 1961), vol. I, pp. 494ff.

But however these critical and historical questions may be settled, I think we can adhere to our assertion that eschatology, though it can be mythological in form itself, is a myth that must end myth. Inevitably it gives way to history, because of the future reference that it has introduced into history, with its sense of urgency and of living 'between the times'. Bultmann is able to claim that in the New Testament itself we see the beginnings of an existential interpretation and demythologizing of the eschatological myth, especially in the Fourth Gospel. So it is not unreasonable to claim that by way of eschatology, mythology tends to transcend itself and to pass over into the language of existence, into talk of the possibilities that are here and now in history. As we have said earlier, mythology bursts into history, and perhaps we can now see more clearly something of the meaning of that remarkable exception that we noted earlier, namely, that the mythical drama of the New Testament is not set in some remote time and space, as is characteristic of myth, but right in the midst of history itself.

We have still to look at the third factor in the analysis of mythical discourse, the factor that has to do with the person or persons to whom the discourse is addressed. Again, this will be a point over which we need not linger, for the answer has become apparent. The aspect of discourse which is important in this connection is communication, that aspect which belongs to the person-to-person dimension of all discourse. Such communication is never a mere transference of beliefs or ideas from one person to another, but rather a sharing of what is disclosed in the discourse, and this sharing is made possible by common interests and presuppositions. We have seen how myth fails to communicate with modern man because in our time we no longer participate in many of the presuppositions on which mythical talk proceeded. But if indeed the anthropological interest is as strong in myth as we have seen reason to believe, then an existential reinterpretation would seem to offer a very hopeful way by which the content of the myth can become once more intelligible and accessible. And what else, it may be asked, does the man of today share with the man of archaic times except his basic humanity?

Let us now pause for a moment and call to mind the steps by which the argument has proceeded. While we saw reason to reject the unqualified identification of the language of religion with myth, we acknowledged that myth is nevertheless the primordial language out of which the more sophisticated kinds of God-talk, including theology itself, have arisen. In particular, we noted that the Bible is saturated in myth (within the sense of the word which we delimited) and that mythical elements have inevitably passed into those theologies which have their source in the Bible. Since myth no longer communicates, there arises the problem of demythologizing, or of translating the essential content of myth into an alternative mode of discourse. We have paid special attention to Bultmann's attempt to translate the content of the myths into the language of existence, and have argued that not only does his procedure lead to results that make good sense but that it carries through to its completion a tendency that was inherent in the mythological ideas of the Bible itself. This procedure, moreover, does not prevent us from continuing to make use of the dramatic stories and evocative images of the Bible, but rather enables us to understand them better, as myths and symbols that have been distinguished from the realities that lie beyond them.

But we have still left unanswered the important question of whether the existential interpretation exhaustively reports the content of the myth, or whether there is a residue still concealed there, and one that Bultmann's approach has missed. It seems clear that a thoroughgoing existential interpretation of the biblical drama would take it simply as a way of life for man, to be expressed in terms that are completely immanent to man's life. Bultmann himself does not go to such extremes, for his demythologizing is complicated by the fact that his interpretation of myth involves not only talking existentially about human possibilities but also analogically about God's action. But we have seen that this is the most obscure and unsatisfactory part of his hermeneutic, though at least the problem has been clarified by the present discussion of mythology and by the discussion in the last chapter of Heidegger's hermeneutics. The translation of myth, so far as possible, into a language of existence is an important step in elucidating theological language and in helping to establish a 'basic logic' for it, but obviously it leaves unsolved problems. To come to grips with these, we must go on to a study of symbolism and analogy.

# 9

## *Symbolism*
## *Case Study: Light as a Religious Symbol*

IN THE LAST chapter we dealt with the question of mythical language and its interpretation, and this discussion brought us in turn to the question of symbolism. Even Bultmann's 'de-mythologizing', in spite of its negative-sounding name, does not aim at the elimination of myth but at its interpretation, and more specifically, its existential interpretation. But we found that, for more than one reason, mythological language cannot be entirely translated into existential language, in spite of the proven affinities between the two. One reason was that, as in all interpretation, there is a kind of reciprocity between the two languages, so that one is not absorbed into the other but rather each helps to throw light on the other. In this specific case, the language of existence helps to light up the obscure expressions of myth, but then in turn the concrete drama of the myth throws light in a new way on the structures of existence. The other reason was that myth is more than just an anthropological language; it has a further dimension, which we might call onto-logical or theological or cosmological. This cannot be translated into existential language, and we find it appearing in Bultmann as what he calls 'analogical' language. In any case, here again the language of the myth is resistant to attempts to get rid of its concrete, pictorial character, for it wants to speak of a level of reality transcending the human level, and if we are to speak at all of the ultimate mysteries of God and Being, we cannot avoid using an indirect language of images.

So we are brought before the problem of symbolic language. We have already indicated in a somewhat rough and ready manner how 'symbolic' language, in the widest sense, is different from myth.[1] The point is, as we have seen, that myth has an immediacy in which symbols and what they symbolize have not been sorted out. But a consciously symbolic language is much more sophisticated, and has some understanding of the complexity of its own logic. In such a language, the symbol and the symbolizandum are consciously distinguished. Perhaps the most familiar and the most profound symbols have their home, so to speak, in myth and in the unconscious, but they can become detached from this 'dreaming' background, as it were, and may continue to be used in very fruitful ways by men who have become 'awake' to their symbolic character.

Apart from making this rough distinction of symbol from myth, and thereby showing how symbols may continue to be useful and even indispensable in a post-mythical world, we have not tried to pin down too precisely what we mean by a 'symbol'. The word has an extremely wide range, and there is a sense in which all language is symbolic—every word is a symbol, and even the letters, out of which written words are made, are symbols. On the other hand, there are a great many symbols that are not words. Since we ourselves are concerned in this study with language, we are more interested in verbal symbols than in, let us say, flags, emblems and the like; yet it is not possible or desirable to discuss a word without also discussing the thing or the phenomenon for which the word stands, and whose properties or characteristics have made possible the particular symbolic use of the language. On the other hand, although we are concerned with verbal symbols primarily, we are obviously not interested in *all* words, though all words can be called 'symbols'. Our interest lies in those words which are 'symbolic' in a narrower sense, namely, words which stand for a thing or

[1] See above, p. 174.

phenomenon which is itself a symbol, in so far as it stands for something else; so that the word, in such a case, refers indirectly through its immediate referend to whatever this may symbolize. If I may anticipate the study of a special case to which we shall come later in this chapter, I may give an illustration at this point. In the Nicene Creed, it is asserted that Jesus Christ is 'Light of Light'. Now this expression is symbolic, that is to say, the words are symbolic. More than this, however, the actual phenomenon of light is considered a symbol of the divine. Thus the words immediately refer to light, but in the universe of discourse in which they are used, they bounce off their immediate referend, if I may use such an expression, and point to the mystery of Christ's deity.

Yet even if we pin down the notion of symbolism in this way, our usage is still very imprecise. What has been described is indirect or oblique language in general. Is all such indirect language to be called 'symbolic'? Or are we to make further distinctions between 'symbols', 'analogues', 'images', 'metaphors' or whatever other expressions may be used? Bultmann, for instance, does distinguish between 'symbol', 'analogue' and 'metaphor', though I have shown elsewhere[1] that his distinctions are never made very clear and that he is not consistent in maintaining them.

If we try to move toward a more exact differentiation among the various terms that we have noted, a first useful step would be to separate metaphor from symbols, analogues and images. The expression 'metaphor' is used mostly in literary contexts; and although 'symbols', 'analogues' and 'images' are all expressions that can be used in a variety of contexts, we are thinking of them here primarily in their religious and theological use. Now, it seems to me that we can separate metaphors from the other three chiefly in terms of our existential response. As far as the metaphor is concerned, our response to it is an aesthetic one. A well-chosen metaphor sharpens our perception so that we notice features of the situation that we would not have noticed

[1] *The Scope of Demythologizing*, p. 205 n. 1.

otherwise. We share in the way the poet has seen whatever he is describing to us. Now surely the symbols, analogues and images of religious discourse likewise sharpen our perception, and the manner in which they do this has obvious affinities with the way in which literary metaphors function. But the response, in the case of the religious expressions, is not an aesthetic one. It does indeed involve feeling, though it would be the feeling associated with the sense of the numinous rather than with the sense of the beautiful. It also involves insight, and our major problem is to elucidate the kind of insight that such religious symbols and the like may bring, that is to say, to elucidate their cognitive dimension. But perhaps the chief difference is that the religious symbol, analogue or image calls from us a response of commitment. When Matthew Arnold writes, 'And still the men were plunged in sleep', this is a vivid metaphor that presents a situation to us in a sensitive and dramatic way, and perhaps even involves us in this situation; but it involves us aesthetically rather than personally or morally. On the other hand, when we think of some of the images that were applied by the first Christians to Christ, these involved a faith-commitment to him. To call him 'Lord' or 'Son of God' or 'eternal Word' or even 'good Shepherd' or 'true Vine' is not so much to light up his being (though this is included) as to respond to him by accepting him and declaring one's allegiance to him or obedience to him. Generally speaking, then, it seems to me that in the way they affect us and in the existential response that they call forth, religious symbols and allied expressions have to be distinguished from the metaphors and other figurative expressions used in literature. That there are resemblances, we need not deny; and that the poet too can evoke commitment, we need not deny, though then he is probably writing as a prophet, rather than a poet pure and simple. But even when we allow these things, we can still see that the oblique language of religion has its own distinctive characteristics.

Can we now make some further distinctions as among 'symbols', 'analogues' and 'images', the three expressions which we have been using up till now? In common usage, I believe that these expressions frequently overlap, so that such distinctions as we make will have a somewhat arbitrary character. Perhaps we could agree to use the word 'image' as a broad generic term that would cover any kind of pictorial language. The question would then arise about how we distinguish between symbols and analogues within the general field of images. It is obvious that many theologians have in fact made such a distinction, although one would have to add that the dividing line is not always a very clear one. Not until we come to the next chapter, which will be specially devoted to the problem of analogy, can we hope to arrive at something like a satisfactory clarification of the difference between analogues and symbols. But there is a rather obvious difference, which although it may seem a trivial matter in itself, suggests a point of departure. The difference is that the best analogues are almost self-interpreting, whereas symbols frequently require much explanation of background before we begin to see where they are pointing. This difference may sometimes be a relative one, and depends simply on the fact that the best analogues assume a background of ideas and relationships that is universally known, while even quite well-known symbols imply a narrower background of ideas, perhaps deriving from the history of a specific community. But I think there is more to the difference than this.

Analogy would seem to depend on some intrinsic likeness between the analogue and that for which it stands. We do not, for the moment, pause to ask the difficult question about what is meant precisely by 'likeness' or 'similarity'. In the case of religious analogues, the likeness would usually be found in some personal characteristic or relationship. For instance, when we speak of God as our Father, we are employing an analogue which depends on an intrinsic likeness, in some respects at least, between the parent-child relation and the relation of God to his creatures. I say that an analogy of this kind is almost self-interpreting (whatever its ultimate difficulties may be) because it seems to imply some straightforward likeness and because also the parent-child relation is universally known in human experience. Such an analogy gains the widest currency and perhaps we could scarcely imagine the possibility of ever dispensing with it. It is true that in some cases the analogue might be less than self-interpreting. There is the case of the child who has never known parental love, and for whom the analogue of God's fatherhood needs to be unfolded through the experience of love in a Christian community; again, human fatherhood is frequently so cheapened and debased that it may afford only a very distant glimpse of what is meant by divine fatherhood, and needs to be itself judged in the light of the God-creature relation, to which it has afforded a clue; or again, one would need to take account of Freud's theories about the projection of the father-image, and ensure that this particular analogue is not allowed to degenerate into something infantile and neurotic. Nevertheless, this kind of analogue seems to have an extraordinary stability and universality, as well as a direct and readily intelligible power of address. Later, we shall have to investigate more fully the whole problem of analogy, and may well find that this problem constitutes the core of the wider problem of God-talk, and that especially we are challenged to give some reasonable account of the 'likeness' which is supposed to make analogy possible.[1]

However, to say that it is 'likeness' (we have not yet defined this idea very closely) that makes possible analogy is not to imply that symbolism is something purely subjective, and that there is no kind of intrinsic relation between the symbol and that which it symbolizes. It may well be the case that there are relations other than likeness that make possible a symbolism that has some ontological validity and is not exhaustively accounted for in terms of existential response. Tillich, for instance, speaks of 'participation', and as an illustration he mentions a national flag, which is said to 'participate' in the being of the nation to which it belongs.[2] Admittedly, this notion of 'participation' is

[1] See below, pp. 219ff.
[2] *Dynamics of Faith* (New York: Harper & Row, and London: Allen & Unwin, 1957), p. 42.

not made very clear, though it seems obvious that it is something much more concrete than the participation of a particular in a universal, the way in which the notion of 'participation' (*methexis*) has usually been understood from Plato onward. But it is also clear that this participation is something very different from 'likeness'. We would never dream of calling a flag an 'analogue' of the country to which it belongs, and even if we thought of it as more than a merely extrinsic or conventional symbol, we would not suppose that the intrinsic relation, whatever it might be, is one of likeness.

Perhaps we may get some help at this point if we recall a much earlier discussion in which a criticism was made of the so-called 'picture' theory of language.[1] According to this theory, our language somehow reproduces the structure of the facts about which we are talking and so, presumably has some kind, of formal 'likeness' to the facts. But we saw that while the proponents of this theory, such as Earl Russell, believed themselves to be championing the cause of science and empiricism, they get no support from contemporary physics, in which the relation between language and facts is much more complex than a relation of simple likeness.

The point has been developed in relation to religious language by Ian Ramsey, who bases himself in turn on some views about scientific models put forward by Max Black.[2] Here we are introducing a new word into the discussion—the word 'model'. I do not think, however, that this need be taken as an additional complication. As the word is used by Ramsey, it has a fairly broad generic range (like the word 'image') and seems to cover both analogues and symbols. Ramsey's point is that there is a big difference between the way scientific models were understood in the nineteenth century and the way they are understood today. In the nineteenth century, these models were supposed to be 'picture' models, reproducing or copying on a different scale selected features of the reality which they were

---

[1] See above, p. 58.
[2] *Models and Mystery* (London: Oxford University Press, 1964), pp. 2ff.

supposed to represent. I suppose that the model of the atom as a miniature solar system, if taken more or less literally, would be an example of a 'picture' model. But the kind of models used in contemporary science are different. It is accepted that the atom cannot be pictured at all, and although we may talk of 'particles', 'waves' and the like, this language is not to be taken literally. We cannot understand the atom in the way the nineteenth century physicist wanted to understand it, that is to say, by constructing a mental model that would reproduce the essential features of the atom. Yet, on the other hand, it is clear that people today do in fact understand the atom better than people did in the nineteenth century. The models that are used today—Ramsey calls them 'disclosure' models—are not pictures based on one-to-one likeness between features of the picture and corresponding features in the original, yet the fact that they enable us to operate with the atom and to harness atomic power shows that somehow they stand in real relatedness to the nature of the atom. These contemporary scientific models are symbols, rather than pictures. One might almost call them 'ciphers', in Jaspers' use of this term,[1] that is to say, words that stand for something that is in itself quite incomprehensible, and yet words that somehow give us some way of coming to terms with the mystery. But I doubt if Jaspers himself would use the term 'ciphers' in this way.

John McIntyre has made an interesting comparison between the non-picturing models about which we have been talking and the so-called 'secondary' qualities given in sense-perception.[2] These secondary qualities, we suppose, do not belong to things apart from our perceiving them—the rose is not 'really' red, or the sky blue. Yet on the other hand these secondary qualities are not just subjective ideas in our minds, unrelated to the external world. This comparison is, of course, itself an analogy, and it must not be pressed too far, but it does at least give us an example of how we may know something through properties or

[1] *Kerygma and Myth*, vol. II, p. 169.
[2] *The Shape of Christology* (London: SCM Press, 1966), p. 67.

characteristics different from but not unrelated to the properties or characteristics of the thing itself.

Actually, we use the word 'symbol' to cover a whole range of possible relations between the symbol and the symbolizandum, extending from something very close to a purely conventional and extrinsic relation at one extreme to something near to the 'likeness' of analogy at the other. A mathematical symbol would seem to be a matter of convention, and to have no intrinsic connection with what it symbolizes. A letter of the alphabet might seem to be just as conventional, though it must be remembered that letters which now represent sounds to which they have no intrinsic relation have been derived from ideograms which originally pictured objects or ideas. A national flag would seem to acquire its relation to or 'participation' in the life of a nation through its association with the history of that nation; but it is hard to know whether this ever becomes an intrinsic relation, or whether Tillich is justified in putting the flag so definitely among symbols rather than among what he calls 'signs'. Such a symbol as the cross might seem to be in similar condition. It is a symbol of God's love within the Christian community because of the associations which it has there with the death of Jesus Christ; but in pre-Christian times, or in a country that knew nothing of the Christian religion, the cross would not be such a symbol. Yet just because of its distinctive shape, the cross has served as a symbol of other qualities in non-Christian and pre-Christian cultures—of immortality in ancient Egypt and of fertility in Central America, to mention only two widely divergent cases. Thus, apart from its historical associations in the Christian religion, one would have to say that the cross has a kind of intrinsic symbolic power, though this has been differently understood in different cultures. Water, on the other hand, seems to be in still another class. Apart altogether from the history of its use in different cults, its everyday use in washing gives to it an almost universal and intrinsic symbolic power as representing cleansing. When we come to such a symbol as light, of which I shall have more to say shortly, the dividing line between symbols and analogues has become very ill-defined, for one could argue that there is a measure of 'likeness' between some features of light and some features of God as he is known in religious experience.

While there is a wide range of religious symbols and while the degree of affinity between the symbol and what is symbolized varies, it would seem that there is always some affinity, and that religious symbols are never just extrinsic or accidental. By its very participation in the history of a community or in the experience of mankind, a symbol establishes itself, exerts its own power and claims its own right. Such a symbol is much more than a mere conventional sign like, say, the plus sign in arithmetic or algebra. The operation of addition could get along just as well with some other sign, though it may be worth noting that even the addition sign does not seem to be entirely arbitrary, for it consists of one stroke added to another, and to this extent is intrinsically related to what it signifies. Still, it could be changed by agreement. But it would be unthinkable for Christianity to dispense with the cross or change it for some other symbol, just as presumably it would also be impossible to discard such fundamental analogies as that of the fatherhood of God.

But if symbols, or at any rate some symbols, are just as much built into the Christian faith as some of its central analogues, why is it the case—as we have asserted earlier—that the analogues have a kind of self-interpreting quality, whereas the symbols may have a kind of obscurity that calls for their reinterpretation and refurbishing, in an enterprise rather similar to the interpretation of myth?[1] To this it may be replied that symbols only remain symbols for as long as they successfully point to the reality which they symbolize, and relate that reality to our human existence. This, in turn, depends like all successful communication on a background of shared ideas within which the symbols can operate.

Even the cross could become an empty symbol, and for this reason we not only exhibit the cross in our churches or make the

[1] Bultmann does in fact speak of a 'desymbolizing' as well as a 'demythologizing'.

sign of the cross in our worship, but also preach the cross and continually call to mind its meaning in the Christian story and the theology based on this story. There is a double activity here, typifying again the hermeneutic circle whereby we move back and forth from one medium to another, and find that each interprets the other. The symbol lights up for us levels of meaning and of reality in ways that perhaps conceptual language could not do, above all, if it is an abstract language; yet without conceptual elucidation of the symbol's meaning, it would lapse into utter obscurity and could not perform its function.

I propose now to illustrate and clarify these general remarks about symbols and symbolism by taking a concrete example of a religious symbol and subjecting it to closer study. We shall try to see what are the dimensions of meaning in this symbol, and we shall consider also how far it typifies the tendency of symbols to lapse back into obscurity, and what kind of interpretation or reinterpretation it demands—in other words, what kind of 'desymbolizing' is called for, if we remember that this expression implies just as positive a hermeneutic as does 'demythologizing'. The example chosen for this case study, if I may call it such, is not so central as the cross in the Christian faith. It is nevertheless a very important symbol, and one that is found not only in Christianity but in many other religions besides. It is the symbol of light.

An examination of a symbol like light is an interesting pointer to those unifying factors which, in spite of all differences, run through the religious faiths of mankind. A study of the shared imagery might turn out to be one useful way of promoting communication and co-operation among faiths. But however that may be, the symbol of light is one that has been known far beyond the borders of Christendom, and it has had a very long history among the religions of the world. The very name of one of these religions, Buddhism, implies that 'enlightenment' is of the essence of religion, for a Buddha is simply one who has become enlightened. Edwyn Bevan, in an admirable discussion[1]

[1] *Symbolism and Belief* (London: Allen & Unwin, 1938), pp. 125ff.

of this symbol, has briefly traced something of the history of this image in the religious vision of ancient peoples. He begins from the sun-gods of Egypt and other countries of the near East, continues through the dualistic world-view of Zoroastrianism, with its depiction of the cosmic struggle between light and darkness, and comes on to the use of the symbol in Hellenistic times, when, as Bevan believed, it acquired a special importance. In this period, light figured prominently in Gnosticism, neo-Platonism, the writings of Philo, and generally in the religion and philosophy of the Graeco-Roman world. To the examples adduced by Bevan, one could now add a mention of the light symbol in the Qumran community, one of whose documents dealt with 'The War of the Sons of Light with the Sons of Darkness'.[1]

But what is important in Bevan's treatment is not so much his bringing together of historical examples as rather his masterly exploration of the symbol itself and its power to direct us into many dimensions of experience. Prominent in Bevan's account is what we have called the element of 'existential response', that is to say, the feelings and commitments which this symbol awakens in us, and which we may suppose are likewise feelings and commitments appropriate to the religious realities which light is taken to symbolize. But there are hints also of the ontological dimensions of the symbol, as lighting up something of the mystery of these religious realities themselves. The problem of desymbolizing begins to show itself as remarkably parallel to the problem of demythologizing. In both cases, existential interpretation is an important step toward elucidating the meaning, but in neither case is such interpretation exhaustive.

Perhaps it is only when one begins to look for it that one realizes how pervasive the light symbol is in Christian thought and worship. Its place in the Bible itself has been well shown by A. G. Hebert. He uses a typological method of exegesis and believes that we can discern certain great images or symbols that

[1] Millar Burrows, *The Dead Sea Scrolls* (London: Secker & Warburg, 1956), pp. 390ff.

recur throughout the Bible; if we follow these up, it is claimed, we find them building themselves together in revelatory patterns. Applying this method to the symbol of light, he notes that there was light in the beginning of the creation, when God said, 'Let there be light'. There was light at the theophany to Moses in the desert, and in the exodus, in the pillar of fire. The light symbol recurs in the New Testament, for it is present at the beginning of the incarnation, at the birth of Christ, just as it had been at the beginning of the creation. There is light too at the transfiguration. In St John's Gospel, Christ declares himself to be the light of the world, while in the First Epistle of St John, it is asserted that God *is* light. This identification of God with light may, incidentally, be cited as illustrating a kind of transition point between myth and conscious symbolism. For many persons in the first century, especially in the dualistic Gnostic cults, God and light were literally one and the same. Presumably in St John's Epistle, the literal identification of light with God has given way to a conscious use of the light symbol to stand for God. Yet it may well have been the case that the distinction between symbol and symbolizandum was still blurred. This seems even probable when we remember that the contrast between light and darkness is one element in the so-called 'Johannine dualism', and that Bultmann and others have seen in this dualism (as well as in other things) evidence of a Gnostic influence in the Johannine literature.[1]

But let us come back to Father Hebert's remarks on the light symbol in the Bible. In this poetic kind of language, one does not look for complete consistency. Sometimes God is represented as the author of light, sometimes he is associated with light, sometimes light marks his presence, sometimes he is identified with light. According to Hebert, the symbol of light 'is used to describe the work of God in the whole order of creation and redemption, and it dwells in the imagination as exact theological definitions cannot do'.[2] Even if we have reservations about

---

[1] *Theology of the New Testament*, vol. II, p. 21.
[2] *The Bible from Within* (London: Oxford University Press, 1950), p. 176.

aspects of Hebert's typological style of exegesis, we can acknowledge the claim that he makes for the poetic, evocative force of symbolic language, as a kind of language that can somehow work upon men and lead them to insight and even action, where a more exact conceptual language might fail.

The importance of the symbol of light in Christianity may be seen further if we consider its place in liturgy and devotion. Right through the Christian year, the symbol of light figures very prominently. In the Anglican Book of Common Prayer, the collect said throughout the season of Advent begins with the petition that God may 'give us grace that we may cast away the works of darkness, and put upon us the armour of light'. Christmastide tells how the 'glory of the Lord' shone round about the shepherds, and also of the 'true light' that came into the world.[1] Epiphany is perhaps *par excellence* the season of the light symbol. In the gospel, we read the story of how the wise men were guided by the star to Jesus.[2] In the epistle, St Paul asserts that the God who had said in the beginning, 'Let there be light!' has shone in our hearts to give 'the light of the knowledge of his glory in the face of Christ'.[3] From the Old Testament, we hear the voice of the prophet: 'Arise, shine for thy light is come, and the glory of the Lord has risen upon you'.[4] Of course, the very word 'Epiphany' is derived from the same root as the Greek word *phōs*, 'light'. Epiphany simply means a 'coming to the light', a manifestation or shining forth in which something that has hitherto been veiled or hidden is now brought into the open. It is not necessary for us to pursue the theme of light through the remainder of the Church's year, but it keeps recurring. We may remember too that on various Saints' Days, the theme of light occurs. Soon after the Epiphany we commemorate St Paul's conversion and recall how 'there shone round about him a light from heaven'.[5]

It is not my intention to try to explore the evocative connotations that the symbol of light carries with it, either in the general

---

[1] Luke 2.9; John 1.9.  [2] Matt. 2.9.  [3] II Cor. 4.6.
[4] Isa. 60.1.  [5] Acts 9.3.

religious experience of mankind or in the context of the Bible or of Christian worship. It would in any case be difficult to add anything worthwhile to the perceptive comments of Bevan, Hebert and others. Rather, we shall consider this symbol in a more general way, hoping that this may help us toward a better understanding of religious symbols as such. The power of a symbol to awaken an existential response must be related to its power to yield insight into some ontological reality. When this fails to happen, the symbol becomes obscure, its power is weakened and it may eventually fall out of use. So we may begin by asking about the power and effectiveness of the symbol for our times, and this will lead us into the question of its meaning and the possibilities for reinterpretation. Even the most powerful symbols eventually grow old and die, so that they can no longer speak to men with their former persuasiveness. There are two reasons for suspecting that the symbol of light, whatever its past power may have been, is no longer one that can easily speak home to men in modern times.

The first reason is simply that our prosaic matter-of-fact attitude to the world gives us quite a different feeling for light from that which men presumably had for it in ancient times. For them, light was a mysterious effluence, already possessed of something like a numinous character. For us, light has become just another physical phenomenon; and more than that, it is something that we have at our disposal, for we now make our own light and use it when we will, and are not dependent on the 'great lights' of the sky that once 'ruled' the day and the night.[1] Like all other physical phenomena, light is for us profane, secular, matter-of-fact. Even if it is ultimately a mystery, we can nevertheless place it in our scheme of the physical universe. We can think of it as waves, whose frequency and intensity we can measure; or as packets of energy, whose very mass we can likewise measure. Even by the most strenuous effort of imagination, we could hardly feel for light as people once did. But without its ancient connotations, light can hardly function

[1] Gen. 1.16.

for us with the power of a symbol, that is to say, with power to shape our lives; at best, it might remain as a metaphor, operating on the literary and aesthetic level.

The second reason suggesting that the power of the light symbol has declined is that, as a symbol drawn from nature, it lacks a personal or existential dimension, even if it has possibilities for eliciting an existential response. When we remember how thoroughly personalized is the Bible's talk of God, it is perhaps rather surprising to find a naturalistic symbol figuring so prominently as does the symbol of light. Even if we agree with those scholars who maintain that the talk of light and darkness in the Johannine literature comes out of a Gnostic background, there are still plenty of other areas of the Bible that speak of light. The light symbol is indeed so firmly established in the Old Testament that one could argue that it is unnecessary to look to near Eastern dualism for the role assigned to this symbol in the Fourth Gospel. But we need not concern ourselves with this question about origins. However, let us notice that the very epistle which makes central the naturalistic symbol of light in asserting 'God is light', also contains the assertion 'God is love', and in this passage makes central a personal image.[1] Most Christians would probably think that this second and personal way of talking about God is much more adequate than the first, because it points to him by employing a symbol—or, to speak more precisely, an analogue—drawn from human existence, not from inanimate nature. We are participants in human existence and know it from the inside, whereas we know nature only from without. But admittedly, the passages about light in the New Testament are given an existential application: for instance, both our Lord's declaration that he is the light of the world and the assertion that God is light are followed by statements about walking in the light. Nevertheless, the symbol is itself an impersonal one.

The question then arises whether we can find some way of re-interpreting this ancient symbol of light, so as to restore

[1] I John 1.5; 4.8.

something of the force which it presumably once had, and keep it from degenerating into a mere metaphor. Is there some expression that might help to bring to life something of the meaning of the symbol of light that belonged to it when light was still a mysterious and even numinous effluence? Perhaps this means finding an expression that will introduce an existential dimension into the naturalistic symbol—a symbol which has been progressively depersonalized as nature has been stripped of any animistic interpretation. We must look for some interpretative idea that will allow us to grasp the language of the biblical writers—and/or allow it to grasp us—as not just a figurative flight of poetic imagery, but as having to do with the 'light of life',[1] our life here and now.

Let me now suggest that an expression which can perhaps help to revivify the biblical symbol of light is 'openness'. We cannot think of 'openness' as simply a word that can be substituted for mentions of 'light', but it is a word that can help us to understand an important dimension of the light symbol, a dimension that has been obscured in the general decay of the symbol that has gone on concomitantly with the secularization of nature. Roughly speaking, one might say that the word 'openness' can do for the symbol of light what the word 'estrangement' has done in much contemporary theology for the moribund word 'sin'. 'Estrangement' is certainly not a substitute for 'sin', but it does refurbish the old word by pointing to a basic structure to which 'sin' refers. In similar fashion, the word 'openness' draws our attention to a basic structure intended by the light symbol, for only where conditions of openness obtain can there be light. In the depth of a forest, for instance, it is where the wood has been opening up that the light comes in, and we call such an open place a 'clearing' or a 'glade', a place that is bright.[2]

The interpretation of the symbol of light in terms of openness is an existential-ontological one, related to the basic logic of all

---

[1] John 8.12.

[2] The German word for a clearing, *Lichtung*, makes even more obvious the connection with light (*Licht*). Cf. Heidegger, *Being and Time*, p. 171.

theological discourse. The interpretation begins from the existential side, for we find the first clues to what is meant by 'openness' simply by considering ourselves. What makes us, as human beings, different from rocks and stars and even animals is just the astonishing multiplicity of ways in which we stand open. We are open to the past through memory and open to the future through anticipation, and so we are open to the possibility of becoming responsible selves. Again, we are open to our world, so that we can understand it and, within limits, transform it and become creative within it. We are open to other human beings (themselves having this kind of openness) so that we can enter into personal relations with them and push outward the horizons of genuine community. Surely we are open also to God, the Being within which we and all that is have our limited beings.

And yet, as soon as we say these things, we see that all of them have to be contradicted. This openness of ours is ambiguous and variable in its character. We have it as a potentiality of our being, but in fact we oscillate between being open and being shut up. We shut out our past by 'forgetting' what is unpleasant to us, and we withdraw from the disturbing responsibilities of the future. We mark out for ourselves a corner of the world that we want to possess. We throw up barriers against the neighbour. Likewise we can go far toward shutting out any ultimate concern by immersing ourselves in what is immediate or even petty.

It is in this ambivalent and even contradictory situation that there is addressed 'the message that we have heard from the beginning', the message that God is light. The statement 'God is light' could be translated into the language of openness by saying: 'Openness is constitutive for being'. The more openness, the fuller being and the more expansion in being; but where openness is obstructed, being is narrowed down and thinned away. Openness is the very law of being, so to speak, because Being itself or God is constituted by openness.

It is not difficult to relate this ontological interpretation of the symbol of light to some of the central Christian doctrines. God is not closed in himself, like, perhaps, the 'uncarved block' of

Chinese mysticism. He does not preserve himself intact, if one may so speak, but goes into the openness of the creation, conferring being, and even, in the case of the creation of man, conferring responsibility for being and a measure of his own creativity. God takes the risk that is inseparable from all openness, for to come into the open is to be exposed. Yet this very coming forth is what makes him God, what allows us to call by this holy name the ultimate Being of the world; for we could not call a self-enclosed Being 'God'. It is true that the depths of God remain veiled, yet there is an openness in God so that he is not merely opaque to us. This openness, which can be called both 'light' and 'love', belongs to his very essence.

But in saying this, we seem also to be asserting an analogy or likeness between God and man, in so far as we have spoken of both of them in terms of openness. The openness of God (Being) is of course prior to the openness of man, and determinative for it. Since this openness is the very law of Being, as it were, then in the case of human existence too, it is the man who would save himself by gathering up his being that actually becomes less in his being and eventually loses it; while the man who loses his being by going out into the risk of openness in its many dimensions is the man who really *ex-sists*, who really *is*.

Christ is the 'light of the world'[1] because in him the full openness of God and the potential openness of man have converged. In the Eastern churches, the Epiphany is specially associated with Christ's baptism and so with its imagery of the divine Spirit descending upon Jesus and dwelling with him. Jesus, we may say, was the man fundamentally open to the Father, and this is the basic openness on which all other kinds of human openness depend. We can think of Christ as the God-man because he moves out to fulfil the openness that is potential in all human existence. What is ambiguous and obscured in everyday human existing is revealed and manifested in the Christ. Here is openness to the world, openness to the neighbour, the manifestation of God's openness in the flesh. This thought of

[1] John 8.12.

Christ's openness, moreover, gives us a clue to the mystery of what we mean by 'incarnation'. A human life that has gone out in complete openness is the manifestation in the flesh of the openness of God. This is possible because human 'nature', as an existence, is not a closed nature but an open and dynamic one.

The symbol of light serves to point to these fundamental structures of openness—in human existence, in Christ, in God. But our consideration of this symbol has already led us to the special theme of analogy, and it is to this that we must next turn.

## 10

## Analogy and Paradox

THE PROBLEM OF analogy is a very old one in theological discussion, but it seems to me that it lies very near the centre of
the current debates, not only about language but about God
and the meaning of the basic Christian doctrines. It is probably
the case that many of those engaged in these debates do not
explicitly recognize the relevance of the problem of analogy to
their work, and may even think that it belongs to an older way
of doing theology. In any case, the tendency nowadays is to talk
of 'models' rather than 'analogues'—at least, this is the tendency
among British theologians, perhaps influenced by Ian Ramsey.
But whatever terminology may be employed, we seem driven to
something very like the problem that has been traditionally
considered under the heading of analogy.

As Alec Vidler has remarked, 'There may be many readers
who are interested in the recent ferment in theology without
being aware that a great deal of this kind of thing has been
going on for as long as I can remember, and before that.'[1] A
few years earlier, John McIntyre had written: 'One of the major
discoveries—it may be only a rediscovery—of recent theology
has been the central place which analogy occupies in theological
inquiry of all kinds.'[2] These words got an unexpectedly empha-
tic endorsement four years later when *The Observer* of London
introduced Bishop Robinson's reflections on the problem of God

---

[1] *Twentieth-Century Defenders of the Faith* (London: SCM Press, 1965), p. 7.
[2] 'Analogy' in *Scottish Journal of Theology*, vol. XII, p. 1.

with the sensational headline: 'Our image of God must go'. The subsequent debate which the Bishop triggered off has turned on this question of images. How can we think and talk of God? What images are appropriate? How can language bridge the gulf between the finite beings about which we talk in our every-day discourse and the God about whom faith and theology want to talk? Can the word 'God', in the last resort, be given an assignable meaning, or must it be judged an empty word that can no longer be used in the serious discourse of our time?

Of course, every way of talking about God has been called in question in the recent discussions. If any way has been felt to be appropriate, then it would be the *via negationis*. However, we have seen that this way, taken by itself, can lead only to silence and agnosticism. In the case of at least some of those writers who have taken up a position of 'Christian atheism', one might attribute this to an exaggerated and one-sided use of the *via negationis*. Certainly this way of negation serves a very useful purpose and is quite indispensable if we are to be safeguarded against immature and over-literal talk about God—talk which drags God down to some idolatrous fiction of our own minds. There is, of course, nothing new in this insistence that God's essential Being transcends our comprehension—it was plainly taught by the classic Christian tradition as we find it in St Thomas and the patristic writers, and is already implicit in the biblical conception of the divine transcendence: 'For my thoughts are not your thoughts, neither are your ways my ways, says the Lord. For as the heavens are higher than the earth, so are my ways higher than your ways and my thoughts than your thoughts.'[1] Yet if there is just total difference between God and man, can we say anything significant about God at all? Can we even say that he exists or has any reality, if he is not like any existent entity?

In practice, the *via negationis* has always been supplemented by some other ways of talking about God, and apart from such supplementation, we do seem to fall into atheism. But what

[1] Isa. 55, 8-9.

other way of speaking is permissible? I have indicated that the problem of analogy is of central importance in trying to answer this question, whether or not this problem is explicitly recognized by those engaged in the current discussions. The reason for singling out analogy for this key role is one that has become apparent from our earlier discussions. We have seen how myth is defective in its communication, and even if it can be partly re-interpreted in an existential language, there is an ontological core of meaning that is not exhausted by the Bultmannian type of demythologizing and that calls for some other kind of expression in an indirect language. When we considered symbolism, we arrived at similar results. A conscious symbolism is an advance beyond mythology. Like mythology, symbolism can be partly analysed in terms of the existential significance of the symbols in the lives of those who have committed themselves to them. But we found that the most important symbols are those having some intrinsic relation to what they are taken to symbolize, and when we probed this point through the examination of a particular symbol, we found that the question of symbol, like the question of myth, drove us inexorably to the question of analogy. The point is that of all our ways of talking about God, the way of analogy is the one that has the most positive content. It is not, of course, a literal or direct way of talking about God, and yet it is a way that seems to give us assurance that our talk is not just empty, and that it does somehow impinge upon God and give us some insight into the mystery of Being. Analogy makes possible that language of scripture and liturgy that is at the heart of the practice of the Christian religion. Is this language really meaningful, or is it just, to put it bluntly, a kind of mumbo-jumbo that we go through because it is a well-established tradition or because it affords us some comfort and enjoyment or because it is supposed to inculcate in us 'desirable' moral attitudes? Unless we can say that it is meaningful, I think honest people would want to get rid of the whole business. This means that unless we can produce some reasonable account of the logic of analogy, there is no support for our other ways of talking about God, except the *via negativa*; and, taken in isolation, this leads straight to atheism.

What I have been trying to say in the last paragraph was already hinted at in an early chapter of this book.[1] We were trying to show then that the question of language occupies a pivotal place in contemporary theology, and in order to do this, we noted how three outstanding theologians of the last generation had all left behind them an unresolved linguistic problem. But we could have gone further, and said that it was not only the question of language but, more specifically, the question of analogy that had emerged as the central problem. What we found puzzling in Bultmann was not his existential interpretation of myth, which was all very clear and helpful, but the trouble began when he invoked analogy so that he could talk about an 'act of God', an 'address of God', and the like. Our difficulty with Barth came at the point where, as it seemed to us, he made an arbitrary leap and claimed that our finite human language can bring to expression God's own word because divine grace empowers it and establishes an analogy between the human and the divine. Finally, when we turned to Tillich in the hope that he might somehow provide a mediation between the other two, it was again the problem of analogy that constituted the major difficulty, though this time the problem took the form of the *analogia entis*. This early indication of the centrality of analogy has now been confirmed, for our discussions of the different modes of discourse, such as myth and symbol, has once more pointed us to analogy as the core of our problem.

In the last chapter, we discussed briefly the distinction between symbols and analogues, and we shall now try to make this distinction clearer. It is interesting to note that Roman Catholic writers have for the most part been suspicious of symbolism, although at the same time they hold strongly to a doctrine of analogy. I believe myself that the distinction between symbols and analogues is not entirely clear cut. There is a distinction worth making, but we have already seen in the

[1] See above, Chapter II, pp. 33ff.

preceding chapter that there are borderline cases and that the problem of symbolism eventually resolves itself into the problem of analogy. The traditional Roman Catholic suspicion of symbolism was perhaps not unjustified, for there have been Protestant theologians and philosophers of religion whose conception of symbols was so far removed from what Catholic writers have meant by analogy that a conflict between the two points of view was inevitable.

Generally speaking, the Catholic objection to symbolism in theology has been a twofold one. It has been claimed that those who talk of a 'symbolic' knowledge of God have reduced this to something entirely subjective. The symbols are said to be prized only for their effects in the lives of those who accept them. This was the kind of charge brought against some of the Catholic Modernists in the early years of the century, for their interest seemed to lie chiefly in interpreting the dogmas of the Church as symbols normative for practical conduct. The other side of the objection to symbolism had to do with the allegedly emotional character of symbols, as contrasted with the claim that analogues have a definite intellectual and conceptual content. Behind this objection lies the fundamental question that persists with us through all these discussions: what is the relation between the symbol (or, more generally, the image) and that to which it is supposed to refer? Does it, perhaps, just evince an emotion that we feel in the face of something entirely unknown, or even something that does not exist? Or does it yield in some manner, even if indirectly, a genuine insight into the character or structure of the symbolizandum?

We made a beginning toward answering these questions in the last chapter. We freely acknowledged that all symbols do have their subjective effects, but we could not admit that this proves that they are merely subjective or emotional in character. In distinguishing religious symbols from mere metaphors, we stressed the element of commitment involved in them. However, we had also argued[1] that the way we feel about the situa-

[1] See above, p. 81.

tions in which we find ourselves implies a cognitive grasp of the shape of these situations, comparable to the sensuous intuition of objects in the world. Thus, whenever anyone wishes to talk about the 'subjective' aspect of symbols, we would prefer to talk (and this would be much more accurate) of the 'existential connotations' of symbols, and these we would consider to be neither subjective nor objective, but as embracing both sides of this divide.

Yet we also agreed that there seems to be a whole range of symbols extending from those that have only a minimal relation to what they symbolize to those for which it is possible to claim an intrinsic relationship and affinity. We could agree with Tillich that a symbol such as a national flag has a much more intimate relation to what it symbolizes than has, let us say, an arbitrarily chosen mathematical symbol, such as the letter *i* for the square root of minus one (something that is in any case 'imaginary' and paradoxical according to the ordinary rules of mathematics). The flag, as Tillich understands it, has 'participated' in the history of the country, and for the citizens of that country, it has acquired a wealth of existential connotations. Yet even at this point, it may be doubted whether the difference is any more than a relative one. It could be said that in the history of physics and mathematics, the letter *i* has also acquired a penumbra of connotations, so that something like an intimate connection has sprung up between this symbol and its symbolizandum in the minds of those who use it. Even if it was once arbitrary, it is now universally used in a given way, and anyone departing from this practice would have to explain what he was about.

It seems to me that Bevan has a real point, as over against Tillich, in claiming that even such a symbol as a flag, whose connotations are social and historical, has an external character and does not really open up to us an understanding of what it symbolizes. Whatever understanding it conveys depends on the habits of mind of a given group of people. On the other hand, the light symbol seems to have an intrinsic relation to what it symbolizes. We ourselves tried to interpret this relation in terms of 'openness', and we claimed that this does point to a 'likeness' or 'similarity' of structure which can be traced through the various entities to which the light symbol is applicable—God, Christ, man. But with this mention of likeness and similarity, we came to that end of the range of symbols where they seem to merge into analogues.

Just as we seem to have a continuous range all the way from symbols that depend on convention to those that come close to analogues in expressing some intrinsic likeness, so we have a range from those that seem to have a primarily emotional content to those which come close to a conceptual content. I would claim that even those that have a strong emotional tone are not devoid of cognitive insights, while I have shown that such a symbol as light does point to a structure, openness, which can be grasped conceptually. On the other hand, we have to be clear that the strongest supporters of the doctrine of analogy insist that our best analogues are *not* capable of yielding a direct conceptual knowledge of God. Indeed, if we could know him in such a way, he would not be truly God. Eric Mascall writes: 'All our assertions about God are grossly inadequate in so far as they apply concepts to him.'[1] Yet both those who talk of symbols and those who talk of analogues claim that, in an indirect way, they do have an indirect understanding of God. To quote Eric Mascall again: 'Here indeed we see as in a glass, darkly, and not yet face to face; nevertheless, we see.'[2] To recall our own example of the symbol of light: the understanding of light in terms of openness does show us a fundamental characteristic of divine Being, and yet what openness might be in God transcends our power to understand, since we know at first hand only openness in nature or in human life.

These remarks on symbols and analogues, taken in conjunction with the argument of the preceding chapter, are meant to show us that symbolism, if it is to avoid the charges sometimes

[1] *Existence and Analogy* (London: Longmans, 1949), p. 120.
[2] *Words and Images* (London: Longmans, 1957), p. 126.

made against it of being an empty and subjective kind of talk, must inevitably move in the direction of some kind of analogy, and in the long run must look for some kind of foundational likeness between the symbol and what it is supposed to stand for. But here, I think, we must pause to define, more precisely than we have done so far, just how we are to understand this notion of 'likeness'.

From all that we have said earlier in criticism of the so-called 'picture theory' of language, it seems clear that we cannot think of our symbols or analogues as 'picturing' God, any more than we can think of the symbolic transcripts of contemporary physics as 'picturing' nature. Yet it would seem that in both cases there must be some likeness between the symbols and the reality. Our trouble is that when we talk of 'likeness', we can hardly help thinking of *looking alike*. However, there are many kinds of likeness, apart from looking alike, and looking alike could have nothing to do with any likeness that we might posit between God and some finite being.

It might even be useful to get away from the word 'likeness' altogether. Tillich, it will remembered, talked of 'participation'. I doubt whether he has anywhere defined 'participation' in any exact way, but those critics who interpret it as the traditional participation of the particular in the universal (as a red object may be said to participate in redness) are far from understanding him. By 'participation', Tillich clearly has in mind something far more concrete, whether he is talking about the participation of the theologian in the subject-matter of his study or the participation of the beings in Being itself. Perhaps the participation of an individual in a community gives us the best idea of what Tillich meant. Now this concrete participation is not simple likeness—we would hardly say that an individual is 'like' a community. But on the other hand, it does imply some kind of likeness, or some measure of likeness, for the individual and his community share certain basic human characteristics. The question gets harder when we ask about the participation of beings in Being. This is basic to Tillich's theory of symbols, for it is in virtue of its participation in Being that any particular being can function as a symbol of Being and become disclosive of Being. Something like an *analogia entis* between Being and the beings is clearly implied, but how could there be a likeness, even the kind of 'likeness' that we might claim to find between a human community and one of its members?

Perhaps the word 'affinity' has some advantages over both 'likeness' and 'participation'. The term 'affinity' gets away from the idea of 'looking alike', but perhaps it brings out the notion of some basic kinship or *analogia entis* better than does the word 'participation'. Let me give an example that may help to clarify the kind of relation we have in mind. This whole book has been devoted to a study of language. How are we to think of language in relation to the person who uses it? We would not normally say that language is like a man, or that man is like language. Certainly we would not say that language is an analogue or symbol of man. Yet on the other hand we do think that language, above all, reveals to us who the man is. We have already defined the relation of the person who speaks to his language in terms of 'expressing'. The language expresses the man; alternatively, he expresses *himself* in his language. But when we consider this, are we not then driven to say that language is indeed *like* man? It is like him, not in the sense of looking like him, but in the more fundamental sense of somehow sharing the personal character of man's being. Language has its personal dimension, and in this lies its affinity to man. Man, in turn, is the *zōon logon echon*, the living creature that has the word, the being whose essence is (to use the current word) his 'linguisticality'. There is a deep affinity here between man and language, nothing in the way of a 'picturing' likeness, and yet an essential kinship that can properly be called 'likeness'. In the same manner, what we call the 'word' of God, wherever this *Logos* may be found, in the world, in history, or in Christ, makes implicit claims to be sufficiently 'like' to God to give us a 'true' (unveiled or unhidden) glimpse of who he is; and in the same manner too, the non-picturing formulae of physics claim to give us some clue to what the physical reality is—in Max Planck's expression, the quantum symbol is 'like a new and mysterious messenger from the real world'.[1]

Provided we are willing to understand the notions of 'likeness' and 'similarity' in sufficiently sophisticated ways, we seem bound to say that there must be some kind of likeness or similarity between God and the creatures if the latter are to function as symbols of the former, at least, as symbols that yield some genuine insight into who God is. But to say this amounts to saying that all symbolism brings us back to the problem of analogy; and that among the kinds of analogy, the analogy of attribution is fundamental.

These comments, however, also bring us into contact with the crucial debates about God that are going on in contemporary theology. There, are of course, many points of view represented in these debates, but one point that seems to be generally agreed is that we cannot conceive God as another being. Tillich has insisted that God is not a *being*, but Being itself, or the unconditioned. In this he has been followed, though perhaps not very consistently, by Bishop Robinson and his supporters; though we have also to notice that at this point some of the more extreme critics of traditional theism have decided that the new conception of God (though it is not really new) is so rarefied as to be hardly worth retaining, and so they have lapsed into a frankly expressed atheism. They have solved the problem of analogy and of God-talk generally by abolishing it. But if we refuse to go with them, and stay with the view that God is Being and not a being, then how can we envisage the possibility of any 'likeness' between God and the creature, such as would make analogy meaningful? Has not an unbridgeable gap been set between them?

On the contrary, I am going to argue that further examination of what we mean by asserting that God is to be understood as Being, rather than as a being, does give us a firm basis for the possibility of analogical thinking. But for a clarification of the

[1] *The Universe in the Light of Modern Physics* (London: Allen & Unwin, 1937), p. 20.

issues, it is once more desirable to go beyond the theologians to the philosophers of existence and being. We concentrate attention on Martin Heidegger, for one of the central points in his philosophy is what is called the 'ontological difference', that is to say, the difference between Being and the beings. How does he explicate this difference?

At first sight, it might seem that Heidegger rules out any possibility of analogy, for he declares that Being is strictly 'incomparable' and that it is 'wholly other' to any particular being. But over against this, he tells us that there is no Being apart from the beings, and that Being can be known only in and through the beings. So if there is a sense in which Being is utterly transcendent of any particular being, there is also a sense in which it is immanent and accessible in the beings.

So the language of 'incomparability' need not utterly deter us, though, like the *via negativa*, it stands as an immediate warning against any familiar and over-literal talk of God. After all, deutero-Isaiah too spoke of the incomparability of God: 'To whom then will you liken God, or what likeness compare with him?'[1] St Thomas quotes this verse in his discussion of the image or likeness of God in man, but he goes on to declare that 'man does bear some likeness to God that is derived from God as its original, though this likeness does not amount to equality'.[2] We have to bear in mind the strong tempering of agnosticism that goes with all symbolism and analogy. The doctrine of analogy does not demand an identity between God and the creatures or Being and the beings, and is indeed far removed from such a view. For to make such a claim, as Father Copleston has rightly said, would mean 'degrading the idea of God and turning him into an idol'.[3] The verse quoted from the Old Testament asserting the incomparability of God is to be understood as a protest against idolatry, and this protest must be maintained if we are not to fall into the error of worshipping the creature rather than the Creator.[4] Yet at the same time, because God has set his

[1] Isa. 40.18.  [2] *Summa Theologiae*, I, 93, 1.
[3] *Contemporary Philosophy* (London: Burns & Oates, 1956), p. 102.
[4] Rom. 1.25.

stamp on his own creation, we must hold that there is a sufficient measure of resemblance to make analogical discourse possible. There is both continuity and discontinuity, and perhaps this has been brought out most clearly among recent writers on theological language by Ian Ramsey, with his terminology of 'models' and 'qualifiers'. It is a failure to consider the function of the qualifiers that leads to taking the language of analogy too literally, and perhaps this lies behind Barth's suspicion of analogy and his fear that it degrades the uniqueness of God.

But if we say that God is Being rather than *a* being, how can there be ground for any analogy at all? I mentioned that this way of understanding God is not really new. Although St Thomas (and other Christian writers before him) may not have explored the 'ontological difference' with the same thoroughness as have some modern philosophers of being, and although some of his ways of talking confuse the issue, so that we might think that God as the *ens causa sui* or the *ens realissimum* was another being, albeit of a different order, from the *ens creatum*—a confusion that specially arises in his proofs for the existence of God—nevertheless, he too thought of God as Being, yet he did not suppose that this precluded the possibility of analogy. In discussing the view of God as Being, as found in Bishop Robinson, Eric Mascall has written: 'That God is Being itself (*ipsum esse*) and that with creation there are more beings but not more Being, are Thomist commonplaces.'[1] A full discussion of this sentence would, I believe, lead us into difficult questions of interpretation, but it is unnecessary that we should undertake it. What we have to consider is how and whether, in the light of the new or, rather, renewed assertion that God is Being rather than a being, and in the light of recent ontological investigation, especially that of Heidegger, a sufficient basis can be found for analogical talking about God.

The discussion will be a threefold one: first, we shall consider the possibility of whether time may provide the required link

[1] *The Secularization of Christianity* (London: Darton, Longman and Todd, and New York: Holt, Rinehart & Winston, 1966), p. 123.

(the element of 'likeness') between Being and the beings; secondly, we turn to the question of whether man, as the existent, has among the creatures a unique kind of being that makes possible analogues such as will illumine the character of God in a manner that goes far beyond such natural symbols as light; and finally, how these points are further illustrated by a consideration of the incarnation as the coming together of God and man, that is to say, of Being with the beings. Formally, this discussion covers the same three areas as were taken into account in the earlier discussion of the light symbol. That discussion, however, pointed us to the central Christian analogues, and the present discussion could be described as having for its theme 'God is love' rather than 'God is light', though in the end these two affirmations are not very different.

The first point, then, is to raise the question of how far time can function as the link or ground of likeness between Being and the beings. Clearly, all finite beings do exist in time, and this is as true of man as it is of the lower creatures. However, man's relation to time is quite different from that of an object which simply persists through time. Man takes time into himself, so to speak, so that we could even say that he is constituted by his temporality, and it might be more accurate to say that temporality is in man than that man is in time. He does not just persist from moment to moment. The more truly human and personal he is, the less does he drift through time and the more he lays hold on temporality, extending himself through past, present and future, through his capacities for memory, judgement and anticipation. Yet even in doing this, he is also transcending time as mere successiveness, for he is no longer the creature of the passing instant, but has the possibility of building up a unified self that remains relatively stable and abiding through changing circumstances.[1]

Now this in turn may furnish some kind of model that would provide a remote but fundamental analogue to the character of

[1] See my essay, 'Selfhood and Temporality', in *Studies in Christian Existentialism* (London: SCM Press, 1966), pp. 59ff.

Being as such. Heidegger claims that time offers 'the horizon for any understanding of Being whatsoever'.[1] A pure Being, conceived as completely unchanging and monolithic, would be indistinguishable from nothing, as has been clearly seen long ago in the history of philosophy. Certainly, we could *say* nothing about such pure Being, for our own experience is tied to time. Therefore, in those eastern mysticisms which do tend to think of Being as utterly immobile and undifferentiated, it is asserted that one can only be silent. But obviously this is not the God of the Christian religion. Yet one could not say that God is *in time*, either. It is rather that God too takes time into himself and extends himself in time. He needs time to create, to act, to make history. He is not a God who, if we could think of him at all, we would need to suppose as some immutable eremite, but a God who goes into the risk of creation and history, as we already saw in considering the symbol of light as openness. Yet he is also the faithful God, the God who has unmatched stability, so that the unimaginable vastness of past, present and future are gathered up in the totality of his Being in a manner of which we get some faint hint from the way in which these dimensions of time are brought into the unity of a self.

In following the leads of contemporary philosophy and thus taking time as the link between creaturely being, especially as we see it in man, and divine Being, we seem to be following a course directly opposite to that of ancient philosophy, for Aristotle thought that it was in the *permanence* of man's soul that one could discern a likeness to God. However, this kind of permanence belongs properly to whatever is conceived on the model of inert, enduring thinghood (the model of 'substantiality') and is appropriate neither to man's temporal yet time-transcending selfhood, nor to the infinitely complex Being of God, as both stable and dynamic; for this is a mystery which cannot be adequately thought of as *a* being, and still less as having the kind of being that belongs to a thing, in time and enduring through time.

[1] *Being and Time*, p. 1.

Our first point, which has concerned time as the basis for constructing any analogy between Being and the beings, has led to our second point, for it has already pointed us to man as the particular being in whom this analogy is to be most clearly read—perhaps indeed the only particular being with respect to whom it is proper to talk of analogues rather than of symbols. According to the Bible, it is man who bears the image and likeness of God.

Can we now then look for that peculiar feature of man's temporal existence that might show us more distinctly wherein this likeness to God consists? In the past, this feature was often seen in man's rationality, but the tendency nowadays is to look for a broader basis. The modern existentialist talks of man as the 'existent' because, in a peculiar way, man does stand out in the world of created beings. His peculiarity is that he not only *is* but, within limits, to be sure, has a responsibility for his being and even for his world. We could put it in this way: Man not only is, he has the power to let be. That is to say, he has a share in the creativity of God. Of God himself, if we think of him as Being rather than as some being or other, however powerful, then it is more correct to say that he lets be, than that he is. As coming before every being, so that he is the condition that there may be any beings at all, it is more correct to say that he confers being than that he is. And in the unfolding of his creation, he has brought forth finite beings who, in a limited way, have a share in his own letting-be and in the shaping of creation.

I use the expression 'letting-be' in an active sense, meaning something like 'enabling to be', 'helping to fulfil the potentialities for being'. Such letting-be is the highest activity open to man, the most 'godlike', we may say; and perhaps its highest is in letting the neighbour *be*, that is to say, in helping the other to the fulfilment of his being. This is in fact nothing but a description in ontological terms of disinterested love or *agape*.[1] But this in turn shows why the affirmation that 'God is love' is

[1] See my *Principles of Christian Theology* (New York: Scribners, 1966 and London: SCM Press, 1967), pp. 310–12.

probably the key analogy that we can have before our minds in any attempt to think of God. For the very understanding of God as Being rather than as *a* being, the understanding which has been discovered or rediscovered in recent theology and which is certainly getting stressed in current discussions, is so far from destroying the possibility of analogy that it gives it a basis that is very relevant to the Christian conception of God. Being is the letting-be that creates, sustains and perfects the beings; and we find the model to this ultimate mystery in creative, disinterested love.

This leads to our third point, the illustration of these matters by a consideration of the incarnation. The coming together of God and man must be understood as the coming together of Being with a being, if we are to be consistent in following the lines that we have already laid down. Such a coming together might seem to be utterly impossible. But is it not the case that the complete self-emptying of Jesus (another theme that is prominent in current discussions) is, on the level of creaturely being, the fullest realization of the divine letting-be, so that in the words of the Epistle to the Hebrews 'he reflects the glory of God and bears the very stamp of his nature'?[1] In Christ, the one who gives up his own being in order to let-be, we see, as it were, the upper reaches of our human nature, transfigured into the divine nature or, if we think of it from the other side, made transparent so that the divine nature is revealed through him. Hence Christ is the living centre that gives reality to our analogies and assures us that they are not merely fanciful. In saying this, we are also acknowledging the correctness of Barth's association of analogy with incarnation.

But when these claims have been made—and without question a strong case can be made for them—we have to come back to the point that God is hidden as well as revealed, and that part of his Godhood, without which he could not be God, is just his incomparability and his transcendence of all human understanding. Yet equally a part of his Godhood is that he has come

[1] Heb. 1.3.

forth from his hiddenness and given us such knowledge of himself as makes it possible for us to worship him and acknowledge his Godhood. The doctrine of analogy tries to combine these truths, acknowledging on the one hand that all our language about God is oblique and inadequate, yet claiming that there is a sufficient basis of 'likeness' to make this language meaningful and not merely empty.

Thus analogical language—and all symbolic language—has a paradoxical character. Simply to affirm an analogue or symbol is to fall into that over-literalness which, if we are applying the image to God, leads into an attitude of idolatry. Whatever symbol or analogue is affirmed must be at the same time denied; or, better still, whenever one symbol is affirmed, others that will modify and correct it must be affirmed at the same time. Thus the New Testament, in trying to explicate the person of Christ, applied to him a number of images—'Son of man', 'Son of God', 'Messiah', 'Lord', 'Word'. It is impossible to 'harmonize' all these ideas, but out of agreements and conflicts something of the mystery of the incarnation finds expression.

The trouble is that when one image has established a kind of monopoly and then someone rebels against its tyranny, he may set up another which is equally unsatisfactory if taken in isolation. What must be done is to have a number of images, each correcting and supplementing the others. A good illustration of the kind of error into which it is easy to fall in these matters is provided by Bishop Robinson. He is very much opposed to the symbol of height when applied to God, for a God 'up there' savours too much of mythology and a false supernaturalism. So he shifts the stress to the symbol of depth. Now, if these two symbols were held in tension, then a big advance would be made toward a more adequate thought of God. But the Bishop tends to set up a new monopoly for the image of depth, and this could become even more distorting and certainly more idolatrous than the height symbol ever was.

The tangle into which the Bishop has stumbled is shown by his very confused ideas on the liturgy. His preoccupation with the symbol of depth has made him an enthusiast for having the celebrant face the people, so that the action of the eucharist goes on 'in the midst'; but on the other hand, he wants the Church to be turned outward from itself! His absolutizing of the depth symbol produces the danger of a Church that introspectively dwells on the depth or midst of its own being, a kind of communal contemplation of the navel. The Bishop seems to have some apprehension of this danger himself, for in spite of all his criticisms of the height symbol, he finds it necessary to talk about 'the vertical of the unconditioned cutting into and across the limitations of the merely human fellowship'.[1] One is certainly glad to read these words, and to know that for the Bishop the eucharist is more than just an exercise in 'relatedness'; but even so, his stress on what happens 'in here' remains far too one-sided.

The purpose of this brief digression has simply been to stress through a concrete illustration the inevitability of paradox in all theological language. Where paradoxes get too easily ironed out, superficiality results; and in periods when this has happened, the Church needs a Kierkegaard or a Barth to come along and to reassert, even in violent fashion, the dialectical necessity of correcting every image of God and every assertion that we make about him. It is true that theology, as an intellectual discipline, cannot rest content just to deal in paradoxes. The theologian has got to show that the various images have their rights, and because they are images rather than concepts, they do not exclude one another as we seek by means of them to light up the mystery of God and his acts—a mystery to which no language can be adequate. But while the theologian has this duty to vindicate the right of his paradoxes and to show that they have a logic, he has always got to be on his guard against succumbing to the temptation to take a short cut and to fasten on one aspect of the truth to the neglect of others.

[1] *Honest to God*, p. 89. The Bishop, by the way, is quite wrong in thinking that in the eastward position of the celebrant, attention is fixed on 'a point somewhere in the middle distance beyond the sanctuary' (*ibid.*). On the contrary, I would say that priest and people are united in having their attention fixed where it ought to be—on the cross and altar.

Let us sum up the findings of this chapter. In the present atmosphere of confusion and bewilderment concerning God and what we can know about him, it has become an urgent task to show what are the foundations for our analogical talk about God, not only in theology but in scripture, prayer and liturgy; and to show too that the apparent conflicts between our ways of talking about God are of the nature of paradoxes, rather than of self-destructive contradictions. I have tried to show that a reasonable case can be made out to establish that analogical language about God is by no means empty, and does indeed relate to the reality of divine Being. Yet if we are not to be misled by our own images, we have always to bear in mind that the best of them must be held dialectically, and that God far transcends anything that our minds can reach. He cannot be shut up in our minds or our theology or our communities.

# II

## Empirical Language

ESPECIALLY IN THE English-speaking countries, but increasingly elsewhere as well, empiricism is a powerful influence, and this is surely understandable at a time when the empirical sciences have made and are still making enormous strides. It seems desirable therefore that we should devote a chapter to the place of empirical language in theology. By an 'empirical' language, I mean one that is in some manner open to testing by experience, or one that relates to some observable facts. The chapter will be fairly brief, because we have already examined some of these problems. A chapter was already assigned to a consideration of the views of logical empiricists on theological language;[1] and in our analysis of St Athanasius' *De Incarnatione*, we saw how he introduced some empirical arguments into his treatise, and we classified these and briefly evaluated them.[2] In many ways, I think we have acknowledged a place for empirical language within the totality of theological discourse, and it would sometimes be hard to distinguish sharply between 'empirical' language and what we have preferred to call 'existential' language; but we certainly have not thought of all theological language as having an empirical character. It will be necessary therefore to clarify further the empirical element in theology.

Before we can go any further, however, we must decide just what can be recognized as 'empirical'. There is a broad usage of this expression, and perhaps in the broad sense the account of theological language given so far in his book is not too far from

[1] See above, Chapter 5, pp. 102ff.      [2] See above, p. 143.

empiricism, for we have stressed the existential element in theology, that is to say, our first-hand participation in the experiences and situations which theology tries to explicate. I suppose one would say that it was empiricism in the broad sense that was characteristic of the teaching of John Locke. He was willing, for instance, to allow the experience of 'inner sense' to stand alongside the data of the senses of sight, hearing, touch and the rest. At the present time, one would see what I am calling a 'broader' empiricism in the work of Ian Ramsey, with which we have indicated sympathy in earlier discussions. If one is prepared to allow as 'empirical' the kind of disclosures of which Ramsey talks, then this is something very like what I have called the 'intuiting' of situations through existential participation.[1] The connection between Locke and Ramsey, incidentally, can be seen from the following quotation from Ramsey: 'Can we find in Locke, as the founder of eighteenth-century empiricism some hints as to where the narrower empiricism of his successors is inadequate, and where also a broader empiricism might do more justice to the reasonableness and distinctiveness of the Christian faith than was ever possible when metaphysics of the old brand held sway? Here is the timeliness of Locke for our own day.'[2]

On the other hand, there is a narrower empiricism, and I suppose one could trace its lineage from David Hume down to the logical positivists of recent times. The stress is on sense-experience, and this narrower empiricism culminates in the verification principle, or something like it. I do not think there is any possibility of making sense of theological language if one accepts this narrower empiricism. Even if one does not dismiss this language as 'nonsense' and allows it some 'use' in psychological or sociological contexts, this is still to deny any cognitive status to theological language, and no theologian could accept this as an account of what he is saying. The tendency in recent times has been to restrict the word 'empirical' to the narrow

[1] See above, p. 76.
[2] In his introduction to Locke's *The Reasonableness of Christianity*, (London: A. & C. Black, 1958), p. 20.

sense, and for this reason I have elsewhere criticized those who want to talk of theology as an 'empirical science' on the grounds that the expression is nowadays misleading.[1] However, it might still be the case that some quite narrowly empirical language, for instance, an assertion about what happened on some publicly observable historical occasion, would have its relevance for theology.

Apart from this distinction of broader and narrower types of empiricism, there are some other characteristics of empiricism that have been very well clarified by J. Alfred Martin in his critical examination of the empirical approach in the philosophy of religion. It will be noted that, in the passage quoted, he alludes to both the narrower and wider kinds of empiricism. He recognizes three meanings of 'empiricism': 'To be "empirical" in the approach to philosophical problems may mean simply to be "realistic" or "tough-minded": to take full account of all the relevant data and to blink none of the significant "facts" . . . Or empiricism may be associated primarily with an "appeal to experience" in the establishment and defence of philosophical doctrines, a deference to the "given", whether "experience" be conceived as consisting essentially of sense-data, or whether it be construed more liberally. Again, empiricism may be viewed as primarily methodological in import, signifying a particular type of inquiry, usually with an emphasis on *a posteriori* hypothesis and induction as over against rationalistic *schēma* and logical or metaphysical *a prioris*.'[2]

When we have regard to these different, though related, usages of 'empiricism', it seems that we have also to recognize a considerable diversity of empirical language in theology. I have already indicated that I do not think that theological language as a whole could be called 'empirical' in any commonly accepted sense, but there are empirical elements within it, some of them more important, some of them less so. I shall instance five distinguishable uses of empirical language, though without claiming that the list is exhaustive.

[1] *Studies in Christian Existentialism*, p. 21.
[2] *Empirical Philosophies of Religion* (New York: King's Crown Press, 1945), p. 110.

1. There are the arguments of natural theology. These arguments proceed from observable facts within the world to conclusions about the character of the world as a whole. By 'natural theology', I mean here the kind practised by St Thomas and his successors, for this had a definitely empirical character and began from the facts of experience, as distinct from the 'rational theology' of St Anselm and others who have begun from *a priori* concepts. The kind of arguments we met in St Athanasius, where he points to structure and differentiation within the world,[1] is a good example of empirical natural theology, and the basic pattern of such arguments has remained essentially the same down to the present. A recent exponent of natural theology, John B. Cobb, who bases his case on Whitehead's philosophy, remarks: 'Whitehead's argument for the existence of God, in so far as there is an argument at all, is primarily the traditional one from the order of the universe to a ground of order.'[2]

This would not be the place to go into all the discussions that have gone on over the question of natural theology.[3] Let it suffice to say that I do not think that one can prove the reality of God or establish the 'truth' of faith on the basis of empirical arguments. The evidence is too ambiguous, and furthermore the logical connections between the premises and the conclusion are too dubious. But this is not to deny all value to natural theology. Though it could not establish a religious faith, it can support one. The point is that any faith must let itself be exposed to the observable facts of the world in which we live. The business of natural theology is to show that these facts are not incompatible with the convictions of faith, and may even tend to confirm these convictions.

2. Another area to be considered is that of historical assertions. These are of special importance in Christian theology, for the centre of its revelation is an actual historical person, Jesus Christ. The New Testament asserts that he lived and died at a

[1] See above, p. 141.
[2] *A Christian Natural Theology* (Philadelphia: Westminster Press, 1965), p. 169.
[3] See my *Principles of Christian Theology*, pp. 39ff.

given period of world-history, that he taught, ministered to the sick, disputed with the religious authorities, gathered around him a community, was put to death and yet, as his disciples believed, rose again and continued as a living reality in his Church. These are empirical assertions, just as much as assertions about Napoleon or Julius Caesar, and there are recognized ways of testing their truth claims.

This talk of the historical Jesus and of his significance for faith and theology raises once more questions much too extensive and complex for us to go into here.[1] But we may say on this theme something rather similar to what was said on the theme of natural theology. On the one hand, investigation by empirical methods of the 'facts' about Jesus could never establish faith in him as the Lord and Word. Not only are the evidences fragmentary, but, more importantly, even if we had the fullest evidence about him imaginable, this could not validate faith's interpretation of him. Yet to deny that historical research can provide a foundation for Christian faith is not to rule it out as of no importance. Because faith has found its centre in this historical person, it cannot remain indifferent to such questions as whether he ever existed, whether he was the kind of person that the tradition has represented him to be, and so on. As I have called it elsewhere, there is a 'minimal core of factuality' that is of importance to theology. So here again, if theology is not going to operate in a world apart, a dream-world or a wish-world perhaps, it must be exposed to the question of how its faith is related to what has actually happened in this world of harsh realities, and this is an empirical question.

3. There have been appeals to the alleged empirical evidence of miracles and fulfilment of prophecies, and we have briefly alluded to each of these matters in our analysis of the *De Incarnatione*.[2] I indicated then the unsatisfactory nature of such arguments, and will not repeat the points here. However, I will make a somewhat different point. It is likely enough that arguments from miracle and prophecy were persuasive at some

[1] See my essay, 'History and the Christ of Faith', in *Studies in Christian Existentialism*, pp. 139ff.   [2] See above, p. 49.

periods in the Church's history, and they were persuasive because people entertained certain ideas of what 'miracle' and 'prophecy' mean. I do not think we share these ideas any longer, and yet I think that the notions of 'miracle' and 'prophecy' can still be meaningful for us—'miracle' as the event which focuses for us God's action in the world, 'prophecy' as the summons to authentic existence. In so far as these converge on Christ, the old arguments from miracle and prophecy can be re-interpreted. These arguments were never purely empirical, and their re-interpreted versions could not be purely empirical either. But there is an empirical element here, for what is being done is to point to certain aspects in the life or person of Jesus Christ and to ask whether, when men are willing to be exposed to these, they do not perceive in them a depth of meaning which is at once the manifestation of God (miracle) and the summons to authentic humanity (prophecy).

4. There are appeals to what is called 'religious experience', and some forms of this would be fairly close to what we have just mentioned, namely, the perceiving of a depth of meaning in some event so that one may claim to understand it as God's action. More generally, religious experience would cover cases of the awareness of the presence of God, the sense of the holy, mystical experiences and the like. The narrower kind of empiricism would reject these, but if one is prepared to accept a broader kind of empiricism, then such experiences have a claim to be considered seriously. It would seem that in this kind of experience, what comes to our awareness is a *Gestalt* or situation in which we are ourselves participants. I have argued earlier[1] that in some of our affective states, we *notice* structures and configurations that normally escape us, and that our mode of intuiting these should be set alongside our sensuous intuitions as together constituting our openness to the environment. This is in effect to claim an empirical status for these affective intuitions. It might be argued, however, that they are not testable in the way that universally observable objects of sensuous intui-

[1] See above, p. 76.

tion are. I think this must be accepted, since this other kind of intuition never is objective, but always implies participation. On the other hand, I would equally deny that it has a merely subjective character, and would suggest that some kind of existential phenomenology might be used for the investigation of such experiences and that this would accord to them a trans-subjective validity.

5. Finally, there are arguments that appeal to the concrete results of faith in human experience. If such faith does indeed conduce to the fuller being of the individual and to an authentic community, then by these very facts it is establishing a claim to validity, for it is hard to believe that if it were merely error and illusion, it could bring forth such fruits. But the argument is not merely a pragmatic one, as if faith were to be prized or judged only or even primarily by its practical consequences. Though faith is not an intellectual hypothesis, it does have its cognitive side and it does make its truth claim, and to this extent it might be compared to a scientific hypothesis. A successful scientific hypothesis is one that is able to account for a great many scattered facts, and the more it does so, the more it establishes its claim. If in following out a faith, one finds that the interpretative power of this faith is an expanding one and that it makes sense of more and more of the events of life, then this faith is empirically establishing itself. I believe myself that the Christian faith does establish itself in this way.

Summing up these points, we may say that theology does not indeed lend itself to entirely empirical modes of expression, but that there are strands of empirical language woven into it, and that for some of its assertions we can point to ways in which these may be tested by experience. The importance of this empirical dimension is that it keeps theology from flying off into a realm of pure speculation, or into a world of wish and fantasy. It keeps in touch with the sometimes unhappy facts of this real world of ours, and any vision that theology frames is rooted in experiences that men have had in the midst of history and concrete existence.

## 12

# The Language of Existence and Being

THROUGHOUT THIS BOOK I have referred from time to time to what I have called the 'basic logic' of theology, and I have also described this as the language of existence and being, or as an existential-ontological language. It has been suggested that the pattern of this language underlies the others that we have talked about. Admittedly, in any actual theology, we are dealing with concrete symbols and images; but when we inquire about their credentials, and about how such discourse functions, we find ourselves driven to consider the formal existential-ontological structures that have, so to speak, clothed themselves in the imagery of some particular expression of theology. Such concrete theological discourse, we have seen, has both its existential dimension, insofar as it works upon the existences of those who use it and evokes their commitments, and its onto-logical dimension, insofar as it claims to afford an insight into the mystery of God or holy Being. Tillich, as we have seen,[1] believed that the language of Being permits one to make a non-symbolic statement about God. We saw reason to believe that possibly Tillich's assertion that God is not less than Being itself is not really a statement about God at all, but a definition of Tillich's understanding of the word 'God'; and we saw too that Tillich came to modify his claim that the language of Being makes possible a non-symbolic statement about God. Yet there does seem to be a formal, conceptual character belonging to the

[1] See above, p. 50.

language of existence and being, that does not belong to the concrete language of theology. It is for this reason that we called the language of existence and being the 'basic logic' of theology.

What seems to be implied in talking of such a basic logic is the claim that the symbols of theology get anchored, as it were, in this conceptual language of existence and being. But I do not think the claim should be pushed too far. Even the language of existence and being includes images and symbolic elements, and many of its concepts have very ragged edges indeed. On the other hand, one set of symbols can be illuminated by another, and both of these sets can in turn be illuminated by a third set. The process of interpretation and illumination can go on without one's ever having to say that symbols have been left behind (if one could ever say this) and that a direct, literal language was being used. But perhaps what can be done is to move from symbols having a greater measure of particularity, in the sense that they belong within a limited historical community, to symbols which come nearer to a universality of intelligibility. Clearly, a language of existence and being would come near to such universality.

Although we have insisted on holding together existence and being, the existential and the ontological, it will be convenient to say something first about the language of existence, and then go on to the language of being. The major problem is one that has come up again and again throughout our study—the question of how one makes the transition from the language of existence to the language of being. This is in fact just another way of expressing our fundamental question—the question of God-talk. We are not asking about how one might talk about God as he is in himself, for we have agreed that he could not be an 'object' for us, so that we could talk about him in detachment. We are asking rather about how, beginning with the existential approach and the phenomenology of faith, one can be reasonably sure that one is not just shut up in the description of one's own mental furniture, and that one can reach an ontological dimension in which we are speaking of transhuman realities, though, of course, only as they impinge upon us. We have already wrestled with this question in many different ways, and now we consider it once more in terms of the formal language of existence and being.

By a 'language of existence' is meant here a language that describes the structures of human existence, and the possible ways of being that belong to such an existence. Nowadays the obvious examples of a language of existence would be found in those highly elaborated terminologies that have been worked out by some existentialist philosophers. The most impressive example is Heidegger's closely articulated scheme of the existential structure of the *Dasein*, in terms of possibility, facticity, understanding, conscience and so on. This scheme is reached as the result of a detailed and systematic phenomenological analysis, and it has a highly technical character so that, among other things, it has been possible to use it in psychotherapy.

But the expression 'language of existence' can be applied not only to the contemporary self-conscious and explicit endeavours of existentialist philosophers to develop a suitable way of talking about our own existence, but to many earlier attempts to find a descriptive language in which to set forth our basic ways of being in the world. In the New Testament itself, one finds, especially in the writings of St Paul, a very well developed 'language of existence'. He had at his disposal quite a rich vocabulary in which to exhibit the structures and the ways of being that belong to man. When one studies his usage of such words as 'body', 'flesh', 'soul', 'spirit', 'mind', 'heart', 'conscience' and various others, it becomes clear that although he presumably never dreamed of carrying through for its own sake a phenomenological analysis in the manner of a modern philosopher of existence, he was nevertheless working with a very coherent understanding of how the phenomena designated by the various words that have been mentioned constitute a unity in any given individual existence. Of course, St Paul in turn was drawing upon the reflections upon man—philosophical and psychological—that were current in his time, just as the theologian of today might draw upon the work of contemporary philosophy or psychology. St Paul's vocabulary might seem to us a very unsophisticated one, for it uses words like 'flesh' and 'heart' which have to be taken in a metaphorical sense. Yet I indicated that the borderline between concepts and images is rather a blurred one, and it will be remembered that Heidegger today uses such metaphorical expressions as 'thrownness'. In any case, St Paul's language of existence was remarkably adequate for the task which he set himself, that of setting forth the characteristics of a Christian existence, and showing what is distinctive in it. As Bultmann has well shown, the whole theology of St Paul can be appropriately exhibited as an anthropology, in which there is set forth first the understanding of human existence in its fallen or sinful state, and then the movement toward wholeness and restoration in the life of faith.[1]

St Paul has had many successors in the use of a language of existence. In the early Church, as we saw in a previous chapter,[2] the language of existence had a central role in St Athanasius' exposition of Christian faith, at least in his early writings. In the theology of modern times also, the language of existence has for long played a notable part. Schleiermacher is the outstanding exemplar. He explored the religious consciousness, substituted for the traditional theistic proofs the fact that there is a *sensus numinis* in man, and tried to expound the Christian faith in relation to man's basic awareness of his dependent mode of being. 'Dogmas', he asserted, 'are a knowledge about feeling, and in no way an immediate knowledge about the operations of the Universe that give rise to the feeling.'[3] Rudolf Otto, an enthusiastic admirer of Schleiermacher, provided a penetrating phenomenological analysis of the basic religious experience of the numinous and showed how complex are the feelings that come into play in such an experience. Wilhelm Herrmann of the Ritschlian school is another figure who should be mentioned,

---

[1] *Theology of the New Testament*, vol. I, pp. 185–345.
[2] Chapter 6, pp. 134 ff.
[3] *On Religion*, trans. John Oman (New York: Harper & Row, 1958), p. 61.

especially since both Barth and Bultmann were among his students. Herrmann explicitly intended to give a statement of Christian doctrine that would be free from metaphysics and that would be understood 'only as the expression of new personal life'.[1] Most recently, Bultmann has tried to explicate the New Testament teaching as a self-understanding, and has been able to employ the existentialist terminology for this task.

All of these endeavours have had their measure of success. They talk an intelligible language with a recognizable logic. They steer theology away from the objectifying language of myth and from the abstruseness of metaphysical language. Theological talk becomes in the main existential talk, and this is a kind of talk that has a secure place within the total field of meaningful discourse.

But we keep coming back to the difficulty that has dogged our steps throughout these investigations. Can intelligibility in theological language be gained only at the price of a complete subjectivizing? But then, have we any right to go on talking about theology at all? A phenomenology of faith, expressed in a language of existence, tells us about the structure of an existence in faith. It describes what it is like to live in accordance with an attitude of faith, and it may show us also how such an attitude differs from that of the secular self-sufficient man. But does this mean that theology has been reduced to a psychology of religion? Or that faith has been reduced to an attitude prized for its own sake, without regard to any content of faith? The description of religious attitudes and states of mind is certainly something of value, and it is something that must be taken into account if we are to understand what a religious faith is and to estimate its claims. But theology is commonly understood to be more than a psychology of religion, and faith as more than a state of mind. Theology claims some kind of transubjective validity for the experiences which belong to the life of faith. In particular, God and Christ are regarded not merely as elements

[1] *Systematic Theology*, trans. N. Micklem and K. A. Saunders (London: Allen & Unwin, 1927), p. 64.

in human experience, but as standing independently over against man. Certainly, theologians of many different persuasions have often declared that we do not know God as he is in himself, but only as he relates himself to us. But they have never intended by this to imply that God is nothing but a factor in human experience, perhaps a focus of values or an ideal creation of the spirit or a projection of man's hidden aspirations into metaphysical space. That is to say, they have not agreed with the neo-Kantianism of Herrmann Cohen, for whom God was only an ideal of the reason; or with the humanism of John Dewey, for whom God was just a way of referring to the hypothetical unity of the values that claim our allegiance; or with the psychological naturalism (however sympathetic) of C. G. Jung, for whom God was an archetype of the human psyche, though he might be more. On the contrary, theologians have said that man is a creature of God. It is God who is believed to be creative and to hold the initiative in man's experience of·God.

But how then, if one begins with a language of existence, is it possible to break out of the subjective circle? Is one just describing what it is like to live *as if* there were a God and *as if* this God had revealed himself in Christ? But if this is merely an 'as if', then the Christian proclamation, as a gospel, falls to the ground; prayer and worship are illusory; grace and judgment are unreal. At best, the Christian faith remains as a cumbrous and misleading way of declaring and inculcating allegiance to some ethical ideals.

Actually, all the theologians whom we mentioned as using a 'language of existence' did indeed reject any subjectivist account of the matter, and tried in various ways to ground the Christian experience in a reality that transcends the human consciousness. Schleiermacher's 'feeling of absolute dependence' was not merely emotion, but was supposed to have its own cognitive awareness. Otto had a complex and rather confused theory which tried to show that there lies in the depth of the human mind a 'faculty of divination' with its own non-rational category of the numinous. Herrmann claimed that communion with God, established by the impression gained from the inner life of Christ, was validated by the positive fact of the historical Jesus together with the judgment of practical reason. Bultmann (who dislikes being associated with the nineteenth-century 'theology of consciousness') holds that all existence is encounter, so that the God-talk that proceeds existentially is talk about a real Other that stands over against the self in encounter. But even those who find most to admire in the theologians mentioned would admit that those elements in their thought that try to establish the reality of God constitute the most vulnerable parts of their theories.

Frankly, I do not suppose there is any way in which one could prove that the assertions of faith and of theology do refer to a Reality (God) that is independent of and prior to the experiences which we call 'experiences of God'. In order to prove that there is an encounter with a real Other, one would somehow need to get behind the experience, or find a second route to that which we know in the experience, and this is not possible. Yet on the other hand the conviction that there *is* a real Other in this experience is extremely deep-rooted.

It is not inappropriate to compare the conviction of the independent reality of God to the conviction of the independent reality of the world or of other selves, though, as I shall point out, there are limits to the usefulness of this analogy. Presumably no one in his senses seriously doubts the reality of the so-called 'external world' or the reality of other selves in that world. It would, I believe, be impossible to *prove* the reality of either. But a proof that there is such a world or that other selves really exist could be little more than an academic exercise, for everybody already believes in them. But how far could we claim that the religious experience of God, the encounter or confrontation or whatever we may call it, provides a roughly parallel case?

We may refer here to the writings of John Baillie. His most distinctive belief was in a universal presence of God of which, he believed, all men would seem to have some awareness, however dim or even unacknowledged. He wrote: 'Though we may not try to prove to ourselves or others that God exists, we may do something to persuade both ourselves and others *that we already believe in him*; just as it is true that although we cannot prove to the solipsist that his fellow-men exist, we can do something to prove to him that he already believes in their existence.'[1] Though Baillie seems to be right in saying that in such matters there is no proof but only the possibility of persuading people of what they already implicitly believe on the grounds of a kind of 'animal faith', to use Santayana's expression, it is not clear that a belief in the reality of God has either the universality or the inevitability that belong to belief in the reality of an external world or of other selves. If we reflect for a moment, I doubt if any of us could recall ever having met a solipsist in real life; but we have probably all met atheists, and it is hard to believe that all of these atheists were, as Baillie seems to suggest, at heart secret or implicit theists.

Of course, Baillie recognized that the three cases, God, other selves, and the external world, are not all alike. The presence of God is, on his view, always mediated through the world or through other selves. We do not indeed infer to the knowledge of God from the world or other persons, but we are aware of him in and through these. But this difference between the way in which we know the world or other people (directly) and the way in which we are said to know God (as a 'mediated immediacy', in Baillie's expression) constitutes a serious problem if the name God is not just to stand for part of our experience—perhaps that part of which Baillie speaks elsewhere when he says that 'human nature is not a simple nature—it possesses an idea of itself which is at war with what it actually finds itself to be.'[2] The atheist might reply that this immanent ideal is just what gets called 'God' and gets hypostatized as an independent metaphysical entity.

The difference between belief in the reality of God and belief in the reality of the external world or other selves may be further

---

[1] *Our Knowledge of God* (London: Oxford University Press, 1939), p. 240.
[2] *Op. cit.*, pp. 22–23.

sharpened by recalling that in the two latter cases we have sense experience to support the belief, whereas there can be no sense experience of God—or, at least, in a post-mythical era, we do look for any such experience. Belief that there is a real river flowing outside of my window is confirmed by everyone who looks out and sees it; but there is no such universal agreement about the reality of God, and no simple way of testing the belief, like looking out of the window. Even with the other human person, there is a physical and sensible relationship, though indeed this physical and sensuous element does not exhaust the content of the relation. There is nothing of the kind in the encounter with God, and it only confuses the issue to say, as Bultmann does, that the absence of a physical aspect transforms the relation to God into a 'purely personal relationship'.[1] On the contrary, since the only persons we know are embodied persons, a purely personal relationship would involve a physical aspect.

It is part of the meaning of the word 'faith' that there cannot be certitude in these matters. Faith is not sight, and so to live in faith is to live with the possibility that the faith may be an illusion, in the sense that it refers to nothing beyond one's own states of mind. But the whole trend of our study in this book has been leading us toward an increasing confidence that God-talk is well founded, and that it does refer to a transhuman Reality that embraces our existences and meets them in grace and judgment. The more we can show that God-talk has a coherent logic, the more it is shown that faith in God is a reasonable faith. We have tried to show this by analyses and interpretations of myth, symbolism, analogy, paradox and so on, and we have backed up these interpretations by empirical arguments which, as I have maintained, at least point to the theistic vision of the world as more probable than the atheistic one. But insofar as we have held that the basic language underlying theological discourse is the language of existence and being, and insofar as our interpretations have consistently assumed an existential-onto-

[1] *Jesus Christ and Mythology*, p. 69.

logical form, we come back to this language as the crucial one for theology.

It seems to me that much depends on whether we accept or reject the account of the transition from the language of existence to the language of being that we find stated in the philosophy of Heidegger, and to which our argument has appealed at several important junctures.[1] I do not say that the case stands or falls with the acceptance of this account, for the forms of theological discourse are many and diverse, and we have seen that there are many ways in which one can seek to interpret and vindicate them. Nevertheless, I believe that Heidegger's attempt to move from existential into ontological language is most important and, if one accepts it, it constitutes a kind of paradigm or prototype for the language of theology.

Heidegger's account of the matter takes two forms, distinct but related. The first, perhaps best expressed in *Was ist Metaphysik?* and its postscript, turns on the notion of affective states, especially anxiety, and their capacity for causing us to notice structures and situations to which we normally remain oblivious. It is through these states that we are awakened to the disclosure of Being which has given and entrusted itself to us.[2] The second version of the matter is one in which he talks rather in terms of thinking. There is a thinking in which we are passive rather than active (though indeed it could also be conceived as the highest activity), a thinking in which we hold ourselves open and in which Being discloses itself to us, and has the initiative in this disclosure, so that one could truly say that this is Being, thinking and speaking in us, rather than that we are thinking and speaking of Being. The parallel with the religious experiences of revelation and grace is obvious. One of Heidegger's latest works expresses the experience in dialogue form as follows:

*Scholar:* So far as we can wean ourselves from willing, we contribute to the awakening of releasement (*Gelassenheit*).

[1] E.g., p. 82, above.
[2] For a discussion, see 'The Language of Being' in my *Studies in Christian Existentialism*, p. 79ff.

*Teacher:* Say rather, to keeping awake for releasement.

*Scholar:* Why not, to the awakening?

*Teacher:* Because on our own we do not awaken releasement in ourselves.

*Scientist:* Thus releasement is effected from somewhere else.

*Teacher:* Not effected, but let in.[1]

And perhaps this is as far as we can go. If we are prepared to have this kind of openness and readiness to listen, then I think we shall find the language of theology and faith convincing; and when, in more critical mood, we subject this language and discourse to such analyses and testings as we can devise, I believe it stands up and comes through with its truth claim unscathed.

[1] *Discourse on Thinking*, trans. John M. Anderson and E. Hans Freund (New York: Harper & Row, 1966), p. 61.

*Indexes*

# Index of Names

Adams, J. L., 94
Anderson, John M., 248
Anselm, St, 234
Aquinas, St Thomas, 76, 100, 222, 223, 234
Aristotle, 136, 147, 225
Arnold, Matthew, 195
Athanasius, St, 15, 16, 123ff, 171, 181, 231, 234, 241
Avicenna, 76
Ayer, Alfred J., 105, 106, 107

Baillie, D. M., 31
Baillie, John, 244, 245
Baker, J. A., 188
Balthasar, Hans Urs von, 21
Barr, James, 63, 120
Barth, Karl, 13, 34, 41, 42, 43, 44, 45, 46, 47, 48, 49, 50, 52, 53, 54, 56, 83, 124, 143, 186, 215, 223, 227, 229, 242
Bartsch, H.-W., 36, 186
Berkeley, Bishop, 46, 96, 104
Bevan, Edwyn, 202, 203, 206, 217
Black, Max, 198
Boehme, Jakob, 53
Bonhoeffer, Dietrich, 80, 81
Bosanquet, Bernard, 103
Bradley, F. H., 103
Braun, Herbert, 39
Bromiley, G. W., 41
Browning, Robert, 106
Brunner, Emil, 13, 135
Buber, Martin, 68, 69, 77
Buddha, 20, 21, 202
Bultmann, Rudolf, 34, 35, 36, 37, 38, 39, 40, 41, 42, 43, 47, 49, 50, 52, 53, 54, 83, 147, 148, 154, 155, 160, 171, 181, 182, 184, 186, 189, 190, 192, 201, 204, 215, 241, 242, 243, 246
Buren, Paul van, 11, 99, 181
Burrows, Millar, 203

Caird, Edward, 103
Carnap, Rudolf, 67, 84, 112
Cassirer, Ernest, 172
Clement of Alexandria, 25, 26
Cobb, J. B., 53, 99, 152, 234
Cohen, Herrmann, 38, 243
Cohen, L. J., 114
Cohn, L., 23
Copleston, F. C., 222
Cross, F. L., 127
Cullmann, Oscar, 188

Dewey, John, 38, 243
Dilthey, W., 147
Dingle, Herbert, 95
Dorner, Isaak, 124

Ebeling, Gerhard, 148
Eichhorn, J. G., 170
Eichrodt, Walther, 188
Eliade, Mircea, 187
Elijah, 20
Eliot, George, 170

Ferré, Frederick, 49, 119, 143
Filson, Floyd V., 188
Flew, A., 24, 88, 109, 115
Frege, G., 55, 104
Freud, Sigmund, 17
Freund, E. Hans, 248

# Index of Subjects